The Whiteness of Bones

THE WHITENESS OF BONES

Sarah Penny

PENGUIN BOOKS

PENGUIN BOOKS

Published by the Penguin Group
27 Wrights Lane, London W8 5TZ, England
Viking Penguin, a division of Penguin Books USA Inc, 375 Hudson
Street, New York, New York 10014, USA
Penguin Books Australia Ltd, Ringwood, Victoria, Australia
Penguin Books Canada Ltd, 10 Alcorn Avenue, Toronto, Ontario,
Canada M4V 3B2
Penguin Books (NZ) Ltd, 182-190 Wairau Road, Auckland 10, New
Zealand
Penguin Books (South Africa) (Pty) Ltd, Pallinghurst Road, Parktown,
South Africa 2193

Penguin Books (South Africa) (Pty) Ltd, Registered Offices:
20 Woodlands Drive, Woodmead, Sandton, South Africa 2028

First published by Penguin Books (South Africa) (Pty) Ltd 1997

ISBN 0 140 26423 X

Typeset in 10.5 on 12 pt Bembo
Cover photograph: The Image Bank
Author photograph: Bobby Jordan
Printed and bound by Creda Press, Eliot Avenue, Eppindust II, Cape

For Nicholas

Let the whiteness of bones atone to forgetfulness.
There is no life in them. As I am forgotten
And would be forgotten, so I would forget
Thus devoted, concentrated in purpose. And God said
Prophesy to the wind, to the wind only for only
The wind will listen.

T S Eliot, *Ash-Wednesday*

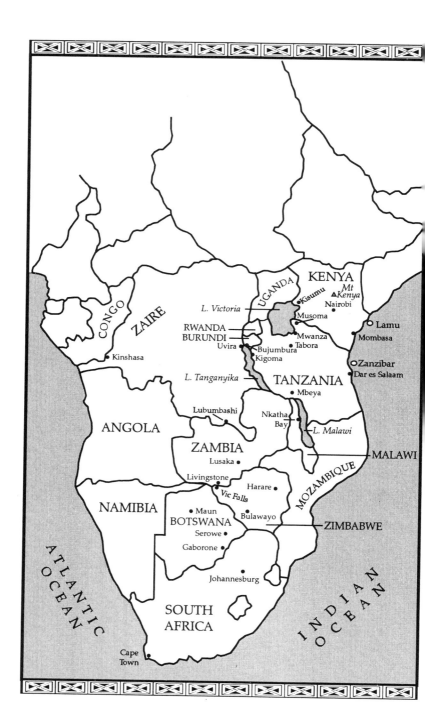

Contents

Journeys

The history of the world is a history of journeys. Journeys of war, journeys of discovery, journeys made by the banished, the inspired, the zealous.

Jesus, they say, never travelled more than three days' distance from his place of birth. Yet successive generations of his acolytes have traversed plains, penetrated jungles, scaled peaks, and generally poked their questing noses into every imaginable or suspected quarter of the globe.

Legend and humdrum Sunday morning Bible classes tell the tale of Moses, who shepherded the weary Israelites across an immense desert, and those ill-fated Egyptians in hot pursuit who met a watery death.

Journeys have echoes. Journeys create complex legacies. Journeys shape and shadow the future. Journeys become eventually tedious compilations of dates and names and circumstances in the dog-eared textbooks of fidgeting school-children.

Cortés captured Montezuma, Columbus discovered a new continent through ignorance and faulty mapwork, and insisted he had not. Marco Polo voyaged from the Polar Sea to Java, from Zanzibar to Japan, thus confusing the origins of ice-cream and spaghetti for ever.

And of course journeys pre-empt other journeys, in the flights of the myriads of the dispossessed. Who can say how significant a journey might be in future millennia? I once met a white American Rasta woman. She was attracted to Rastafarianism, she told me, because it brought her back to her African roots.

'Yes,' I protested, 'but you're from the United States.' And I gestured with vague emphasis at her skin which was a livery pink.

'Oh my dear,' she responded earnestly, 'we're all from Africa, if you study scientific prehistory.'

I suppose, as a white African, my heritage is specifically about journeys. According to neo-Darwinists, my prehistoric ancestors trekked up and away to the colder reaches of the north. Eons later, a more immediate ancestor came trailing back again, in the form of my great grandfather, who had a stern chin and very blue eyes. He bequeathed me his eyes in a genetic legacy. Although we never met, we used to gaze at each other with a familiar blue intensity throughout my childhood, he from his portraited vantage point upon the wall, and myself in the cool polished gloom of the hallway, three feet tall, wondering why he left Home.

Home was England, referred to as such with great nostalgia until my grandfather's generation. My great grandfather arrived in Cape Town as a colonist, but he came bearing neither Bible nor weapons. If he carried anything, it must have been a ledger or perhaps an abacus.

We were business people. We still live in the same city and we still live by the same business. Perhaps consistency was another behest of that questing great grandparent, who left Southampton to settle in Africa.

This is not the story of an epic journey, although it was for me a seminal journey. A journey between child and adult, between the outer and the inner selves, between points on the map, between cultures, between theory and practice, between pain, despair, anger and salvation, between refuting and believing in oneself, between loss and gain, death and life, negation and affirmation.

This is the story of my journey.

Preparations

It began with not wanting to go to England. I was dimly aware as I entered my final year at the University of Cape Town in 1991 that almost everybody else did want to go to England. English-speaking South Africans have this perennial love affair with England. The pathos there is that it is almost wholly unrequited.

All my crowd were gearing up for London. Maps of London could be spotted on the passenger seats of cars. London stories abounded. London was radical, London was happening, London was nineties, London was everything that Cape Town patently wasn't.

Then there were the London consultants, those who had been and returned. They painted glorious pictures of a garish, fast-paced, kaleidoscopic capital. In London you lived on beans, but you clubbed all night. In London you were offered an astonishing medley of drugs practically upon arrival. London was your oyster if you opened yourself up to the experience.

'Big Ben on acid,' recalled one of the returned. 'It was like . . . arcane.'

But I didn't care. I hadn't wanted to go to England for A-levels and I hadn't wanted to try for Oxford and nor did I yearn for Big Ben to be arcane on acid. My life at this point had assumed a particular flow.

The 1960s had arrived in South Africa at around this time, after having been on hold for thirty years. I had fallen in with the Beautiful People. We loved nature. We perceived and treasured the unique form and beauty and soul of leaves and waves and motes of sunlight. We were pantheists. We frolicked naked in the ocean. We talked endlessly about consciousness and meanings and purity. We had love-ins and hair-ins and people-focus. People-focus was sitting in a circle as someone displayed their writing/poetry/art/photographs and told the story of their life. We spent weeks setting up camp in nature reserves and then subsisted on mussels and rice and drew intricate designs in the sand that the tide would have erased by morning. We danced expression-dances in the moonlight.

I knew London was not a place befitting a pantheist.

Africa, on the other hand, had a tremendous allure.

My problem was finding someone else who was feeling the allure. Several of the Beautiful People felt the allure, but they didn't feel it sufficiently.

I was beginning to despair when I met Cyril. He was not feeling the allure, but he was infinitely open to suggestion.

I tracked him to a meeting of the Hare Krishnas and kept him in my sights.

We knelt and rose and knelt and did little sideways dances and up-and-down dances and chanted 'Jai Prapupadha'. We covered ourselves with marigolds and blessed ourselves from the flame and sang the Hare Krishna Hare Rama mantra.

Cyril was a man, so he was up front in close propinquity to the deities, whereas I was lurking around near the back. However, by the time the holy prasad was served some of the younger and flirtier devotees had begun to mingle gender, so I managed to approach. Cyril was in the *corps de ballet* and he had come directly from a performance of The Merry Widow. His lips were still scarlet and his eyelashes heavy with traces of mascara.

'Hey you,' he said indistinctly, through a mouthful of

cauliflower tandoori, when he spotted me.

We ended up on the roof of my block of flats, with a bottle of Amarula liqueur that someone had given me for my twenty-first birthday earlier that week. Marula is an African fruit that ferments quickly in the sun and has an astonishingly narcotic effect on elephants, baboons and people. Elephants and baboons are reduced to eating the fruit as it rots on the ground, having dislodged itself from the parent tree. We were imbibing it from a shapely little bottle with elephants in graphic design on the label. And we were on the roof because somehow, in those days, one always seemed to be on the roof. It was considered good manners.

'Hello, do have a cup of tea. Shall we go up to the roof?' an efficient hostess might ask.

And then the perilous ascent would begin, shinnying up the drainpipe, crawling along the corrugated iron, clinging to the chimney. Inside the house itself, you would know if the roof was vacant or occupied by the rate at which bits of plaster and peeling paint would detach themselves from the ceiling. There was a strict code of conduct – only such and such a number on the roof at any fixed time, priority to courting couples, and so on. To this day I will unexpectedly come upon packets of my own hair, or stray bits of memorabilia wedged in the crevices of chimney-stacks across suburbia.

As a writer, I felt the roof was the only truly omniscient geographical position I could occupy, because of the greater insights it offered into the mystic communications of the neighbours.

Now the roof had become a proposal zone.

'I'm going up Africa,' I offered shyly. 'You can come if you want to.'

'Cool,' returned Cyril, as I had known he would.

I had a tenuous framework in my mind of what I expected to do.

Whilst the borders of many countries were still closed to

South Africans, everything was in flux. Two close friends with British passports had crossed overland as far as Chad. Moreover, my elder brother Nicholas, who was a collector of African art and artefacts, had made an extraordinary odyssey, completely alone, through Namibia and Angola, the latter still embroiled in a civil war in which South Africa was covertly involved. His Land Rover had been burgled and all his funds stolen, and he was detained in jail for some weeks in Angola.

Eventually released, he had arrived in Zaire in time to intercept a particularly bloody military uprising and revolution, and had to go into hiding for some months in the jungle, abandoning the truck. After several months of hearing nothing from him, he had recently reappeared with a collection of masks and kuba cloth. He was characteristically both unassuming and uncommunicative about what to me was a fascinating and perilous series of encounters.

'Weren't you *terrified*?' I pressed, on a sunny afternoon in the Christmas season. He had recruited me for servile purposes, to hold the bolt of intricate embroidery still whilst he measured its length. The kuba cloth itself was a series of squares. It gave off a musty, strange odour.

He grunted, absorbed in the work. Between us stood a decade and three siblings. I was the little one, the *laatlammetjie*, as they say at home, meaning literally the late lamb. I was mollycoddled too and resented it fiercely.

'Look,' he said at last, 'it's not random. This cloth is their script. Every cloth is an heirloom. Every one is different.'

He moved his fingers along the patterns, exploring, tracing the alien contorted designs. The cloth sprawled in its entirety along the spread of our brick veranda, ourselves crouched next to it, in the shadow of the old colonial house in which we lived. A weird cabbalism was arising from that cloth, to battle against the oak tree, greening again for the summer, and the gaudy banks of my mother's agapanthus.

My brother's touring finger had located a smear of dirt on

the border of the piece.

'I need a dishcloth,' he said abruptly.

I headed off in search of one. He was a powerful man, and I never cheeked him; my resistances were too effete. Besides, our family operated on what could loosely be described as a hierarchical system of dictates. I was afraid of him, but I also adored him. I would adhere to his more whimsical requests.

When I reached puberty, he was in military service working as an adviser in the remote homelands of KwaZulu/Natal and he had begun to collect Zulu beadwork and pots. I was a young girl, returning from my day school with a satchel of books. He was home on a pass with a moustache.

'Here,' passing a string of scarlet and azure beads around my neck. 'You're not to take that off, you hear me?'

'Yes,' I said timidly. 'What's it for, Nicholas?'

'A protection. For virginity. A man gives it to his sister.'

I cringed to hear that word – a *sexual* word – said publicly. In South Africa in the eighties we did not refer to prurient topics. Moreover, there was little to fear from the polite private school boys whom I met at dancing class and supervised school discothèques. Nevertheless I wore the beads underneath my powder-blue school uniform and fingered their smoothness as we rested painfully on our knees during prayers. A talisman.

*

The Africa game began to take on immense proportions, as my undergraduate degree drew to a close. I began a stubborn refutation of the various suggestions that were being bandied about regarding my future.

No thank you, I didn't want to do a course in advertising, although I was creative and good with words. I didn't want to go to language school in Paris. I didn't want to go to the Courtauld Institute to learn about fashion. I still didn't want to try for Oxford.

What did the child want to do with her life? It seemed to be a mystery. A mystery, remarks Mr Fielding in *A Passage To India*, is only a high-sounding term for a muddle.

My parents' attitude to Cyril was one of partially restrained horror. When he appeared, my mother would cry. My father was deeply depressed for days after a sighting. They seemed singularly obdurate in their inability to perceive Cyril as a free-spirited individual of great spiritual intensity.

I put their hostility down to the religious and class differences between us (Cyril was Jewish and lower middle). They didn't approve of ballet as a suitable career option for a young man. They approved less when he resigned.

'I didn't like him much when he did that,' wailed my mother, with devastating honesty. 'But I like him less now that he does nothing at all.'

I tried to smooth the waters, to pour the oil lavishly when I could.

'They don't mind you very much really,' I told him comfortingly from time to time. 'If you could just try not to speak when they're around.'

'Oh, they dig me! Your parents are groovy!' Cyril had a great optimism. Additionally, my mother's ineffable politeness to strangers was extraordinary, even in the face of severe provocation.

The crux of the matter was that Cyril did not know how to appease parents. He would never concede that it might be deeply alarming for the elders of a young woman to learn that her beau wanted to live in a forest, grow vegetables and never pay taxes. He had little concept of their mixed feelings when they learnt that he was devoted to the chronicles of a thirty-thousand-year-old Persian deity called Ramtha, who channelled himself rather fortuitously through the body of a now handsomely wealthy blonde American housewife.

Cyril explained patiently to my doubting forebears that the reason he absolutely never could or would read another book in his life, was because this Ramtha had revealed the Divine Truth, and any further literary explorations were quite redundant. The most *amazing* thing was that he, Cyril, was going to live for ever and ever, because . . . he had discovered the secret of eternal life.

My father acquired a ghostly pallor. He became haggard.

I devised a little memorandum.

SUITABLE CONVERSATIONS FOR PARENTS

Topic One: Economics (good for father)
Communism versus capitalism. Refer knowingly to recent events in the Eastern bloc. Remember to praise the free market system. The argument can be rendered more contemporary by references to corporate responsibility for environment, social welfare etc. Some allusions can be made to laissez-faire policies in America in early twentieth century, and resultant social misery of depression, but only with great sensitivity.

Topic Two: Art and Culture (good for mother)
Validity of modern art. Express puzzlement at developments in last century (not Picasso, Picasso is sacrosanct). Say something along the lines of: I'd be the last person to stand in the way of true artistry, but some of these things look like a child's doodling. Widen argument by evoking the flaw-lessness of the old masters, Van Gogh's passion, Da Vinci's precision etc. Mother will take it from there, she's an excellent conversationalist.

Topic Three: Weather (good for mother, father, and any other visiting friends or relatives)
Boring but dependable. Comment on present conditions. Make light conversation regarding past weathers of your own experience. Absorb the opinion of conversational counterpart and then agree.

I backed up this strategy with a number of mini lectures on the various subjects and a system of flashcards for when he was on the spot. But he wouldn't have it. My memorandum was consigned to the rubbish tip.

A sample conversation between Cyril and Father:

Father: What do you intend to do with your life, Cyril?
Cyril: I'm going to grow *vegetables*.
Father: Her-hmmm. You would like to be an agriculturalist?
Cyril: No, I wanna grow *vegetables*.
Father: You understand, Cyril, that even a small-scale market gardening venture would require a large capital investment initially.
Cyril: Yeah, I'm gonna get some *seeds*. I'm gonna be self-*sufficient*.

Cyril retired from the *corps de ballet* and we moved in together. By now we were living in the coastal town of Knysna where I had been offered a job as a hotel employee. Cyril did not need to work because of his ballet pension and unemployment benefits. I learned to make Hollandaise sauce and to process telephone bookings and minister to corpulent, fractious German visitors. From time to time my parents would send newspaper clippings, advertising posts for ballet dancers in remote parts of the country.

*

I loved to dress up. As children we had had policemen suits and nun outfits, we had had the sartorial provisions to be fairies or doctors or nurses. Now the Africa game was a minefield of potential. Cyril and I went shopping. We bought matching turquoise backpacks and matching broad-brimmed scout hats and all-encompassing rainwear in navy blue. We bought rubbery mats and slept on them experimentally as a simulation exercise.

We acquired little yo-yos and folding scissors and other knick-knacks to trade with the locals. We exchanged our guitars for a tan Kestrel tent.

In our respective ways we tried to be practical. I persuaded Nicholas to give me one of his Michelin maps and ordered visas for our passports. Cyril took the wider view. He made an exception to his restricted reading policy and began to devour bush survival manuals. In theory, he was rapidly able to skin and eat a decaying baboon carcass, like the Selous Scouts of old Rhodesia. He learnt how to trap a meerkat, encourage it to gorge itself on a salt lick and then scurry after it to its hidden liquid resources. By the end of the month he had perfected the art of erecting a bridge over a swollen river, using the bathtub for practice. He could tie a variety of intricate knots.

He was also able to trap rain water in a square of plastic mackintosh. I looked doubtfully at the sagging plastic mackintosh. The still-falling raindrops were spritzing outwards from its overloaded bowels. It seemed to me that the operation was weighted in our favour, by dint of our residing in the highest rainfall catchment area in South Africa, in the rainy season. Bush conditions would be starker, possibly. I also did not intend to enter a state of abandonment in any waterless climes.

On the other hand, I followed the theory that boys will be boys, and if Cyril wanted to cast himself as David Livingstone, then all to the well and good.

I would have found the situation comic, except that I had begun to experience an extremely oppressive feeling. A heavy, anxious sensation had settled on me. I couldn't shake it. It was stalking me by day, as I served the guests their breakfasts, as I wandered through the thick concealing foliage of the forests. At night I churned on my pillow, ugly, formless voices whispering in my ear.

My parents had withdrawn from the fray. They said very little.

Nicholas watched our mounting devices and strategies with

amusement. He gave me an old penknife and a selection of antibiotics. I met him one afternoon in Cape Town city centre, got up experimentally in the garb; the sturdy leather boots, the broad scout hat, penknife on a thong around my neck. Cyril had gone in search of compasses with inbuilt convex magnifying lenses for starting fires. These were recommended by the survival manual.

Nicholas was dressed in faded jeans and a checked open-necked shirt. We squared off against each other, innocence and experience. I dared him to challenge, to be patronising. He absorbed the apparition that was me. Apart from the Africa gear, I had paid some unemployed farm labourers' wives to plait my whole head of lanky blonde hair into tiny interwoven strands. Cyril and I had made and painted clay beads and affixed them to the ends of the plaits. After all, I had reasoned, there won't be any *shampoo* in Africa.

Two siblings, a busy street in late autumn, the sheer north face of the mountain rising like a monolith at our backs. His eyebrows lifted in greeting. He didn't mock. He tugged lightly on one of my gaudy little plaits.

'You two will have a great time.'

I tried to believe it.

But the sourceless, voiceless dread had become a clawing panic.

I said my goodbyes and left.

We travelled to Johannesburg to spend a few days with Cyril's parents. The turquoise backpacks were in a state of readiness.

Clothes	*Necessities*
Socks	Map and compass
Boots	Sleeping bag
Underwear	Methylated spirits cooker
Rainmac	Water filter
Trousers	Selection of novels
Scout hat	Diaries and pens

Jersey	Camera and film
T-shirt	English and French dictionaries
Shorts	Cosmetics, hairbrush, toothbrush

The novels were John Fowles' *The Journey of the Magi*, and a complex series of diatribes on American life by Joan Didion (hence the English dictionary). I was stumped by words such as *metastasis* and *teleological*.

Cyril, too, was fine-tuning his literary diet. He had spent weeks reducing the several chronicles of Ramtha to a series of spidery scrawlings in a pocket notebook. This notebook was to contain only the most vital philosophies, but Cyril was agitated by the following discovery, which can be expressed in mathematical terms:

Number of pages in pocket notebook $= Y$
Number of pages needed for terribly important Ramthic portions $= 3Y$

I had a look. It was apparent that the Ramtha quotes had been transferred without modification.

'Look, why don't you summarise?' I suggested. 'No, honestly, I used to summarise all the critical reviews for university, otherwise I would have had to buy the books. Look at this sentence here: "Know ye, I am the great Ramtha, the ancient deity from days of yore, and you are sovereign beloved entities and as you are possessed of a great, immortal ageless soul, know ye, know ye, that very same soul can leave and enter the wonderful isness of the body through the orifice of the pineal gland." Most of that is just repetition and redundant labelling. The actual information contained is "Soul enters and leaves through pineal gland".'

I paused. 'Where is the pineal gland, anyway?'

Cyril stared at me, outraged. He had the air of a Talmudic scholar who had been presented with a *Reader's Digest* version of the Torah.

We were due to leave in the morning.

I scrutinised my face in the mirror. The foreboding continued to pulse slowly in the pit of my stomach. Something, somewhere, somehow was terribly, terribly wrong. Feel excited, I told myself. For God's sake, what's the matter with you?

My mother's phone call, when it came, was not wholly unexpected.

Disaster

It is difficult to write about the circumstances of my brother's death. It isn't that recalling the events themselves causes unbearable pain. It is more that the narration of them has become factitious.

Once you have been required to discuss a horrible tragedy a number of times it becomes a story. Once you've replayed the unfolding drama, shot by shot, scene by scene through your mind's eye, it becomes cinemascope. It loses authenticity. It becomes hackneyed.

The trauma persists as a deep unalleviated scar, but a reference to the dramatic action itself does not necessarily reduce one to fragments. You learn to manage it when it surfaces in conversation. There's a posture, an attitude, a show of resigned fatalism, a smile and a sigh to show the (often unsuspecting) interrogator that you've dealt with it all. To spare him the grinding embarrassment of sympathy.

Briefly, then, my brother, who was always a daredevil, dared once to go too far. He went tyre-rafting in bad weather, against advice, and did not return. He had begun the ultimate journey, hidden and untraceable, in the vast secret Witels mountains which abut the Cape Peninsula. We never saw him again.

I flew home to wait out the search. The pilot was a jaunty

fellow. As we traversed the jagged pinnacles, his disembodied voice informed that 'Ladies and gentlemen, here below you can see the mountains where the search is being conducted for the lost hiker.'

There was a releasing of seat belts, a scrambling to the left hand side. Far, far below were those silent, pristine peaks. The seasonal snows were brilliantly white.

'The poor thing!' exclaimed a middle-aged lady, inflating her plump cheeks and craning her head. 'He must be so cold.'

Our family tragedy became public property. The press loved it. It had all the pickings of a fine news story. They seized on my brother's physical beauty and the extraordinary narrative of his life. Old Etonian, Rhodes Scholar, Fulbright Award to Massachusetts Institute of Technology, Wall Street merchant banker turned African art collector. And from an old Cape Town family. His dark, restless eyes gazed out from the front pages.

Perhaps they would have liked a happy ending. So, too, would the phalanx of crackpots and self-promoting psychics who ceaselessly rang our number to report their garbled visions. So, too, would the intrigued family groups who arrived at the search site with folded rugs and picnic hampers of marinated chicken, to show the kids the choppers and search squads in a blessed respite from the monotony of small town life.

In the end there was a memorial service, in bodily absentia, and the press came crawling out of the naves and up the aisle for their booty, popping off their blinding little bulbs at my father's stony physiognomy. They were waiting outside afterwards. I was on the front page, suitably stricken and pathetic, in the protective clutches of a relative. A funereal tea. There was weak Ceylon and eggy sandwiches. There was mother, father, remaining brother, married sister, unmarried sister. We were bleak and speechless. There was nothing to say.

After the funeral was the denouement. There were the old lives waiting. My married sister had a small child to nurture, my unmarried sister a medical career. My brother, who worked for the Anglo American Corporation, had diamond mines to manage. Unanimously, they felt I should cancel my trip.

Unfair under the circumstances, they implied. I prevaricated in the impenetrably empty vacuum that had become the world in the last few days. Astonishingly, it was my mother, having unfailingly opposed the trip, who stepped into the breach.

'Of course the child must go,' she told the detractors fiercely. 'It's what she's always wanted. She's been working for it for months. What good will it do her to sit here mourning with us?'

As a goodbye present she gave me Kuki Gallman's *I Dreamed of Africa*.

So the die was cast.

*

Each successive day passed as a flat, grey, weary passage of hours. Cyril, who had come down for the funeral, hitch-hiked back to Johannesburg, where I was to join him later in the week. He disappeared for five days. His mother and I exchanged anxious, mystified phone calls. We assumed the worst. I cancelled my flight.

The problem was that Cyril had never really come to grips with that compass with the inbuilt convex magnifying lens for making fires. Instead of bearing north north east, he had travelled north north *west*. When he reached the Augrabies Falls National Park on the Namibian border, he realised that the level, planing semi-desert, the dwarfish halfmens shrubs, the tough, rubbery aloes, had little in common with the skyscrapers and teeming boulevards of his birthplace. About turn, thought Cyril, at this point. But now he was stranded on the outer limits of civilisation.

I sympathised with his mistake; map reading can be a tricky business. However, it wasn't politic. My mother put things rather succinctly.

'How is that boy going to travel through Africa,' she demanded, 'when he can't even find his way home?'

'I'll take care of us, Mum,' I promised.

Cyril's little roadside peccadilloes had whetted his appetite for foreign travel. He arrived at the airport to meet me in a condition of bouncy anticipation. He disregarded my persistent gloominess. This was not because Cyril was given to *schadenfreude*. He genuinely regretted my loss. At the funeral he had been kind, considerate and, to my relief, diplomatic. But he had no concept of grief. He had been a child, that was fun; he had been a ballet dancer, that was fun; and now he was going to be an African adventurer and that would be the most fun of all.

In trying to comprehend my sudden encounter with the dark side, Cyril aggregated his own bad experiences and attributed the net result to me. He had survived teenage girlfriends who wouldn't answer his phone calls in fits of pique. Then there was failing to be promoted to a soloist role in the ballet and arguments with his mother who tried to keep him in for dinner. But Cyril had rallied. He assumed I had rallied too. Besides, there was Ramtha philosophy to back him up. Death happens, explained Ramtha, smiling gently from beneath her bouffant hairdo, *because we desire to know the experience*. The experience of the death of those we love helps to release us from the material world.

There was an up side to his attitude. It did not compromise the approach I had adopted. I was in denial, as the Americans say. We did have fights. He was annoyed by my failure to embrace the philosophies that would so clearly cancel my doldrums.

Most of the time I watched him moving and gesturing on the far reaches of a dry, silent, fathomless space. But sometimes he would spill into my head. I would dissolve into hysteria – but unspoken, noiseless hysteria, bloodshot gaping at the effigy of myself in the bathroom mirror, hunched night-time walkabouts in the neighbourhood, watching the shadowy forms of the African servants who congregated on the street corners after their work hours. When I returned he would be asleep, or have shut up.

My father came to visit during those last days in Johannesburg. We were invited to an Anglo American dinner party and sat like two corpses amongst the jovial guests. At the end of the evening we took our leave of each other.

'Goodbye, Dad.'

'Goodbye, girl.'

'I'll write then, shall I, Dad?'

He nodded. He was so terribly tired, casting his eyes over the exterior of Cyril's modest, comfortable house. How impossible it is to comprehend one's children, who will offer themselves to the most malignant influences. We hugged each other and he eased himself into the driver's seat. He was almost sixty, but still a strong, severely handsome man.

I felt suddenly stranded. I always was a Daddy's girl, trailing over the mountains in childhood, holding on to the loose cords of his rucksack, prattling.

'Why is that shiny rock inside that rough rock, Daddy?'

'Why doesn't baboon crap smell bad, Daddy?'

Or struggling through the endless stanzas of *The Rime of the Ancient Mariner* wanting to impress, in his study at night, with the bound volumes flanking the wall and the bank of fire snapping and blazing at my back.

My father has a dry, backhanded humour. In my eyes, he would cover himself with glory at the most appropriate moments. At my boarding school, he once asked the headmaster what educational advances he might implement, after the head man had returned from a tour of British schools.

Our headmaster was a man who wore a polyester suit and liked to reminisce about his soldiering days in the Rhodesian war. Astro turf, it transpired, was what had captured his imagination.

'How terribly *necessary*!' said my father.

The headman concurred.

These memories scoured my mind as I watched his BMW turn the corner and disappear.

Keep Moving in a Forward Direction

The sleeping child was lifted on to my lap. He moaned faintly, tensed his lithe little body against the incursion, relaxed against me. He was the apogee of a desirable Afrikaner child. A flat, open face, burnt clear skin, soft white blond hair cut round the rim of a pudding bowl. His little mouth was agape and some sticky confectionery had been retained in blobs. I watched his chest rise and fall as the breath hissed between his reddened lips.

This car had halted for us on the open road beyond Pretoria. We had left Johannesburg at dawn and were headed for Gaborone in Botswana, where an old friend of mine lived. The car geared up again into a steady rhythm. It was a rickety old Toyota, a family car. The driver had his window open, one meaty forearm resting on the sill. Inside it was bakingly hot, the midwinter sunshine was superbly indifferent to any seasonal reduction. Endless fields of ripe golden maize shimmered in the heat. We were in the Groot Marico, the heartland of the North Western Transvaal, made famous by the tersely funny stories of Herman Charles Bosman.

There were two men in the front of the car, or one confirmed man and a youth verging on manhood. Maybe he was sixteen or seventeen. Manhood came early here on the land, without larking about after the quests of the young. The driver looked to be in his early thirties. He had coarse pinkish skin, livery with sun damage, and a moustache which showed efforts at containment. The boy still had spots. It was possible to tell from those ravaged hillocks that he had been picking.

At first they said nothing to us. They had a desultory exchange about some third person. The younger addressed the elder as Kommandant, deferentially. I guessed they must be members of the Afrikaner Weerstandsbeweging – the Afrikaner Resistance Movement – the right-wing army who opposed the recent volte-face of the ruling National Party. They were not wearing the armband of the three sevens, but they were also clearly not from the South African Defence Force. Incognito renegade rural guerrillas. For the time being, all these activities were still legal. There were rallies and mobilisations and surreptitious arming. Training camps were held on the isolated farms. The wives were taught to shoot a rifle. I had heard that in bygone years the women would hand out condoms to their African labourers, to stop the Prolific Procreation. They were supposed to have ceased these social services after realising the implications of Aids.

There was an air of grim purpose in the car. Nevertheless, Kommandant was a funny fellow. When a *boeremusiek* love-song trilled through the static of the car radio, Kommandant accompanied the singer for a verse or two in a shrill falsetto. The youth chuckled gauchely. Their eyes flicked to me in the rear seat. I smiled. The channels of communication sprang open.

'What are you chaps doing?' queried the Kommandant, in Afrikaans.

'We're going travelling, *Meneer*,' I explained.

'Travelling where?' he pressed.

'Don't know exactly, *Meneer*. In Africa.'

'*Yissus*,' exclaimed the boy irreverently, with a doubtful lift of his pale blue eyes in my direction via the overhead mirror.

Cyril remained silent. He couldn't, or wouldn't, speak

Afrikaans, despite the years of intensive study required for passing the national examination. This was not uncommon.

The Boer War between Imperial England, spearheaded by Cecil John Rhodes, and the Afrikaner guerrilla fighters led by Paul Kruger, grizzled President of the Transvaal, had been waged at the turn of the century. I supposed that those Afrikaner Nationalists were not very different from the men with whom I now conversed. The Boers, wily, mobile, and with a generations-old knowledge of the veld, ran circles at first around the slowly advancing and highly visible columns of British troops. Their women worked the farms and provided supplies for the duration, enabling the men to continue fighting.

But Afrikaner gains were reversed with the strongman tactics of the British army chief of staff, Lord Kitchener. Kitchener's 'scorched earth' policy permitted the wholesale burning and looting of farms, creating a proliferation of women and children refugees.

The concept of the concentration camp was established in South Africa under the British, although the camps were only intended as a makeshift measure. Notwithstanding, twenty-six thousand women and children died in the camps, largely from cholera and typhoid. Of these, twenty thousand were under sixteen years of age. Kitchener was a handsome if iron-willed man, but he had a notorious aversion to women, and his attitude to the refugees was one of expedience.

Even after the war the Afrikaners were inadequately compensated for their losses and were forced into humiliating concessions. This left a bitter legacy and the echoes resounded, even touching my own generation, the great grandchildren. It was mutual. Cyril did not like Afrikaners on the whole; he called them by the Yiddish expletive *ghatis*.

I spoke the Afrikaans language fairly fluently because it was the mother tongue of my childhood nanny and lifelong family servant, a Cape Coloured woman. It was a brown people's language as well.

The younger man had been eyeing me with a great circumspection. Eventually he spoke up.

'What's the matter with *Mejuffrou*'s hair?'

'It's the new style!' I met his sceptical gaze in the mirror and pulled down the corners of my mouth in a little gesture of self-mockery. The two men blinked at each other. Ah, a joke! There was a barrel-chested explosion of guffaws. Bugger the Boer War.

The little boy woke up. He stared at me in frozen distress from the depth of his electric blue eyes and began to howl.

'Japie!' said the Kommandant. 'You shitting yourself because you're on a strange aunty's lap!'

'*Toemaar!*' announced the burgeoning youth with courageous ribaldry. 'If it was me I would really enjoy the experience!'

Another round of laughter. I clumsily handed back the squalling little boy. The Kommandant rested the child on his squashy belly, behind the steering wheel, reducing his speed slightly. His arms were two massive columns around the small body. Japie drifted off again. I was fascinated by such softness in a hard man.

The Kommandant became embarrassed by his own sentimentality. He shook his heavy jowls and drew his lower teeth over the not unimpressive moustache.

'*Warm, nè?*' he announced gruffly.

The smell of sweat was rank.

Presently we drew up alongside one of the numerous signboarded turn-offs, which heralded a dusty road running off into the distance like a brown river between the golden spread of crops.

'*Meneer* can drop us here?' I asked rapidly, to forestall him.

The afternoon was well settled already, the oppressive heat dispersing and a greater stillness whispering on the furrows of the dry earth. I knew there would be an invitation. That is the kind of people they were; the Kommandant and his subordinate and his Japie. There would be a plump wife making pastry in an enamel basin. There would be creeping servants with fat ankles and their tight woolly curls bound in *doeks*. There would be a massive meal of venison, a fresh springbok, picked off only yesterday by the subordinate, who was the age for blood sports. My mother's people were farm people and went in for hunting. I could fire the rifle just for fun, the body backthrusting painfully against my shoulder. I never hit anything, I hadn't an aim. My brothers now, in khaki bush shirts, could follow that leaping pronk in focused concentration until . . .

I veered away painfully.

They pulled our rucksacks from the back of the vehicle and settled them on the roadside amongst the stiff fragrant grasses. An immense panorama of maize-covered rises soared to the horizon. Some of the unlevel ground was not cultivated and the low tufty bush ranged unevenly amongst the rocks. Clearly we were in the boondocks.

The Kommandant was speaking.

'Watch out for those kaffirs, *Mejuffrou*,' he said. '*Mejuffrou* is an attractive woman.'

And nodded at his own injunctions.

The jalopy set off down the farm road in a nebula of browning dust.

'What were they saying?' asked Cyril.

'Have a happy holiday, more or less,' I answered.

*

We spent the night encamped on a square of grass that flanked the railway siding at the small town of Swartruggens, which means Black Backs, named in honour of the nearby range of low hills. By mid-morning the following day we had cleared customs and were on the dusty swathe of tar that leads to Gaborone in the car of a man who installed swimming pools. Having no local money, I swapped him a rand coin for the equivalent value in pula, the Botswanian currency.

He left us at the local mall. Needing change to make a call, we entered the mini supermarket. There was a price reduction on household essentials and the aisles were crowded with well-dressed African women, skimming through the sale baskets with expert precision and dropping sundry articles into their wire baskets. We stalled, looking for some small purchase that we did need. The crush was stifling in the heat.

'Keep moving in a forward direction,' urged the aproned assistant, eyeing the produce anxiously.

I bought a vial of lip balm, pocketed the small change and located a street telephone. Dropping a coin in the slot, I waited for the dull pealing call to arouse its target.

'Hello.'

'Tiddles.'

'Skini! Where are you?'

'At the post office.'

'Fantastic! I'll be there in five minutes.'

Skini was my hippie name. It came out of nowhere and stuck. The full appellation was Skini Ready For Any Eventuality. I never threw anything away and I never emptied any of my various reticules or my car boot. A skirmish with the contents of the grimy interior of the latter would inevitably yield up the object of desire – anyone's desire – at any time. Apples, woolly jerseys, hairbrushes, nineteenth-century romantic novels, illustrated charts of the chakra points – I could produce them all after several minutes of fierce rummaging.

'Just wait a moment – I'm quite sure it's in here. I bought one last week. There it is! Oh, sorry, it's got a bit of something on it. Honey? Oh no, it's Vaseline. Don't worry, there's a dishcloth in here *somewhere*, I'll give it a wipe.'

Our particular nucleus of the Beautiful People was known as the Purple Bubble of Consciousness. We delved deeply into metaphysics and all fell utterly in love with one another. Reviled by our private schools, and alarmed by the exigent Calvinism that was South Africa in the eighties, it was an incalculable relief to recognise the existence of like-minded people. We released ourselves from the mind-forged manacles, from the demoniacal legacy of prep and pull up your socks.

I was one corner-stone of this group. Tiddles the Wombat was another. He studied painting, I studied drama and literature. We believed in art and personal liberties. Some time had passed since the heyday of Purple Bubble, but the bonds created were still in place. Tiddles was now living with his parents in Gaborone because he was suffering from myalgic encephalo-myelitis – or yuppie flu – a debilitating condition which leaves the sufferer in a permanent state of exhaustion. After increasing disillusionment with allopathic medicine, he had begun to study naturopathic healing.

I awaited the arrival of his car, a red and white hatchback, the Candy Striped Electronic Whizzmobile. The Whizzmobile had swallowed many a mile of coastal road, throbbing to the noisy decibels of Bob Marley, congested with our sunny young bodies in two-piece bathing suits, or baggy surfing shorts. If we chanced to spy Rastafarians we would skid to a halt and pile out to squat in the dust with the coloured Rasta men, who had eschewed Society and wore their matted hair in dreads.

'Going to Babylon,' the Rasta men would say sagely of the beefy sunbaked policemen who crawled past in their yellow vans. We knew whose camp we were in. No ways were we going to Babylon (an unspecified location, but clearly not nirvana).

'Skini!' said Tiddles the Wombat, against a backdrop of rectangular metal cubby-holes, under the awning of the post office in an African shopping mall, in the erstwhile protectorate of Bechuanaland.

We had not seen each other for a year. The illness had taken a toll – he was pale and his voluminous burst of nutty brown curls had been cropped short. We held on to each other. Life had mauled him too – he had lost his own brother by suicide only a few months before.

'Oh.' I released him. 'This is Cyril.'

They shook hands.

'Hey man,' said Cyril.

The Wombat looked at Cyril equably enough. I regretted Cyril, who belonged to a later world, after Purple Bubble. It seemed a travesty that there should have been a later world, especially this world where there was nothing but a shifting perception of chasms down which one might plummet with a straying thought. There were serpents in Paradise. There was nothing but serpents. African dancers had begun to gyrate and stamp their feet in the roofless quadrangle of the mall. The skins shook on their hips. A semicircle of stalls around the dancers sold plastic hair clips and waist belts of fake crocodile skin. In odd contrast, a Chicken Licken outlet was doing business in polystyrene buckets and Barclays Bank displayed the cool gloom of its carpeted interior whenever a client emerged through the hinged front doors. I let my mind absorb these exterior things, these safe things.

'You must have had one hell of a week, this last week,' said the Wombat later. 'How are you anyway?'

'Not great, actually.'

'We'd better have a love-in,' advised the Wombat sympathetically.

The next few days were a hiatus. I clung to Tiddles and shrank from Cyril. Neither of them seemed to mind. There was an eye of the storm quality around me. I couldn't think about what was past, wouldn't think about the things to come. The love-ins, shared by the three of us, were reassuring. While crouched in a circle, with the drowsy chanting – love love love love – peace peace peace peace – I let my conscious thought drift away.

Tiddles was glad to have us there and he needed someone to practise his healing techniques upon. The healing seemed to consist of hours of tapping on the ribcage and lifting and lowering the left forearm. Large wall charts confirmed the gnostic secrets which my physical form was releasing. Tiddles sifted busily through his copious manual. I learnt that I had felt active guilt for the first time at eighteen months.

I was reclining on a piece of plank, watching the wispy cirrus cloud scud across the sky. I tried to recall the parental smack which would have heralded the onset of that first spasm of culpable feeling. The lore of Tiddles' copious manual was that all infant memories were entrapped in the body tissue.

The healing was administered to Cyril as well, but he did not take to it. He emerged from his first session looking blackly furious and lolloped off down the street.

'Oh *dear*,' I said, delighted. 'What's the matter with him? When did he have his first guilt experience?'

'I can't think.' Tiddles was clearly mystified. 'I regressed him to a past life and it turned out he was a French countess beheaded in the Revolution. He didn't seem to like that.'

This revelation was very galling to Cyril. Ramtha principles stated unequivocally that man was ever man and woman ever woman. Reincarnation was not a gender-bending experience unless one was prepared to embrace unnatural passions. Homosexuality, explained the Ramtha texts, was the result of the aberrant desire to experience life as the opposite sex.

This trite syllogism satisfied Cyril, as a self-styled theologian, because homosexuals disturbed him, despite his having worked for years amongst gay men. I suspected that attempts at seduction in some stage dressing room had forged his initial contempt.

I could picture him as Marie Antoinette rather easily. His grace, his flightiness, his air of feminine command; how had these qualities descended upon a boy from Johannesburg? Could they not be the residue of a past existence?

'I could regress you too,' offered Tiddles helpfully. 'You could locate the source of some of your problems. They can go terribly far back, you know.'

'Thank you, Tiddles,' I said humbly. 'But I think most of my problems stem from the present incarnation.'

Following the regression incident, the Wombat was not deeply impressed by Cyril. Cyril's excitable chatter or the sight of his bobbing curls on the horizon would produce a brow furrow of acrimony not dissimilar to my father's. Also, Cyril had a habit of giving out sharp, high-noted yelps when he discovered something he liked or appreciated which set one's teeth on edge.

'Is he all right?' Tiddles asked me once furtively. The man in question was engaged in a headstand at the bottom of the swimming pool.

'No, he's really weird,' I answered truthfully. 'He's just not like other people.'

'I suppose you've got him now though.'

'You can't get rid of them once you've got them, can you?'

'Not very easily,' concurred Tiddles. We both sighed with philosophic resignation. Late adolescent romance was a mine-field, our sagging shoulders suggested, and life itself was a quagmire.

'Water's *great*!' yelped Cyril, shooting out of the pool like a sky rocket.

An invitation arrived, to the home of Miriam and Ian. Tiddles had met them through the healing network. They were tremendously spiritually advanced. And they wanted to have us for tea.

Their garden was surprisingly verdant, in that dry town where everything had to be eked painstakingly out of the flat ungiving dirt. Hibiscus flowers bared their scarlet petals to the sunlight and bluebells bordered the lawn. Wooden carts and whirling whorls on a stick lay about – the playthings of children who were napping now. Miriam and Ian had welcomed us at the door and led us to their back lawn. There was no mention of tea. They gestured to us to sit down. Another love-in, I thought. But it wasn't. It was a Meditation.

'Don't know how to meditate,' I said grumpily. The eye of the storm was passing and scouring winds were beginning to buffet me again. We were leaving the next day.

'Imagine you are travelling in some way through some dimension.' This was Miriam speaking, and very earnestly. She had loopy earrings of woven cotton. 'Imagine yourself in that place, a safe place, and feel your way into it.'

What place is a safe place? I wanted to scream at them.

I smiled. But the others had their eyes shut and were beginning to rock gently on their heels. A faint humming issued through the parted lips of Ian, to join the thrum of the bees in the forget-me-nots and the throb of the heavy afternoon sun.

I imagined a boat cutting along the swell, a trailing wake behind, the sunside of the waves reflecting in a myriad points of light, the low undulating line of the shore running parallel. Dip and rise, dip and rise. The briny scent thrown off by the ocean filling the lungs, the pink underneath of flamingo wings in unfettered flight. Five children and two adults.

'We're turning about. Turn about! Get your head down, girl! Catch that rope, boy!'

'Dad, there's water in the bottom!'

'Bail it out, bail out. Move back, girl, you're unbalancing the whole boat.'

'Mom, Sarah's crying again.'

'Oh, pass her to me. Quiet now, shhh now, the boat's not going to fall over, Daddy's in charge. Nicholas, *don't* lean out like that. Peter, tell him not to do that.'

'Get down from there, boy.'

Hello, Miriam was shaking me. Come back, we're going to have some tea now. Oh yes, tea, that's what we came for. Honey lemon tea, served as is. The napping children had awoken and spewed on to the patio. We sat in the shade on white iron-worked chairs, beneath the awning. Ian was expansive and garrulous. He told about his life. Or lives. He was following a spiritual movement called Eckenkar and claimed to be leading eight lives simultaneously.

'Oh, I was into Eckenkar,' recalled Cyril.

'Eight!' I thought dazedly. 'I've got one and I'm making a mess of it.'

Ostensibly, Ian seemed only to be leading one life. The other seven were peripheral, he explained. Some of them took place on the astral plane. At night, whilst his body remained rooted to his bed, his spirit would soar forth, meeting new people, encountering new lands. Once he had even met the Eck Master himself.

'A phenomenal experience,' recalled Ian.

'Do you go too, Miriam?' I asked her.

'No,' she replied with unconvincing serenity. 'No, I stay right where I am.'

I tried to imagine their sex life. Ummph, darling, that was wonderful. Haven't lost your touch at all. Well, have to go now, love, you know how it is. I'll see you in the morning. Were there women in his other lives? Did it count as bigamy?

'And sometimes the Eck Master speaks to me in the most unexpected ways,' continued Ian. 'For example, last week I was in a shop and the shop assistant – *the shop assistant* – became the channel for the Master. She said to me, "Keep moving in a forward direction!" which in fact was a piece of advice that I had been searching for at that time.'

'Amazing,' breathed Cyril.

We left in the morning. Tiddles drove us just out of town and deposited us at the side of the road. We were en route to see my brother Gareth, who was living in the village of Serowe. Fortuitously, Cyril wandered away to practise waves at trucks and to investigate the scrawny bearded goats that browsed on the plastic litter. Tiddles and I managed our goodbyes.

'I love you, Tiddles,' I said emotionally.

There was so much to say, it couldn't be voiced, or we had already said it all during the Purple Bubble years when our inhibitions were temporarily suspended. Cyril bounced back from the goats, looking insanely cheerful. Tiddles ducked back into the Whizzmobile, gunned up the engine and drove away.

*

The village of Serowe was the seat of power of the Bamangwato, the dominant tribal group in Botswana. Botswana has an interesting history in that its people, the Tswana, were not summarily colonised like their immediate neighbours. In the late nineteenth century the great Zulu chief, Shaka, was in control of an enormous army which had subordinated numerous other tribes and appropriated vast tracts of land. One of his captains was Mzilikazi, clan leader of the Matabele. The two chiefs fell out when Mzilikazi refused to surrender looted cattle to Shaka. Mzilikazi, forced to flee, marched his men to what is now south western Zimbabwe, routing, killing or enslaving the Mashona tribespeople as he went. Mobilising his troops, he was soon poised on the border of the Tswana territories.

Simultaneously, there was disruption in the white camp. The Boers refused to accept subordination to the British Empire and trekked in their covered ox wagons away from the Cape, over the apparently impassable Drakensberg mountains to the Indian Ocean where they declared the independent republic of Natal. This area was promptly annexed by the British, who arrived in boats.

The Boers moved north and west to the Orange Free State and the Transvaal, but were again subject to British interest once gold and diamonds were discovered there. Resuming their endless trek north, they were soon converging on the Tswana.

Now the Tswana faced invasion by two militant and dispossessed peoples. The chief of the Bamangwato, Khama, who was a Christian convert, appealed to the Crown for protection, which was granted. In 1885 the Bamangwato and the closely related tribes of the Bakwena and the Bangwaketse became part of a British Protectorate. The area at that time was known as Bechuanaland.

Khama's grandson, Seretse Khama, was to cause a great stir in the African subcontinent in the 1940s by taking a white woman as his wife. Educated at Balliol College, Oxford and the Inner Temple in London, the young lawyer and future chief fell in love with Ruth Williams, a twenty-four-year-old from the home counties in England. This interracial match caused consternation, both amongst the British and the Bamangwato.

Whilst the Bamangwato accepted the situation fairly rapidly, Britain was hampered by its diplomatic relations with South Africa. My country was at that time evolving the tortuous, virgin policies of apartheid and saw the union as a perversion against God's laws and the dictates of their own regime. Britain, on the whole, did not behave terribly well. The Bishop of London, the Right Reverend William Wand, refused to marry the couple. They were married instead, rather furtively, in a registry office. Britain now conducted a judicial inquiry into the young Seretse's suitability to fulfil his position as chief and consequently exiled him from the nation for five years. Later he was reinstated and Botswana continued as a haven of calm amongst the bloody internecine struggles conducted by its neighbouring states of South Africa, South West Africa, Rhodesia and Angola. Ruth Khama, now widowed, still lives in the village of Serowe.

Gareth, the younger of my two older brothers and the second eldest in our family, had been there for two years, during which time he set up a diamond polishing factory for Anglo American. I had never been to the village before. Having caught a ride with a truck as far as Mahalapye, we hailed a pick-up truck taxi and squeezed in amongst the dozen other passengers huddled in the rear. The truck bounced at high speed along the road whilst we clung with some trepidation to the rim of its sides. The other passengers were not similarly affected.

Serowe is the largest village in Botswana. We arrived at a massive expanse of circular mud huts. Gareth's house stood back from the road. He had managed to create a small garden, which was thrown into relief against the brown dust. His Rhodesian ridgebacks worried at the brave little shrubs that were battling against the odds. The interior of the house was cool and ordered. He had prepared a welcoming dinner of roast leg of lamb.

'We're vegetarian,' I said apologetically.

In and around the village there was beautiful walking. One morning I plunged into the thickets of thorn trees a few kilometres beyond the house and pushed deeper and deeper into the bush. For hours there was nothing but dust and the muted mid-morning whirring of insects. Little hard-backed dung beetles rolled balls of excrement across the path. Goats worked their hairy soft mouths along the stark limbs of the thorn trees in search of a bud. Now and then I would see a goatherd, and he would nod and I would nod.

'*Dumela rra.*'

'*Dumela mma.*'

Slight gullies criss-crossed the terrain. Towards late afternoon I was at the base of a hill. I scrambled up until I had mounted the high ridge at the summit. The countryside fell away in all directions, in perfect silence. Thorn bush, mopane trees, the spreading acacias, dust, grass, gullies, cirrus cloud, horizon. A vulture was circling in the distance – a carcass must have been rotting there. I watched its slow encircling sweeps. My body was spent and streaked with sweat, the dirt coursed in funnels down my legs. I leant my cheek against the face of a granite rock, where the warmth of the day was conserved.

The tremendous tension had ebbed from my mind. Everything was still and quiet and I was still and quiet and I was a part of everything. The sky reddened, the lambent, pulsing sun hung there, incarnadine and impossibly close. I could not cry, I had not cried since the funeral, there were no tears in the dry gullies of my own heart. But the gibbering panic was allayed. I could have been swallowed for ever into that dun earth and the savannah grasses closed over my weaknesses.

It was very black by the time I returned; I had difficulty tracing the outline of Gareth's European-style house in the gloom. He had been worried and now he was annoyed. He poured me a gin and tonic.

'I can't help what you do on your own.' Looking at me with

36

exasperation. 'Please try and keep yourself safe whilst you're here.'

'I'm sorry,' I said miserably. A muffled shriek arose from the interior of the house. Gareth blanched and we both scowled in the direction of the fading notes.

'I'm sorry about him too,' I added.

'Why does he make those noises?'

'I've no idea. He gets excited by things.'

'My God!' reflected Gareth gloomily, nuzzling his own glass. 'You do know how to pick them, Sarey.'

'Perhaps I'll improve as I get older,' I ventured hopefully.

Waking at dawn the next morning, I saw the first crimson streaks. I threw back the bedcovers. It had been a restless night with jarring, sporadic, violent dreams. I was not able to sleep through the nights any longer. I would wake up and pace or huddle in a corner of the bed, fighting my ghoulish imaginings.

I struggled with my clothes. The bedroom was a prison. I wanted to be outside, in that crisp invigorating light. I wanted to recover the momentary serenity of yesterday.

As I was knotting my bootlaces, Cyril appeared from his bedroom across the hallway. He did not enjoy being in a separate bedroom, and resented the lengths I would go to to accommodate the wishes of my family, which were invariably an inconvenience to himself. He sized me up accusingly.

'Where are you going?'

'For a walk.'

'I'm coming too.'

'I want to go by myself.'

'You went by yourself yesterday!'

'Cyril, I really need to think. I have to think about everything that has happened.'

'You can't keep going on and on about that for ever. Nicholas is fertilising the ground now. He's part of the Earth Cycle.'

I gazed at his pretty little curls. How delicate you are, you crass bastard. And how long is for ever? Longer than ten days, surely.

'All right,' I said resignedly.

'Wait for me, I need the bathroom.'

There was the sound of urination. I opened the bathroom door and caught a glimpse of his upright back. My hand found the key, and extracted it from the lock. I slammed the door, inserted the key, turned it. The lock slid into place.

'Hey!'

But already I was vaulting the low garden wall. The sound of hammering became a thudding and then I was out of earshot altogether. The fawn dust was springy beneath my boots and the morning air cool in my nostrils. Only the birds fluttered and sang in the dispersing darkness. The shadows of the night began to dissipate. I made my way to a small hill beside the village, where I was able to watch the dawn break from a high vantage point. A spearhead of swifts flurried overhead and circled back again in ecstatic avian celebration. A hornbill glared at me balefully through fringed yellow eyes. Up came the sun, ready to scorch the slumbering huts; magnificently, relentlessly African. I wormed my way into the lee of a pile of stones and pillowed my jersey under my head. I drifted back to sleep.

It was much later when I awoke. I was conscious of being hot and hungry. The sun had climbed half-way to its zenith, a mighty Vulcan with absolute dominion. I trudged down the far side of the hill and came upon the royal graveyard itself, where Seretse Khama is buried. The grave is set apart, with a large plaque and a cordon around it.

'Seretse Khama is buried here,' said a voice behind me. It was a young policeman in a blue uniform. I wondered if he minded my being there.

'Would you like to see the grave?'

'Yes, please.'

He released the cordon. Below the gravestone were baskets of fresh flowers and artificial flowers in glass containers. The grave site commanded a view of the village and the *kgotla* site, where men met to discuss village affairs and policy.

'A very great leader,' said the smart young policeman with pride.

I assented. He offered to show me a closer view of the *kgotla*, where women were not permitted. I assented again. The *kgotla* consisted of several wide tree trunks laid horizontally along the ground with a square of earth in the middle. I would have liked to see a session convened. On the policeman's advice, I went to look at the Serowe museum and the early photographs of the Khamas, taken during the time of their trials with the British Empire. I found it difficult to believe that Britain, who would not buy our apples, could have been so Machiavellian within this century.

It was nearing noon by the time I returned. Needing to use the bathroom, I found it was locked. A dim memory of the dawn altercation arose. Oh, *shit*. I turned the key gingerly.

Cyril was slumped against the side of the bath, staring morosely at the wall. He turned his head to the hovering form of his captor, shot up and slapped my face. I slapped him back. An exchange of poisonous stares. He flung himself through the doorway and left the house.

'How dramatic,' I thought without contrition. 'A string of pearls and he might have been Scarlett O'Hara.'

The White Bamangwato

Bacon and eggs were spitting in the concave bowl of a gas *skottelbraai*. Peter, the Belgian, was stirring the contents, humming some Northern European ditty to himself. Anna, his plump, pretty wife, buttered a mound of bread slabs on a plate resting on the collapsible kitchen table in the shade of a sausage tree, with its enormous suspended sausages of dense vegetable matter.

The children lay on their stomachs on the ground with a game guidebook, trying to name the buck that we had seen in the sunrise. They were astonishingly wholesome, these children, with their predilection for game watching and their helpfulness. In their clear accented little voices they had told me about the village school and their recorder lessons and their soccer games on the dusty pitch. The little boy was very acute – he would perch on the bonnet tyre of the Land Rover and cry:

'Look, Papa, it's zebras, beyond the trees there.'

Peering through the binoculars we would eventually trace the black and white distinctions and the browsing animals would separate from the matrix of their habitat.

Cyril re-emerged from the reed bank where he had gone to relieve himself. I averted my eyes as he looked up. We had not spoken since the incarceration episode, except for a brief argument about money. Gareth had arranged for us to go on safari to the Moremi with Peter and his family, who were employed by the Anglo factory, and he paid my park entrance fees. He was unfailingly generous. Cyril had assumed that since we were as one, I would split it with him. I refused.

Cyril was hurt. If I did not give him the money, he was not going to pay to stay in a game reserve. Why should he pay for what was natural? He would go into nature and animals would come to him.

Good luck, I said. St Francis did it and so can you.

He changed his mind and sulked.

'If you're really serious about living a life of anti-materialism, you should embrace the opportunity to experience poverty,' I suggested.

The sulking did not abate.

'Unless you're going to be a mendicant,' I added as a joke.

But he didn't laugh. He didn't know what a mendicant was.

For two days we had exchanged only one sentence, or several variations on one sentence. The sentence was:

'Give me the binoculars.'

I had a pair of binoculars and he hadn't. They had become the cipher of all the tension and acrimony between us.

'Binoculars!' Cyril would bark.

'Do you think I could have my binoculars back, if you've finished with them?' I requested with all the vicious mannerliness of my impeccable upbringing.

I could make no sense of myself, of my inner world. I had never been bellicose; even when I was angry, I would back down or concede the other person's point of view. But now it seemed that every fibre of my body was a storehouse for a limitless fury. I could not alleviate that stark, constant anger. Was it that Cyril was so very odd? But he had been just as odd when I first met him, and I had managed to coexist peacefully with him.

Beyond the anger there was guilt. I reasoned to myself that I was feeling no sorrow. There was no weeping; I eradicated the memory of my brother the moment it crossed my mind. How could I be so preoccupied with such minor annoyances at such a time? How could I be so selfish? How could I be so insane?

'I am in a position of torment and conflict,' I wrote with self-aggrandising mournfulness in my diary, in the branches of the desert acacia where I had crawled for solitude.

The Moremi in the winter was particularly magnificent. It was not the rainy season and the thirsty animals congregated around the water holes, impervious to their human spectators. The species abided with one another uneasily, the numerous impala and the tsessebe, the deft waterbuck and the lordly kudu. In the muddy flats lay the crocodiles in whose savage maw they could so easily be interred. There were ugly marabous with their raw-wound throats, and comic pelicans who are rendered so spectacular in flight. The flag-pole tails of officious little warthogs retreated from the invasion of our Land Rover. Hippos oozed their vulnerable rumps under the mud to ward off the sun. I saw a lion kill – something I had never seen before and had always wanted to, the cubs playing inside the gaping cavity of the giraffe's stomach and the adults tearing powerfully at the ribbons of flesh. A noisome cub, drenched in blood, came gambolling under the paws of a feeding male, and was propelled several yards with a backhanded swat.

I still could not sleep in the evenings. Lying on my back in the Kestrel tent, staring up at its apex, I became aware of a soft padding. Something was circling us. I followed its progress: clockwise, change direction, anti-clockwise, the almost noiseless shuffle of paws in the dust. An inquisitive nose thrust into the side of the tent and was rebuffed by the ungiving canvas. It circled again and again. There was a sound of heavy nasal breathing – a *schnaff-schnaff-schnaff.*

It must be a hyena, I thought. I opened the flynet to shout at it to scare it away. Hyenas are cowardly; they scavenge on the purloined remains of other carnivores' kills, hardly ever killing for themselves. I had heard that a hyena had recently bitten off the face of an African who had fallen asleep with meat smears on his cheeks. They were odd beasts, massive shoulders, sloping backs, a strangely disturbing cry. As my head emerged, the hyena came loping abruptly around the front flap in his circuit of investigation. We both recoiled in fright.

'Aaaaah! Fuck it! Fuck off!'

He released a putrid blast of breath and retreated into the darkness. The ghastly vapour flooded full into my face and churned up my stomach. I stumbled outside and was promptly sick against the sausage tree.

The following day, by coincidence, we met some rather idiosyncratic people. We had gone to the river to wash; there was a clear sandbank where the water was lucid and you could see for some distance. One would wash and the other would scout for crocodiles. I was feeling a little more cheerful; it was late afternoon and the cool wind was evaporating the dampness from my body. Rounding a corner, we encountered a siege. A family of baboons had lighted on a large green family tent and were romping joyfully on top of it. They had managed to open the flap and had extricated an incredible medley of belongings. Cutlery, clothes, rope and food were strewn the length and breadth of the campsite. A hoary old male was treating the tent roof like a trampoline, whumping up and down on the springy canvas with huge energy. His harem were diverting themselves with the merchandise, much of which had already been borne up to the treetops. Vervet monkey spectators gibbered in a frenzy of excitement.

'These poor people! Chase them off!' I seized a saucepan and clattered a spoon back and forth on it.

The smaller baboons were alarmed by the noise and withdrew to the trees, with wild squeals of disapproval. But the male had no intention of abandoning his new-found sport. He made a feinting lunge forward and the front pole popped outward. The whole structure collapsed. For a while the tent appeared to be fighting with itself and then the baboon emerged, much chastened, and scrambled to a low bough from whence he continued to snuffle at us and scratch meditatively at his pink bottom.

'*Voetsek!*' I admonished him, in the South African idiom which means be off with you.

He gave me a red-eyed leer and sat tight.

We collected everything into a pile and sat back against a sausage tree to wait. It seemed a bit dim to leave the place unattended. The baboons' demeanour made it clear that they regarded our intervention as half-time.

Within the hour an antiquated green Bedford truck of vast proportions came rattling down the sandy track. It slid to a halt in the dust. A Goliath of a man descended from the cabin and regarded us with blank, blue eyes. At his heels was a dapper character of more likely stature who was evidently the master of the twain. Nevertheless the situation had him stumped. He stood perplexed, scratching through his blond moustache. The bemused arcs of his eyebrows soared away into a hairless pink pate, as he surveyed the disarray. He did not seem to find the presence of Cyril and me remarkable. He had the air of a man searching for an elusive explanation.

'What the fuck!'

'Baboons, *Meneer*,' I proffered, rising graciously from the foot of the sausage tree. I explained that we had chased them away. A self-satisfied chuckle from the grotesque simian on the branch confirmed the veracity of my brief narrative.

'*Skelm!*' The man aimed a stone which stung the baboon on its hairy haunch. The whole troop swarmed noisily into the bush.

The Goliath made a wet sound in the back of his throat and shifted from foot to foot. A string of spittle was sluicing its way into the tangle of his beard. He seemed to be not right in the head.

'Good afternoon, *Meneer*,' I said to the vast pectorals, which were on a level with my eyes.

'This is my brother Fanus,' said the other. 'And I am Marius. Marius Vosloo from Serowe.'

I returned the polite introduction but Marius, or his flourishing moustache, was rootling after a deeper truth. His eyes rested on Cyril. He took the measure. Cyril tittered. The rather shrewd azure gaze swung back to me.

'*Soutpiel?*' he enquired, with a jerk of his shining head at Cyril.

Soutpiel is also a South African idiom, but one that requires a more delicate explanation. *Piel* is slang for a penis. *Sout* is salt. The *Soutpiel* is also known as the *Engelsman*, or English-speaking South African. We have not given ourselves entirely to Africa as the Afrikaner has; we still yearn after England and English custom and tradition. Therefore we have one foot in England and one foot in Africa. The penis hangs in the Atlantic Ocean. It was my favourite Afrikaans sobriquet, so coarse and yet so subtle.

The Bedford had discharged the remainder of its contents. There was a lady of indeterminate age and a teenage boy and a small boy.

'Nessie!' said Marius. 'Clean it up here, man. Look at the messing of those buggering baboons. Everything alluvver the place.'

Nessie shuffled forward obediently, in a supermarket dress and flat sandals, and began to gather the effects. The two boys were ordered to resurrect the tent. The teenage boy was dour and the small boy was chirpy. The tent was a heavy military affair and much exertion and sawing back and forth of the ropes was needed. I helped Nessie to restore all their possessions to the false bottom of the Bedford, where they would be less prone to attack. Cyril and the men had gone away to locate Peter and Anna, whom it transpired they knew from Serowe.

Soon things were shipshape. Nessie and I squatted in the shadow of the sausage tree. She lit a cigarette. I noticed that her teeth were either blackened or missing.

'*Jislaaik!*' she exclaimed, offering me a smoke. 'Those baboons. Allus messing, allus getting in everything.'

'Always doing that,' I agreed, lighting up and inhaling. The smoke gave me a dizzy headrush. I lay on my back and looked at the cylindrical sausages and the great blue sky. I liked Nessie. I liked her black teeth and her bunions and her sagging bosom which shifted beneath the supermarket dress. I liked lying on my back beneath the sausage tree, with a Peter Stuyvesant cigarette, not moving and not thinking, watching the drifting clouds. I felt tranquil, suddenly.

'Funny animals, the baboons,' I said dreamily.

*

Supper was a raucous affair. As dusk fell upon our sequestered camp, as the shadows lengthened and the rustlings of unseen life began to echo amongst the spellbound fronds of grass, all non-human things became poised and timeless. Those that were nocturnal began to lift their noses to the coming night and those that were not to shroud themselves against it, girded within their own breathing skins. What were we, demanded the encroaching night, as we laid out the trestle tables and blew the fire up into a living conflagration. We might have answered that we were partly beast and partly some other anthropocentric thing, that must have diversions. Because now a jarring differential whine pre-empted the arrival of the green Bedford truck. Peter and Anna had invited our new friends from the baboon camp to *braai* with us.

Marius had a great big coolbag in a kitchen curtain pattern, with a dismembered springbok inside. Great bloody slabs of meat, with the blood streaking down the outside. It could not be contained. They had also brought *sosatie*, which is skewered meat cubes, perhaps with onion, and chops, and *boerewors*, the spicy sausage. Yes, we were going to have a *lekker braaivleis*, a lovely barbecue; it was detectable in the quivering facial hair of the men.

Whooeee, whooeee, bayed the close hyenas who didn't dare approach, but for whom the extravagant smells of the cooking meat was torture. My own stomach was tightly closed in on first principles, as I washed the grit from our little bag of lentils.

Colours were violently abandoning their former positions. Everything that had been brown in the day – the grass, the trees, our own burnt bodies – now became scarlet under the falling sun, and the bloody meat which had been so red, was browned in its minute reflection. But for us the fire was colossal – it blazed and crackled and threw out a circle of light which drew us in.

The fire mellowed Marius and made him affable. He told a number of funny stories, sitting on his bottom in the dust, ballasted by his two stout legs with bush socks to the knee and velskoen on his feet. His fingers encircled successive cans of Castle beer.

'How long have you lived here, Marius?' I asked.

'Since for ever! Man, we're White Bamangwato now.'

It was axiomatic, he could have sprouted out of the dust itself, like the sausage tree over our heads. I had heard that the Afrikaner had trekked this far, and now I was conversing with a descendant. If I was fascinated by Marius, Fanie was enthralled by me; the lights of love were in his eyes. He was very moved by our pot of lentils, which finally stewed themselves into an edible pulp. Here was Fanus, easing his powerful body on to the sandy puddle at my side with an offering of a venison steak in his hands, the blood running between his broad fingers.

'Jukebox is talking!' said Marius hilariously.

I scrambled away from good intentions and took up with smoking Nessie, whose ten wriggling toes were turned towards the fire.

'Are you always in Serowe?'

'Oh no! Sometimes I go to Pietersburg to the co-op.'

She said it as one might say 'Sometimes I go to Florence to

the Uffizi Palace'. Pietersburg is a rural Transvaal town with suburban housing developments and some chain stores and some fast food outlets. A co-op is a co-operative, where farmers go to buy grain and fertiliser. There seemed little to recommend either. Still, I supposed it was abroad, in a manner of speaking.

'Who do you go with?'

'With my brothers.' She indicated with the tip of her cigarette the raconteur Marius and the gigantic Fanus, who had once again stolen to my ungiving side, where he seemed happy to recline, as a Hindu bhakt might at the foot of a malevolent shiva lingam.

This was a thing! If these were unanimously brothers, who then was the co-parent of the youths? Surely it was not possible, even in this remote place, that . . . I looked uneasily at the prostrate Fanus.

'Where is the father of your boys?' I asked, too bluntly in the face of these conjectures.

'I got them in Pietersburg,' announced Nessie obscurely. She smiled at me comfortably, at peace with the haphazard contents of her mouth.

I began to understand her reverential attitude towards that town. I observed that they did not look much alike.

'No, well, I got them off two men. That man' (pointing at the small boy) 'was very nice. And that man' (fag-end moving to the dour youth who now stared with morose absorption into the fire's heart), 'I didn't like him as much.'

The convivial Marius had overheard our womanly confidences.

'Nessie,' he elucidated affectionately, 'got herself in jukebox trouble.'

Where I came from, illegitimacy was a scandal of insurmountable proportions. Here in the bush, I reflected, begetting seemed the sole prerogative of women. Of those who worked in my brother's factory, very few were married and most had children. I wondered if this forsaking of marriage relations had crossed the colour bar.

The night grew blacker, the men drunker and louder, their bellies distended by meat and beer and good cheer. The women became surreptitiously employed; poking the steaks away from the embers, gathering the paper plates, submerging the greasy cutlery in buckets of cold water. The children dropped asleep in the dirt, with open, snoring mouths. It was very late. Even the slavering hyenas had ceased their crying. A distant lion grunted – somewhere on the level savannah that magnificent creature was signalling. Some of the nearest hanging sausages were smoked on their undersides.

'Yes,' said Marius with final jollity, shaking the sloth from his plump form. 'If a sausage falls on a man's head, he'll still be all right. But man, if a sausage falls on his jukebox . . . !'

Ah, it was clear. I understood what a jukebox was.

*

Peter and his family had to return to Serowe, it was the close of the weekend. The White Bamangwato, who lived from their land, had no such compunctions. They were moving to a fresh camp, on the far side of the Moremi and said we might go too. I was glad, I wanted to stay in the bush and so did Cyril. I had worked out by now that these White Bamangwato spent their days roaming between their cattle lands in Serowe and this wild land – perpetual pioneers, framed and explicated by the dry veld they encompassed with their confident, sun-strained eyes.

I woke early and eased out of the tent. I had found a copse of mopanes nearby and I could sit amongst them and write up my diary. This morning I didn't write, because a martial eagle had alighted on one of the top branches and I was entranced by its fierce immobility. I looked up at the snowy chest with the distinctive spots. At intervals it snapped its brown head commandingly in another direction.

After breakfast I said goodbye to Peter and Anna and their

children and gave them the French and English dictionaries and the Joan Didion to deliver into Gareth's safekeeping. Joan Didion's abstractions about Nixon's America were too remote from this wild place. Closer to the bone was the narrative my mother had given me – *I Dreamed of Africa* by the Kenyan conservationist, Kuki Gallman. It was an autobiographical book about the loss of her son and husband. As for the dictionaries, they were an unnecessary weight; the English was a whimsy, and I would cope without the French once we were in French-speaking territory.

We boarded the green Bedford truck and set out across the tracks until we reached the new camp, passing a lonely and very geriatric male lion en route. He had paused in the shadows of a camelthorn tree, facing away from us, gathered on the points of his mangy buttocks. He sadly surveyed the limitless veld of which he had once been lord. One sensed that even routing an impala was a taxing feat these days. The Bedford pulled up short and threw its superannuated gearbox into reverse. We shuddered back a few yards for a better gape. This whiskery and senescent feline Methuselah inched round on his arthritic forequarters, blinked in bald disgust, and resumed his reverie. The flick of his white-tipped tail made it clear: you might be a huge, green, noisy, overstuffed Bedford truck, but you're nothing to me.

The new camp was more central and populous than the previous one, with an ablution block and communal sinks for washing dishes. The inmates were returning from dawn game drives in their four by fours. The camp was punctuated by purposeful would-be breakfasters whipping up their powdered milk formulas for immersion in the scrambled egg mix. You might hear that someone had seen a serval cat; someone else claimed to have come upon a leopard, in the gloom, just before the dawn broke.

'*Kak*, man,' said a detractor.

'No, seriously, I did. As I said, just before dawn.'

Now a leopard is a magnificent creature of tawny yellow,

buff on his underparts, and his back and shoulders are a mosaic of black rosettes. But he detests the sight and sound of man, and it's very rare to come across one; I have never seen a leopard in the wild. So, you see, it might take the wind out of your sails that you had only seen a serval cat when your neighbour had seen a leopard.

'Maybe yours was also a serval cat,' challenged the detractor. 'A small leopard can look very much like a serval cat, particularly in the dark.'

'It was a leopard! I can tell a blerry serval cat, man. A serval cat has spotty lines from its ears to its arse. This was a spotty arse, no lines. Dinkum blerry leopard, no two ways about it.'

In itself, it is a grand thing to have seen a serval cat, which is also a timid creature and sleeps all day in an aardvark hole. But the serval cat proponent was humiliated, and fried up his *boerewors* with a bad grace and was fierce to his wife when she came from the ablutions with her head wound up inside a towel.

'What side of the bed were you born in?' she enquired, fluffing an old idiom in her indignant surprise.

We set up camp again, and erected our tents with a low level of warfare between Cyril and myself, because this was one of the numerous things we fought about. Cyril insisted that tents and fires were a man's task. I felt the indignity deeply, because I had grown up in a family where camping and the outdoors was a way of life, and Cyril was a fresh recruit from the urban entrails of Johannesburg. His sole exposure to the natural environment had been an annual teenage visit to the umbrella-infested beaches of Clifton in Cape Town, where he had stayed in the high-rise holiday apartment of a former girlfriend whose stepfather was a television comedy personality.

'Let him play his damn games – it's so nugatory,' I would urge myself, but then he would taunt and I would rise to the bait.

We were making preparations for another game drive. Nessie declined, she was tired, she would like to *uitspan*, to relax.

Drifting smoke, she sat down on the root of a marula tree. It was an attitude I recognised from my own mother – a vaguely requesting defiance in the face of an imperative male world. Nessie was indulged, because the Leopard Man had come to pay his respects.

He was a Boer, this Leopard Man, and very polished with smooth black hair. His safari suit was pukka, there were no sweat rings below the armpits, nor did the tips of his velskoen speak to the outside world, as Fanie's had begun to. Away from the bush, he might have been a sales representative for a pharmaceuticals firm. He and Marius got along famously. They plonked their khaki bottoms on the vacant marula roots and stripped the tabs from cans of beer and swapped jokes.

There was no dearth of beer. The false bottom of the Bedford was awash with the stuff, we hoisted it to the upper levels for easy access. Then bumpity-bump, across the scorching veld; a series of stalling jerks and smelly deluges of petrol – someone had installed the unsmiling teenage boy in the driver's seat with his small brother as co-pilot. In the back there were the *rooinek* hitchhikers (Cyril and myself) and Fanus and Marius and the smooth-talking, black-haired Leopard Spotter, whose name was Van Rijneveld. Van Rijneveld had acquired a wide-brimmed hat against the sun, with a gaudy little hatband. Everyone embarked on the serious business of getting thoroughly legless under the mid-morning sun.

'Fanie, Fanie, chuck us a Castle! Have another one, man, wozzamatter, you a Tem'prance? Nyuk nyuk nyuk nyuk. Hey, Van Rijneveld, catch, there's it – hell, he's firewarm.'

'Thanks, *jong*.'

'Don't mention it. Where's that *Engelse* chick with the *lekker* blonde hair. Did you dye it like that – natural? But shame – you should let it loose, not all tied up like so. Nessie dyed her hair like that once – she looked bladdy funny, let me tell you. Hey – whoa! – *jong*! Not over the bladdy *middelmannetjie* – bladdy watch out. Take the bladdy axle out. Hey, Sarah, have a Castle, man, wozzamatter with you, you look like someone died. Smile – life is short, then you die, *nè*, Van Rijneveld?'

'It's the truth. Marius! Tell the boy to go that way – over the bridge. There were lion this morning.'

'Hey, *jong*. Whoa! *Vok*! Make a left! *Yissus* – I need a whizz now!'

An arc of urine streamed into the sky; fell, fell away through the pure air, spattered in a cascade of droplets across the hard earth.

We drove through herds of impala with striped bottoms, through zebras, giraffes browsing regally on the treetops; kudu bulls turned their heads towards us and their great antlers made a Gothic V against the impossibly blue sky; we saw hartebeest with their sloping backs, and the grey gemsbok, and buffalo, the symbiotic oxpeckers buffeting at their hides with neat beaks. Once I thought I saw the coppery pelt of a bushbuck slipping away amongst a grove of trees. Wildebeest looked down their noses at us, as only wildebeest can. And well they might – because our teenage driver was appalling. When there was mud he slithered in it, when there was a *middelmannetjie* he bounced on it, and when there was no impediment at all he proceeded with great velocity.

We came to a lioness, dozing in the shade of an acacia tree.

No scabby old-timer this one. Her muscles were a symphony of flesh and sinew, her golden coat was on fire, feral self-possession exuded from the black points of her tail to her fluffy white chin hairs. Her muzzle was square, her back linear, her sleek ears flattened back against the apex of her neck. She lay along her forepaws, motionless but not dormant, the exhaling breath fluttering her pale whiskers. The lion is my totem – for those who doubt the existence of God, nothing could rebuff as much as her animal divinity, anchored in the dun dust in the slim shade of an acacia; there could be nothing as exquisite, as deitific, as unimpeachable as a fully grown lioness in repose.

'Wozzamatter! Having a zizz, Miss Lion! Hey, get up, we

wanna have a look! Move the truck closer, *jong*!'

Oh God! Mentally, I closed my eyes.

'Hey, Van Rijneveld – look, a *lekker leeuwyfie*.'

We bore down on her, matting the golden pelt with our raised dust. She took us in through intent yellow eyes, not friendly, not baleful exactly, as if she was trying to extricate the meaning of us, and finding a contradictory set of statistics.

'Geddup, we wanna have a look at your belly. Rev the engine, *jong*.'

The senile inner workings of the truck blared up protestingly. Everyone was intoxicated and pissing. Van Rijneveld was pissing, Cyril was pissing, Marius had never stopped pissing. Even the teenage boy who had been quaffing on the sly, abandoned the accelerator and relieved himself through the window aperture. A miasma of uric liquid hissed from the steaming earth.

The lioness did not move an inch. But her poise had altered radically. Before, she had been at ease, a mantle of peace had rested over her tawny body. Now she seemed frozen but alert, as if her long body was a compilation of tiny springs.

'Marius,' I couldn't help saying. 'We're getting her cheesed off and we're in the back of an open truck!'

'Silly girl! She's only a bladdy *leeu* – she doesn't know that we're not inside. They never go for trucks.'

'Never go for trucks!' echoed Cyril raucously, but I saw he had retreated to the far side of the White Bamangwato.

'It's all right for you,' I said nastily. 'You're immortal.' (One of the Ramtha tenets and possibly the maddest.)

We exchanged a Look.

The lioness slowly flicked the black tip of her tail.

'Wanna see your belleeee!' pleaded the ingenuous Fanie, who was now very much the worse for wear. He dropped his can on to the score that already littered the back of the Bedford.

The lioness closed her yellow eyes, opened them, bunched her taut body and . . .

'Move it, *jong*!' bawled Van Rijneveld with great presence of mind, and we streaked off over the veld, flung together like so many skittles in a froth of dented beer cans, banging against the sides in a collective panic, my handcrafted hair bobbles pattering furiously against the sides of my face, my mouth dry, my heart pounding in a drumbeat of adrenalin and terror.

The bush was casting its geriatrics into our path, the faded lords of yesteryear. Now it was an old bull elephant of massive stature with yellowing tusks. He turned impassive eyes towards our truck. Age cannot wither me, nor custom stale my infinite variety. His creased trunk continued to probe the stark mysteries of the veld.

'One helluva jukebox,' observed Marius, slapping Van Rijneveld on the back. Van Rijneveld was in his cups. The lioness escape had knocked his wide-brimmed hat to a rakish angle and the sun leaked in and pinked his nose, or maybe it was the beer.

I had other preoccupations. For some time now, I had been battling a mounting urge for release. It had been two beers and four hours since we left base camp; my abdomen was a taut and unwilling gourd. Crouched over the painful swelling, I had jealously watched the insouciance of the men and their careless fountaining from the sides of the truck. They were such *masculine* men, I did not want to ask them to stop, they would jeer. But now things were accelerating to a stage where prompt action was called for.

'I really need to go to the toilet,' I whispered to Cyril, in desperate euphemism.

'So go,' he said predictably.

Our wanderings had become aimless, but we found purpose at the hippo pool. The hippos were partially submerged, one or two were wallowing in the shallowest water with their backs exposed, yawning with their great jaws. The White Bamangwato descended from the truck and staggered to within a few metres, where they gathered an arsenal of mud clods. It was a clear case of fools rushing in where angels fear to tread, if Cyril and the more timorous Van Rijneveld and myself could be called angels. Hippos look docile, but they can be quick and savage. They can break a person in half with one snap of their formidable jaws, and are responsible for more human deaths every year than any other wild animal in Africa.

Thwack, went the first mud clod. The hippo didn't seem to notice. Fanie released another clod, executing a half-circle on one leg like a professional shotputter. *Schplut!*

I had my legs jammed together, the pressure in my abdomen was searing, my eyes rolled like marbles in my head. The truck was stationary, the men were diverted. I licked my finger and held it in the air. I was upwind of the hippos. I would take my chances with whatever else was out there. In the distance I could see a tree, I climbed down from the truck and ran across the land, boots thudding on the dry grass, until I reached the tree. All the while I kept an uneasy watch on the scrub at my back.

The game of stone-the-hippos was over by the time I regained the truck. The hippos had refused to be riled and had gone sliding back into the muddy pool. Only their ears, eyes and nostrils remained visible above the surface of the water. Marius became paternal.

'Just like a woman!' he scolded, shaking his shining head with its sparse wings of growth. 'Running around in the bush. It's not a picnic park out there, you know.'

'Not a picnic park,' echoed Cyril.

'Sod off, you berk,' I said to him, under my breath.

Back at camp, more game enthusiasts had arrived. It was a terrain of tents in a rainbow of colours: red, blue, green, fawn, tan, purple-and-silver, and the military monstrosity of the White Bamangwato. Well-heeled game vehicles came and went; white Land Rovers outfitted with extra water carriers and petrol tanks, and the trendy and outrageously expensive Toyota landcruisers which the expatriates could afford. In the middle of the camp stood our own green carbuncle. The vervet monkeys scampered around its gargantuan tyres.

Nessie had gotten up a repast of bully beef and beans; Cyril and I made tomato sandwiches. Fanus came a-courting, his fingers besmirched with bully, and wanted to hold my hand.

'Marius!' I complained.

'Leave that girl, man,' admonished the big brother.

*

The following day the White Bamangwato returned to the family seat in Serowe. Nessie and her children had been offered a ride in the relative comfort of a Land Rover and accepted, so Marius and Van Rijneveld, who had become a fixture, were in the cabin and Cyril and Fanus and I were in the back.

Fanus was in his perpetual good spirits. He did not seem to mind being deposed by the self-promulgating Leopard Man. Some mattresses had been extricated from the false bottom to cushion our journey and protect our bottoms. In the event, my bottom barely grazed the mattress. We were all quite consistently airborne as Marius whizzed over the numerous ruts and gouges that marred the Moremi access track. The trick was trying not to concuss oneself on the iron bar which traversed the back of the truck. Fanus did it once or twice, but seemed not to notice.

We drove into Maun, the small town on the edge of the Okavango swamps and the next leg of our journey, passing square mud huts and scrawny donkeys tethered to posts. Cattle, the scourge of Botswana landcover, nibbled fruitlessly on the stripped sands. This was the end of our time with the White Bamangwato, who would travel onward to Serowe. We thanked them and I watched the Bedford pull off regretfully. I would have liked to stay on with them a while, secure in the certitude of their good humour, both appalled and delighted by the exuberant dissimilarity of their universe to mine. But now there was only Cyril and me, so I hoisted up my pack and started to trudge.

Lay Down the Law, Mate

Once more we were on a tar road, shielded by our broad-brimmed scout hats. These were now encircled by hatbands made from Indian scarves that we had dredged up out of our turquoise backpacks. Cyril's was pink and mine was lilac with silver embroidery. We had been inspired by the fashion sense of Van Rijneveld.

We had come from the north. To the south lay Maun, to the west huts and scrub, and the bush beyond that. To the east, there was a broad river and a river bridge. Flanking the river, on our side, we could see the signs of settlement – the roof of a European-style house.

'We'd better find the campsite,' I said. 'Let's see if we can find someone to tell us where to go.'

A large property opened up on to the road. I slipped the catch on the farm gate and we wandered inside. There were a number of jeeps and game vehicles of the kind used for conveying tourists, covered on four sides by canvas that can be rolled up and lashed to overhead iron railings. Some of them had their bonnets open. Assorted spare parts lay on the ground, suggesting that someone had lately been at work. Beyond were some outbuildings and the back entrance to the house. To the left there was a sturdy canvas tent home of the kind that conservationists live in whilst conducting their field research. As I was absorbing all these minutiae, a red-headed girl emerged from the far side of the tent home. I asked her for directions and she invited us to have a cup of tea with her.

Sitting on her front porch, drinking mugs of sweet rooibos tea, she told us the story of her life. She was arrestingly, but not commonly beautiful, blue-eyed with a tumbling mass of titian hair. Her name was Katie, and she was second generation South African. Her people had come from Ireland, now she had moved up here; she needed the bush, she couldn't bear to live in cities, they clogged her. Her pale hands traced out the story on the teak table-top. Maun was so small, sometimes it was constricting, but at other times you felt such peace. It would be difficult to leave. She was a schoolteacher, she had been offered the work whilst at university, two years ago now, the children were sweet, they belonged to the local tour operators and merchants, the school was about half white, half African.

Katie's house was the kind of place I had always dreamed of living in. It had a life that was intertwined with the life of the bush. The walls were plastered mud, painted with a whitewash and supported with wooden trunks. The thatched roof left a space between the walls and itself; there was no ceiling so the breezes travelled through the interior. It was simple and clean. As decoration she had colourful woollen mats and African masks and trays on the wall. The chairs and benches were woven from rushes and some soft wood, perhaps marula. Kerosene lamps stood on the tables and window sills, in readiness for the nightfall. The porch opened up on to a spectacular view of the river which wound past, confined within its wide sandy banks. I could see a pump which must carry water into the house.

'Do you swim at all?'

'Not here. There's a crocodile. Last month it carried off an African child who was playing there.'

We must go, I said at last. We had to find somewhere to stay, and also we needed to see if someone would take us into the swamps the next day for the amount that we could afford. Katie protested no, we could stay in the tent home. It was her boyfriend's. He was a tour operator and he had lived there before he met her. Now he barely used it; besides he was away on safari. And she had a friend who ran the cheapest swamp company in the business. She would drive us in, she had to go to Maun Fresh Produce anyway.

I was touched by her candour, and her friendliness and her generosity; this strangely beautiful girl who was not much older than I and lived in a bush house on the river.

The name of the friend was Bert, we found him at the nursery gardens near Maun Fresh Produce. Bert had a ram-shackle bakkie. He took us on a caper through the countryside, through trees and tracks and straying cattle until we suddenly arrived at a suburban villa in the middle of absolutely nowhere. There was a house with electricity and a tiled roof and a green lawn – *green* – with hydrangeas. The house belonged to his mate and business partner, Dan, who should have been there but wasn't. A small boy came bounding out and cried, Shoot you dead – pointing a wooden gun at me – and then fell in a heap himself. A second small boy leapt on top of him and there was a scuffle, which was terminated by the arrival of a large black nanny who gathered them both up into her vast bosom. It was all so *normal*. I sat down cross-legged in the grass and plunged my hands amongst the spongy fronds for security.

'Tea please, Celia,' said Bert to the portly nanny.

After tea, we wandered over to the garage, where the absent Dan was cultivating a tank of goldfish, and Bert propounded the advantages of his tour company. A marvellous thing to do, confided Bert, was to set your alarm clock for four a.m., wake up, swallow a cap of acid, and then go back to sleep. When the sun stirred you and you came to, you were *absolutely raging*. Nothing like the swamps on acid, we inferred.

All this while he had been dragging on a sizeable joint; now he held it out. We demurred. During the Purple Bubble time there had been a lot of dope around, it was one of the spiritual requirements, but things were different now. Cyril had also smoked, but had quit following a divine instruction from Ramtha. There was a mild competition between us as to who had smoked more during their dopey days. Bert didn't mind our refusal; he continued to inhale and reminisce about his past.

'The most incredible thing I ever did,' shared Bert, 'was flying over the Makgadikgadi pans in a hot air balloon, *whacked* on acid. It was phenomenal.'

We watched him stub out his joint with an air of great panache on the goldfish tank.

*

I was suffocating. On all sides were the limitless swamps. Rushes conceded waterways, waterways disclosed islands, islands gave way to more islands and more waterways, meandering in upon themselves in a snaking infinity. The night itself was vast and black and open. The wandering clouds had thinned and now I could distinguish a pale quarter moon throwing her remote, cold light on the billion leagues between us.

But I suffocated. Devilish harpies had risen inside me, to gnaw at my defences, to break me, to wither my strength. The past weeks were surfacing, were storming my barriers. I would have liked to panic and throw myself into someone's arms. I threw myself into my own arms, and wrapped up my rocking body; fingertips gouging at taut shoulder flesh, biting at the soft inside of my elbow.

Go away, go away, everything, let me be still.

I was not alone. Here were the two men, sleeping on their backs, on mattresses, with their sleeping bags secured under their chins against the night, which was bitter. Cyril had made a friend, an Antipodean air force man, and they had been wagging chins. I found it disagreeable and withdrew.

'Yer sheila giving yer grief?' the air force man had asked, in dulcet tones.

Cyril giggled.

'Yer give 'em a holiday,' extemporised the pilot, 'and yer don't get any thanks. They'd rather be back in their kitchen, won't they, mate? Bloody sheilas.'

'Bloody sheilas,' agreed Cyril.

They swaggered off to the river together to take a bath, laying bare in their collusive mutterings the mysteries of sheilas. The pilot was older than Cyril and had had a great many more women. His words of advice came drifting back to me through the mopanes.

'Gotter lay down the law, mate. Right from the word bloody go. If you let her have her head yer dead meat, mate.'

Nevertheless, their own flesh was alive and tingling, as they sluiced their naked bodies on the river bank in the waning sunlight. I dug my toes into the dust; angry, but without avenues for my anger. The morbid depressions, which my fascination with the White Bamangwato had diluted, were going to assail me once more; there were no ramparts in my feeble psychic protestations which could withstand them.

The men returned. They had become something apart from me now; Cyril was pink-cheeked with jollity and the splash of cold water, the pilot was made complaisant by his own offerings. I went to wash, to be away from them.

When I returned the fire was made; once it was smouldering they cooked. Cooking inside is women's work; cooking outside is men's work. Perhaps it is the danger of being burnt that redeems it, I thought, watching the sparks fly. I picked up a pot holder to move my billy. Cyril laid down the law and took it away; waves of approval proliferated from the pilot. After we had eaten the pilot went to sleep, on his side, and succumbed at once, the heavy breath issuing regularly from his military lungs. Cyril was enraptured and snuggled up to the staunch pectorals.

But only a moiety of me was riddled up in pain for the struggles of women against men. I was wrapped up against loss, and the loss had a name and a history, but I did not want to recognise the name and I did not want to relive the history.

I am suffocating from the things that are rising and yawing me from my course.

I took out my diary and wrote about Cyril.

How can I maintain a perfect state of ongoing calm in the face of his provocation, I wrote. *In the end I suppose it is impossible for me to expect him to cease his insults and corrections. It is within my power to simply live with them in the best integrity of my spirit.*

Is it, is it? whispered the mopane trees, in derision of my prim sentiment. Perhaps you will go completely mad first. And a restless dementia had crept into my body; I could not stand to remain here among these callous, breathing men.

I would go wandering through the mopane trees.

The black night became closer, the pale moon shrank; nothing was clearly visible. I felt my way among the trunks. A bleak memory broke the surface, night wandering at boarding school amongst the unconscious bodies in their iron beds, or lying on the washroom floor in the wee hours listening to the water gurgle in the pipes, dreaming of redemption.

I found a hammock and lay there for an hour or two listening to the night sounds – a rapid scuffle in the growth, the hooting of an owl. Then I was rigid with cold, and made my way back. The fire had burned itself out. I took an armful of brushwood a little way off and made a pile of chaff and twigs. They caught easily and soon I had a good blaze. Inside the fire was an endlessly variegated pattern of smouldering lights. I lay on my side and watched them change and die and revive.

The night was in its deepest element. I myself was a remote, unattached, fraught thing, unafraid of the obvious, petrified by the insidious. Only the fire was reliable and had to be fed, and there had to be me to feed it. I warmed a little, and huddled in the flickering light. Now and then I would replenish the brushwood. My eyes felt strained and tired from too many hours of wakefulness, and the frequent invasion of smoke as I blew into the embers. My body was sore. I felt drowsy, not drowsy enough to sleep, but sluggish, staring ceaselessly into the baking depths.

The black night turned an asbestos grey. I put a twig here and there and snapped a branch on my knee. Little cuts and abrasions all over my hands and legs were the legacy of bush life. I put my head between my knees and closed my smarting eyes. My cotton trousers were deeply imbued with the piquant scent of woodfire. The grey dawn became red and magnificent, each mopane a distinct silhouette. Rosy clouds billowed in the sky. Out flew the busy stonechats, and twittered through the bushes on their tiny wings. Birdsong was swelling in the mild morning air. Everything was new and clean; I was ancient and tired. The taste of fire smut was in my mouth.

The air pilot woke up and shook himself. Cyril stirred and blinked sleepily.

'How about some eggs?' offered the Australian. 'I feel like cooking up a storm.'

'Great.'

The pilot freed himself from his sleeping bag and moved towards me with the staggering gait of the freshly awoken. He noticed the severely diminished woodpile and frowned doubtfully, pulling down the sides of his mouth and distorting the shape of his eyes. He rubbed the corner of one eye with a forefinger.

'Where's the wood?'

'I burned it,' I said, standing up and retreating. I was stiff and my eyes were bloodshot. Tiredness crowded in on me, the right kind of tiredness that might numb me into oblivion for a few hours. I crawled into my sleeping bag, and pulled it over my head.

'Yer sheila burned all our wood,' said the pilot disgustedly to Cyril.

'Tell her to fetch some more.'

'Aw, bugger it. Let's go and get some ourselves. Leave her.

We'll have a cook-up on the bank.'

I heard them breaking through the undergrowth, and then silence. And then I fell asleep.

*

A swamp boat is flat-bottomed and made of wood; they call it a mokoro. A man punts a mokoro by standing on the end, and pushing against the shallow floor of the swamp canals with a light wooden pole.

Our man was Killibele. He was tall and silent and severe. I liked him for his silence and severity. He passed it on to us, even Cyril, so that we drifted amongst the islands in a wordless vacuum. His watchful eyes would infer the bush enigma; a red lechwe buck, a drinking giraffe with her forelegs splayed, the shadow of an elephant. He never seemed to speak; his forefinger would follow its own path into the bush and then we would see.

We gave him our paltry things in return; isotonic drink mix, or chocolate, or fruit. He accepted everything unsmilingly; he was never servile.

In the mokoro the bush was unrepulsable, it came crowding in upon my senses. The spiky leaves of the African grasses betrayed the direction of the flow; the undersides of the water lilies carried a slimy gel. Wet ferns snapped back against my face and the blue earbuds of dragonflies hovered on ephemeral wings just above us.

Nosing through the intricate channels, we surprised grey herons who rose up from the water in an ungainly flurry of wings and settled on the far bank, drawing pink necks into an indignant retreat of feathers. Indistinct patterns of moss and algae moved under the dark water; at infrequent intervals a clump of tangled rushes would betray the spine of a baby crocodile. A hippo blocked our path, the bubbles flooded upwards and then a snout appeared and a pair of suspicious eyes. We took another route.

Other mokoros passed, floating tableaux of family groups. I was reminded of the travelling wagons of medieval religious theatre. The man would be punting, the woman arranged in the midst of baskets and blankets, a pair of wide-eyed children would stare unblinking. As we drifted by in our stately procession, the men would grunt, the woman fluttered a hand; at her breast nestled an impossibly tiny head, bright black eyes unfocused on an undiscovered world.

We spent several days in this way, moving every evening to a different island. At night we would cook. Killibele made putu – the African maize meal porridge. We ate bread patties, which I made from flour and water and fried in margarine over the fire. Sometimes I added peri-peri powder to the dough or wrapped it around nuggets of cheese. We were restricted in what we could eat, because Cyril would not have monosodium glutamate or e-numbers. I did not know what these things were, but they seemed to exist in all the usual things that one might eat whilst camping.

Killibele was the fire god, Vulcan. Fire seemed to issue from his careful hands with extraordinary ease. He would gather some chaff or dry grass and make an elaborate little mountain and strike a match. Exhorted by his soft breaths, the fire would spring up, an incandescent eruption. I watched him, and tried to copy, but I hadn't his grace.

We made the fires for cooking, and to keep the elephants at bay. In the dusk they came to the outskirts of the camp and butted their broad foreheads against the tall doum palms, bringing the fruit raining down. They scooped it up with their soft trunks and shovelled it into their hidden mouths. The deposits they left behind were fibrous and earthy, with whole seeds undigested that might still germinate and take root.

One morning, rounding a blind corner, we saw that our canal levelled out into a muddy depression. We began to punt backwards, to find an alternative forward route, when a colossal matriarch broke the forest cover with a nursling at her side. And then another and another – a stream of elephants poured out from the trees and ranged along the fringe of the mud pan. A matriarchal cow and satellite bulls, and smaller cows, some of them with calves. Their rumbling communications were quite clear. They plodded amicably through the mud and sluiced themselves and each other with successive squirts from their trunks. The little ones jostled playfully, waving the tiny shoots of their incipient tusks, backing up in defeat under the bellies of their mothers. Elephant young are extraordinarily like human children; despite their size, their infantile games touched a wellspring of tenderness in me. The whole gamut of childish emotion was so transparently visible on their quizzical faces – challenge, bravery, uncertainty, retreat, a cautious check on the mother's position. I counted twenty-three – the largest herd I had ever seen.

The herd resumed its march across the mud flats, in a beeline for the rush bank where our mokoro lay. Killibele's back stiffened. I reached for my boots which were lying on the rush matting on the bottom of the mokoro and crammed them on to my feet, without socks. The elephants were closer now, swaying in an inexorable line towards the rush bank. I found the bootlace, it was knotted. I tore the knot apart and began to thread it through the eyelets. Now the herd was close enough for the mosaic of dried mudstains on their round foreheads to be clearly visible. The chain of bodies churned up the mud, a spreading ripple touched the mokoro and unsteadied it. My fingers were seizing up with fright, but they managed a clumsy knot in my bootlace.

'Run!' cried the august Killibele.

He and Cyril scrambled out of the mokoro and fled through the golden field behind us. I paused for a few seconds trying to conquer my bootlace. The titanic mass of elephant bodies continued to advance. I gave it up and leapt through the grass, losing a boot en route, dodging behind the trees where Killibele and Cyril had flattened themselves. Individual sounds hung in the air: the muddy squelch-squelch of tramping feet; our quaking gasps for air, feebly suppressed.

The herd nosed at the mokoro with inquisitive trunks, found it to be an insignificant intrusion, and resumed their upriver march, disappearing into the tree cover a few hundred yards beyond our refuge.

We emerged into the open, shaking like leaves. I retrieved my boot. The sole of my foot was torn up and bloody from the grass stubble.

'Elephant can be very dangerous,' advised Killibele, unnecessarily.

At the end of five days we were due back at the base camp. I was looking forward to it. I wanted to return to Maun and have a shower with soap. We floated past a flotilla of mokoros resting on a bank, with a sandy track leading off into the bush.

'I recognise this,' I mentioned to Cyril. 'We're pretty close now. I saw it about a half hour after we passed under the wire.'

Not far from the base camp, Killibele had told us to lie on our backs and we had slid cautiously under a wire barrier. At the time I had thought that perhaps this was one of the reasons why our mokoro safari was significantly cheaper than the competition.

We continued to punt slowly along the waterways, stopping now and then to swim in the deeper channels, keeping an eye out for the crocodiles. Killibele did not swim. Most of the swamp Africans had never learnt. They stayed in their boats. It was midday, we had hours to spare. The sun burned with unmitigated fierceness overhead, and I arranged a kikoi over my shoulders. Presently another row of boats loomed up, another village; it could have been the same village. There was an astonishing unity here in the swamps, everything flooded into everything else, the streaming water, the numerous islands, the drifting, ubiquitous mokoros.

Another hour passed and another, the sun became less

extreme and the wilting grasses rallied. A row of boats, paddles and mounds of damp rushes stored in their bases, a sandy track melting into the distance.

'Would you like to see my village?'

'Yes!' said Cyril.

We hauled the mokoro on to the sandy bank and tethered it with a rush. Killibele strode off along the path. We trailed after him.

'Cyril.'

'Yeah?'

'He's shamming.'

'What?'

'We've passed this exact same village three times. We've made two identical circuits. He wants to delay until tomorrow so that we'll pay the extra day's fee.'

'Really?' Cyril looked thoughtful. The mokoro fee was not as much as the rivals', but it was not negligible either. We had about nine hundred pounds each for the seven months, and no recourse to any more if it ran out.

'Yes, and I'm not going to have it. I'm going to tell him we want to go home once he's had a chance to see his people. We're awfully close.'

A ripple of welcoming enthusiasm ran through the huts when the villagers spotted Killibele. Round-bellied children ran out and squatted in the dust, staring. Women became coquettish and laughed and smoothed their skirts over generous hips. Along came an elder supported on a stick. He put his arm around Killibele and drew him off into some private confabulation.

We were left alone.

The village was made from mud and rushes, the hut roofs were thatched and the village walls were interwoven reeds. Several carved stools made of a dark wood stood about in the centre of the circle of huts. The children watched us curiously, but didn't approach. The floor was uninterrupted sand; there were no rocks in the delta. A wiry dog slid on its stomach through the grit and snuffled.

The elder had finished his business. He spat in the dust and went away. Now Killibele was in a laager of young men. He regaled them with a story and everyone laughed and coughed and shifted on their feet. It was all very serene, but the night winds were building.

'Killibele, it is getting late, we had better get along.'

He surveyed everything; the huts, the reed walls, the other young men in their shabby trousers.

'Ah, but the time is finished,' he said sadly. 'Tonight you must sleep in the village.'

'We don't want to sleep in the village; you must take us back, it's not far.'

The other young men were silent but attentive, they seemed to be on nobody's side in particular. They were just young men from the village, waiting for the sun to set. One of them wore a stylish fedora hat.

'Hippos,' announced Killibele succinctly.

I became annoyed.

'You might have thought of that before you took us wild goose chasing all over the delta. It's too bad now; we must go and you must take us.'

He looked doubtfully at me and the gaggle of men and the distant trees. The fedora hat also considered the issue from all angles and drew up his lip and slid his tongue along the rim of his upper teeth meditatively.

Killibele sighed and set off towards the mokoro. We loped after him along the sandy track and jumped into the mokoro. He poled us away from the edge. A new set of dictates now informed his powerful body. His shoulder muscles bulged, and the mokoro moved in rapid thrusts along the confined channels.

But as swiftly as we cut through the rippling water, the closing night was swifter still. The evening air brought out little dwarf bitterns to splash at the shore, searching for frogs. The frogs themselves released a noisy symphony of croaks. The cerulean intensity of the sky was diminished, and pink cirrus clouds began to streak it.

Killibele sweated and strained, the mokoro was a lumbering, unwieldy thing. It would not glide like a kite in the wind, but had to be propelled laboriously through the maze of river. The night fell and blackness cancelled every other shade.

Suddenly a series of throaty hippo grunts broke through the night air. A hippo grunt is a powerfully primal noise – unthinkable that it comes from the belly of a ruminant. We stared all around us. Were there malevolent eyes in that black water? Killibele didn't pause, didn't look, his shoulders and arms kept up their steady rhythm. We entered a canal, I breathed more easily, and then a dark pool and every muscle was alert and strained. The grunting seemed so close, but no shadows were discernible on the bank. They must be in here with us, with us in their territories in their feeding hours. They would see and smell our paltry little mokoro; the legendary choler would be aroused. The frantic poling would draw their attention.

A splash on the banks, and then another in the water. The plunge of a heavy body. We were downwind, Cyril's back was rigid, Killibele's arm was a blur of motion.

'Down,' he barked. We flattened ourselves and passed under the wire. Presently we slid into the camp jetty. Killibele slumped exhaustedly on to the grass, trembling with fatigue and anxiety. His dark eyes followed us with subdued rancour as we tethered his boat. We paid him and looked apologetic and escaped.

We weaved our way back through the mopane trees. A fire was blazing and pop music issued from a ghetto-blaster.

I'm walking on sunshine, yeh eh.
Yes, I'm walking on sunshine, whoah oh.

A rousing welcome; a resettlement of bottoms in the sand to make space for us. The odious Australian was gone. Instead, there was Bert and Dan and a couple of other white Africans.

One was a Swazi with a plastic bank bag of Swazi heads marijuana – everyone looked quite stupefied in the firelight and very genial.

We told the story of the hippos. Naturally everyone else had a story too. The Swazi told one about a croc-hunter who had gone out at night and had his mokoro tipped by a hippo. Unable to swim, he had held his breath and dragged himself hand over hand through the weeds until he reached the far side.

'Didn't a croc bite him?'

'Nope. He climbed out, and he ran upwind from the hippos and he was OK.'

Bert had the best story. It was his own story and he told it in a low, gravelly voice, rolling a spliff in his calloused thumbs, squatting in the sand in the shadowy firelight with the night breeze gusting through the mopane leaves.

'Once Dan and me and a Bamangwato boy who was working for us went into the Moremi to see some game and we went over a log in the road that we never saw. There was this crunch. We got down to have a look and we saw, damn, we'd busted the whole underside of the truck. We didn't have any water with us.

'We waited until nightfall for another truck, but nothing came. So in the morning, Dan said he'd walk back to the camp with the Bamangwato boy and get someone to winch us out and tow us back. I said I'd stay and look after the truck. I was pretty thirsty by then and so were they, but they had to walk. By mid-morning, it was so damn hot, I got down and lay in the sand under the truck in the shade. My mouth and throat were burning to pieces. Even breathing hurt. By the afternoon they hadn't come back, and I was so desperate for water. I looked in the battery of the car, and the windscreen water, but everything was dry, everything had burned up.

'I wanted to die, I couldn't think of anything but water. When the night came I just lay on my back with my mouth open and my tongue was all furry and swollen up. I thought I might die.

I just lay there, dreaming and dreaming about water. Felt like blood was running in my mouth, but there was nothing, even the spit had all dried up and gone away. The next day it got hotter and hotter. I thought I'm gonna damn die underneath this damn truck so the vultures don't get me. Then I heard the truck arrive and it was Daniel. I came crawling out from under there and they had two fucking cokes. I drank them down so quickly and then it was two hours back to town. I was still so fucking thirsty, two days in the Moremi without a single drop. I couldn't wait to get home. I said stop at this garage and I ran into the toilet and filled up the basin with water. I stuck my head in there and I just drank and drank and drank.'

He paused and laid the completed joint in the sand; his dark eyes were intense with the recollection. We leaned forward to hear the culmination, our own throats parched with empathy.

'I never went into the bush again without taking a huge damn tank with me,' said Bert.

*

We were on the northern road beyond the town of Nata, leading to the Kazungula ferry which connects Zambia and Botswana. We sat on our bags beneath a mopane tree. Everything around us was a bare flurry of loose dust. Once this land had been grassland but animal husbandry had eroded it. The cattle ate away the rich grasses and the poorer ones came creeping through. The extent of thornbush had also increased; the scrappy trees sprouted along the length of the roadway. Nature had made Botswana a dry country, but man had made her arid. The first white settlers, arriving in the early nineteen hundreds, had found the country interspersed with natural springs and small pools of water. Now these had vanished from the bare wasted tracts.

The mopane tree itself did not offer much protection from the sun. The mopane is an arrogant tree and does not live for the well-being of man or beast; at midday it turns the sharp edge of its leaves to the sun to retain their moisture, and the shade falls away.

The heat made me drowsy and thoughtful, and my mind flowed over the last days. We had gone back to Katie's, but the serenity was shattered. Her boyfriend had returned from safari. He was a big man with a set, determined mouth. His bush-hardened, decisive eyes assailed her tranquillity; the lights of her auburn hair were dulled, her eyes were stained with tears and she was robbed of her gentle spiritedness. She no longer seemed magnificent, just plain and unhappy and having to contend with this powerful man.

I lay on the camp bed in the tent home that night, thinking of the tragedy of men and women. I was reminded of D H Lawrence and his concept of men and women as perfectly balanced poles who might lift one another to the highest experience of happiness. Why then do we drag each other down, to wallow in the dregs of our inadequacies?

My thoughts came crowding in upon me. I was going to an unknown place with a boy who seemed to me to be as mad as a hatter, and I did not know what to do about it. I was falling to pieces. I had lost. I had lost. My panic was surging. I wanted to touch a human face, to talk to somebody – I felt if I could do that I might feel human myself, but there was only dust and loneliness and insanity.

Cyril scuffed his boots and squinted through the mopane leaves. I stared bleakly at his back. Impossible to know what fairy thoughts chased through his impenetrable head. I tried to construe him in terms of my own psychological composition, but he might have come from another planet. We barely spoke the same language.

As the forceful heat gathered I grew quarrelsome and critical. How could he live without literature, without philosophy, without thought, I demanded. The most blighted human being must still be a vehicle for learning. Why should he be exempt from the quest that dogged the rest of us?

'Because I know everything there is to know,' he said patiently.

'You don't! You cannot! You know nothing, you're only silly and young.'

He exasperated me beyond endurance; I could not bear the sight of him. I ground my knuckles in the rufous dust. *Perhaps he is an idiot savant and does know some essential axiom*. No, it cannot be, it would make a travesty of the universe. Was there one truth in this universe, or a multitude of truths?

I had run the gamut of religious enquiry. My family was Anglican and we had been churchgoers. My father said it did not matter whether you believed or not; the Anglican church was a social cement. My mother was more conventionally religious. As a teenager I was briefly a born-again. After boarding school, I left the Anglican Church. It had become a vision of smirking sacristans in green blazers, dispensing the host and ticking you off afterwards for daring to receive the sacrament without your white hair ribbon intact. I became a Catholic proselyte. Then there was the interest in Hare Krishna, and since I had met Cyril I had been learning this and that about Judaism. Verily then, I had shopped my way through some of the major faiths.

The zealotry of the born-agains intrigued me, but I was horrified by their image of God. He seemed capable of a petty vengefulness that could not reconcile with my intimations of His numinousness.

'*He's a kind God, but he's a jealous God too,*' they would say, as if they were speaking of the next door neighbour or someone who might appear at any moment. Theirs was a God of testosterone, of mighty male strength, prepared to patronise me if I was a good girl.

Cyril drew the same comforts. He did adore the bouffanted American heiress and her diabolical imaginings; they filled his dreams and kept him happy for hours in the dust, while I was savage with misery and confusion. Who was I to say any of them was wrong? Was I wrong? Was anybody wrong? I might detect God with sudden clarity on the fading colours of a sunset, but invariably he would slip from my grasp. When Nicholas was lost I had prayed in the conventional manner, but I had not reaped any rewards.

A sick, shrivelled thing, my soul is etiolated, my instincts diminished. The suffocating dervishes will rise again and crumple me. We were in the dust under a mopane, we were in a car, we were at a border post, I am feeling for my documents, everything is a blur. A man is pointing; ah, it is the man who picked us up. He is pointing at a kudu on the roadside, how extraordinary. And a giraffe, two giraffes, go galloping by with arresting grace. Life is an unfolding motion picture with exquisite effects, I am a part of the picture, yet I wish I knew more about it. Life should be more voluntary than this. When did I relinquish control and if I have, who has assumed it? People sometimes told me I was funny or clever, horrid when they did that, because I had to be more funny and clever and became lumpish in consequence. I had another life, I had my people, where were they? I had lost. I had lost. Give me back my people, give me back my lost, take away these new circumstances, let me go back, take away the madness.

'Are you all right?'

I had been breathing very heavily and clawing on the window handle. The driver was looking at me oddly.

'Yes, I'm terribly sorry. I haven't been sleeping much lately. Catching up a bit, I think.'

'Ah, burning the old candle,' commented the driver kindly. He was relieved to tag the situation; the lines of discomfiture were erased from his face. He was a white man, a Zimbabwean, in a very neat Ford GTI.

Everything was greener here and more densely wooded. The late afternoon air was mild and cool. The car took the narrow roads easily. Presently we came into the small town of Victoria Falls. Here were banks and a Wimpy and a crowded campsite.

People stood in groups along the pavement, chatting easily. It was a Saturday; necks had been liberated from their binding ties and leisures were pursued. A dull thundering hung in our ears and a miasmic cloud rose up on the far side of the town; spray raised by the Zambezi river as it cascades over its numerous cataracts. I stood in the cool air watching the bank of moisture, willing myself back into the world of logical consequence.

We had arrived at what the Africans call Mosi-Oa-Tunya – The Smoke That Thunders.

You Should Read Wilbur

On reaching the Victoria Falls, David Livingstone is said to have remarked: 'Scenes so lovely must have been gazed upon by angels in their flight.' But his bearers fell back and were afraid and said the gods were in that place, African Gods who are not as antiseptic as our own. They wanted to make a sacrifice. Livingstone laughed and told them that the place was beautiful and that God was benevolent to provide it; their eyes were shackled by ignorance and atavism.

The Falls are an immense, savage plummeting of water. The lazy Zambezi has its source in the wooded hill country of Zambia, a tongue of which lies between Angola and Zaire. Forty miles away is another spring which joins the Congo and will eventually flow from its mouth at Banana past the Ponta do Padrao and into the Atlantic Ocean.

But the Zambezi is a dilatory stream. First she meanders north and then west and then loops to the south. Finally she settles on the east and broadens and eddies and drifts towards her own mouths at Quelimane and Chinde on the Indian Ocean. Her journey takes her from those Zambian hills through the war zones of Angola and back through the Zambian wildlife reserves. The briefest of acknowledgements to Botswana at the Kazungula Ferry and the spectacular deluge at the Mosi-Oa-

Tunya. We call those various plumes of water the Devil's Cataract and the Eastern Cataract, the Main Falls and the Rainbow Falls.

On through Zimbabwe she travels; she is dammed at Lake Kariba where the wealthy can sail pleasure boats on her, and dammed again at Cahora Bassa in Mozambique where there are no pleasure boats. Now she is the Rio Zambeze and ultimately she spills into the ocean – 2 200 miles from her source.

But the Victoria Falls is undoubtedly the apotheosis of her beauty. I stood on the bank under the dense evergreens, in a mist of spray which gathered and dripped from their mossy boughs, and watched the falling mass of the river churn and surge through the rapids and the delicate rainbows that shivered in the midst of it all.

Victoria Falls – what a *stiff* little name. Lead powder on the face and loving one's own husband; these things were Victoria. Of course I was indebted to the monarch; her colonial cupidity gave me an African childhood, but this was not an altar at which to evoke her memory. This carnage of liquid – quintessentially African – could only be Mosi-Oa-Tunya, the thundering smoke.

Perhaps dark gods did inhabit that place. I was strangely affected, and then I had a vision, of sorts.

Cyril pre-empted the vision. We were wandering by the roadside, gathering fuel, and he lost his temper.

'You're no fun,' he cried suddenly. 'You used to be fun and now you're not.' He was not eloquent, but his grey eyes were casting after some principle that he was determined to express.

'You should . . .'

He lost the point and chased it and served it up. Now his narrow shoulders swelled with a queer triumph because there was a thing that needed to be said and he was going to say it. All his physiognomy was in agreement, the red lips, the blond, bobbing curls, his cheeks drained by a concurring passion.

'You should get yourself right!' said Cyril.

And turned his back.

The vervet monkeys that loitered on the pavement were

attentive. They watched with glassy eyes, perhaps anticipating some lobbying remark. I stopped amongst them, in my tracks, and watched him go. The black-faced monkeys peered up with a wry interest, but I was not alive to them. I was in the clutches of my vision. Ridiculously, I was remembering an old Woody Allen film.

In *The Purple Rose Of Cairo* Mia Farrow plays a waitress in the American Depression. Mia's character is an abused wife whose one outlet is an infatuation with the cinema. Miraculously, one afternoon a celluloid hero, played by Jeff Daniels, descends from the screen and announces that he is in love with her and he wants to be 'real'. The waitress is a delightful ingenue. She feels badly for her horrific spouse but, on the other hand, she is very taken with this fetching young man from another realm. For a while it looks as if the two of them are destined for a lover's paradise. But it cannot last. The man isn't real and he can't comprehend the real world. He tries to pay for an astronomically expensive restaurant dinner with monopoly money. When they kiss he is astonished that there is no fade-out. Ultimately the waitress has to resign herself to the tragedy that her lover is not real and she must relinquish him. She returns to fisticuffs with the oaf and her tired old humdrum existence. It was all very deep and postmodern and unlikely. I think I wrote a rather wordy paper about it for university, but ultimately it was the pathos that took me in.

But was it so unlikely? A self-confession amongst the vervet monkeys. I was as naive as Cissy and had embraced the same deceptions. The problem between Cyril and me was that it was Act Two. It had been Act Two ever since we left Johannesburg and I hadn't known it. An undetectable curtain had fallen and risen, sweeping away Act One. And of what import was Act One? It had only the faintest chronological bearing on Act Two.

I tried to recall the framework of Act One. A boy and girl meet. She is at drama school; he is a professional dancer. So fitting, they watch each other's performances, they are young and brilliant together. If there is a gulf in reality then reality must be relinquished. In classic art, who looks for the mundane provisos of daily life? An effigy of Odette flaps frantically from the back of the stage whilst her poor heart is breaking. Why doesn't she march into the princely realm, boot out the cunning Odile and her scheming father Rotbart and reclaim the erring Prince? It is quite obvious the poor chap hasn't a clue and has fallen foul of one of those *doppelgänger* machinations. But we don't look for common sense in Odette. What we need from her are her thirty-two *fouettés*. These are what make us hold our breath and proclaim the world exquisite.

And death? In the classic arts, death is never squalid. It isn't even nasty. A palpable afterlife ameliorates its irrevocability. Odette and the Prince kill themselves, but then they sail away merrily to a better world.

Even death coupled with madness is quite equitable. Giselle is a happy peasant girl who falls for a dissembling nobleman, Albrecht, and rather takes leave of her senses. Alas, she dies. Then she resurfaces as a Wili, a wood spirit, and saves Albrecht in defiance of her Wili boss, who doesn't like him at all. I believe she dies again after that, or continues her previous death in a more tranquil form.

One does not expect the proponents of a classic ballet to subsist in a real world, as one knows it and suffers it. One values them for their grace and their abstraction.

When I had rallied for Cyril, I had rallied for an art of great conventions. I had never taken stock of him as a human being. I could not blame him now for being unmalleable, for raising protests. Without a stage and a score and a choreographer, the boy was drifting apart, his various pieces were disassembling, he had no unity. Because Cyril was old art, he was ballet before Ballanchine, theatre before Stanislavsky. He could not bend to the sudden realism which tragedy had inflicted upon my role. He was still awaiting the *pas de deux*; if hostile forces had seized his partner he must twist her back into the required forms.

I hunched my shoulders up into the muscles of my neck and dropped them. I was culpable. I had plucked a conventional art from its natural setting. At whose feet to lay the charge if he now seemed unauthentic? Now we were bound together and it was poor art and all the clear, uncompromised light of the bush vaunted the ungainly shadows. I could not push the pair of us back into a proscenium arch. Here we were, a conventional artist and an unwilling tragedian, taunting each other with our youthful selfishness. Here I was, with a bundle of logs in my arms, learning that art is not life, or bad art makes a bad life. Everything had been deconstructed.

I dropped my twigs and backed away. Cyril was a faint figure in the distance. In my bitterness I might have mocked the mincing steps, but how can you mock what you have yourself incurred?

I stumbled to the upper reaches of the Zambezi, before the Falls, closed in on my extraordinary stupidity.

'Excuse, Madam. Buy an elephant.'

'Buy a giraffe.'

'This big one is rhinoceros. Forty dollars.'

A huddle of African men had converged on me. In their hands they held bluish soapstone carvings. Now they pressed closer, thrusting out their handiwork, a closing semicircle of demand. The air became acrid with the smell of sweat and rank poverty.

'Take this one, Madam.'

'Buy, buy rhinoceros!'

I looked at their faces and I was afraid. Upriver was a line of baobab trees. Downriver the water gathered its surging momentum, in a few hundred yards it would tip over the edge and become the body of that churning inferno. I had walked by myself down a side road and now I was alone, or had thought I was alone until these men seemed to emerge from the trees.

'I don't want anything.' I backed away.

They began to jostle, each other and me. An elbow, a hand,

the sharp nudge of a ludicrous elephant trunk, wrought in stone. Their faces were unreadable.

Back, back, the water slopped into my boots. A mad thought of crocodiles, but the fear was at my front and sides. I continued to retreat and they to advance. My boots ground up against a rocky island and I saw that I had waded through a metre of the rippling water.

They looked silently at the flow and at me. Now they were ranged along the bank. My breathing was hard and high and forced. I scrambled on to a further island. They continued to watch silently and moved neither forwards nor back. It was a blank scrutiny of impenetrable motives.

Rape in Southern Africa is not a remote construct. In my girlhood, the older women were obscure on the subject of sex, but graphic on the subject of rape. The statistics say that one in three South African women are raped in their lifetime. But that doesn't hold true for whites because the whites are watching their backs and making themselves invulnerable. The whites maintain a severe code of laws, not juristic laws, but personal ones.

Before I fully understood what sex was, I knew the code of laws against rape. Don't walk alone, don't be in a strange place, don't speak to men in the street. Later, it was open the gates by remote control, don't get out of your car, carry a spray. Before you go to sleep check the doors and windows, bolt everything, set the burglar alarm. If you hear something – a footfall, a cough, the scrape of furniture – hit the panic button, call the armed guard. Some women slept with a pistol under their pillow.

The sternest law of all was intractably racist.

Beware of the black man.

At university we examined the code and scoffed at it and declared it scurrilous. The mind vowed not to harbour it. Yet the body, so precious in itself, would not submit to political correctness and continued to maintain its generalised defences. Walking on the mountains, I would always be alert. If I heard the clamour of men's voices I would melt into the treeline until they could be scrutinised. We were no longer the goddesses, we were only the enemy and the enemy at its softest element. Africa – angry, poor, discarded Africa – was only behind the next tree or on the other side of the door.

One met the victims and felt their pain. Their sordid details were disseminated softly at tea parties like informal police briefings.

'Poor Mrs Wetherton . . . yes, he came over the garden wall. So unfortunate, but she's bearing up, the poor thing. So brave.'

'And Elaine's mother – absolutely ghastly, she's in her eighties after all, you would have thought he'd have some sort of compassion. No, he actually worked for the old age home, some sort of porter, needless to say no one's seen him since. Tied her up for hours, made a complete mess of her. Luckily she's a bit gaga – she doesn't remember it too clearly.'

Horror stories were served up regularly in the papers and lingered on in the conscious mind: a six-week-old baby, the revenge raping by two men of their four-year-old daughters. Of course it wasn't the preserve of black men, white men raped too, but their inflictions did not summon the same blanket terror. We could comprehend whites, we could draw all the instantaneous conclusions that women do draw about men to preserve their safety. Additionally, amongst the English there were precepts of class structure that kept us in narrow but reliable confines. But black society was a mystery. Across the enormous gulf, black society was alien and incomprehensible. Its members had been offered up to us as servants and now we feared that we would be offered up as victims.

For the victims themselves there was sympathy, but there was also hardness. However much you pitied them, you had to impute a mistake. If you could not find their flaw, their oversight, what prevented you from being the next woman to go crawling to the police station? The selection process could not be arbitrary. So it was discovered that they had scrimped on the burglar wiring or opened the door to a beggar or stopped at a traffic light after dark. They had broken the code of laws, but you had not, so you would be all right.

But now I had broken the code and here was nemesis – a silent line of it. Were they quarrying, was it a rout, why did they stand like that, with that loose intensity, watching everything I did? Something was said in Matabele, they laughed, resumed the watching.

But at that moment a Range Rover came barrelling along the road. I waved and saw the incline of a shadowy head inside. The car braked abruptly and disclosed a portly white man with two small children. He seemed to remonstrate. The men vanished into the baobabs as rapidly as they had appeared. I scrambled back to the bank.

'Thank you,' I said weakly, much relieved.

He let me ride in his car back into town and let me out at the camp. I could see Cyril doing his *barre* work using the edge of the metal sink as a support. *Ronds de jambe à terre*, I recognised. The weight on his far leg, the nearer in second position, *en dehors*, sweep through to rest in first position, *en dedans* and to the side. His hips were level and his legs turned out, chin aloft, one slim arm extended.

I rested my elbows on the sink, turned on the tap, washed my face under the running water.

'Working hard?'

'Uh huh.' His face was set in concentration. He started on *battement frappés*, the rubbery ball of his boot lightly striking on the damp sand at the base of the sink. I felt a return of affection, because he did seem pretty at that moment, his cheeks flushed, absorbed in the *battement frappés*. Above all he seemed safe and of manageable manhood.

'I'll make some sandwiches,' I offered with vast docility. 'You can eat them when you've finished your class.'

*

'Now give me the American dollars.'

'Wait, I'm going to count yours first.'

I shuffled awkwardly through the little pile with one hand, because in the other hand I clutched my own unrelinquished dollars. *Ouf* – a sudden thud in my stomach, not really painful, but enough to make me stagger back against the brick wall in surprise, and then he snatched and ran. His back weaved through the crowd and it swallowed him up. I glanced at my hand. The dollars were gone.

I walked dejectedly back through the Bulawayo station terminus, looking rather hopelessly at stray heads in the throng. A few hundred black faces coursed on either side of me. Anybody could have been the thief, or nobody. I could not tell.

'Did you see someone running this way?' I asked a suited businessman who was opening the boot of his car.

'What did he look like?'

'Ummm – dark hair, dark eyes, well built.' The businessman was an African, and he eyed me with some amusement. Dark hair, dark eyes, well built – the white man's dilemma of recognition. I could have been describing any one of the several score of young men in that bustling crowd.

'Don't worry,' I ended lamely. I had left Cyril in a tea-shop, guarding the bags, and had gone to change money with an amenable young man who had befriended us as we trudged across the platform. The police were everywhere, he had intimated in a low whisper. I can give you a very good rate. We went creeping round the corner and I got a mild slug in the solar plexus and a few crumpled five dollar notes.

Cyril was slumped over a china mug, clearly exhausted, his chin resting on the back of his hand. He wasn't cheered by my news.

'But how could you have let him run off?'

'He walloped me,' I pointed out aggrievedly. 'It didn't look enough and I wanted to count and . . .'

'All right, all right, enough already. I heard the story once.'

We had been on the trot for twenty-four hours and were feeling filthy and enervated. Rising at dawn to stand on the road, there had been a lift on a goods lorry for several hours. The lorry left us on the roadside and there we sat until late afternoon. The worst nightmare – I had turned the final leaf of *I Dreamed of Africa* and had nothing to read. A triple century of disconsolate minutes wasted into oblivion. Itching with boredom, I became feverish with the need to absorb something.

I stared at Cyril.

How does he manage to do absolutely nothing all day long?

The red ants had gotten into my shorts and bitten my bottom into streaky welts. I scratched at them savagely. My leg had succumbed to the tedium and gone to sleep. I noticed that the sole of one of my boots had come loose – the speaking boot. I wiggled the flap and improvised a nonsense conversation between Leg and Boot to fill the dragging moments.

Boot: Wake up what, young leg!

Leg: Why must I? You're just jealous because you can't sleep.

Boot: Be that as it may, I'm not going to let you sleep either. I shall be like the ghosts that haunt Macbeth (strikes an attitude). 'Still it cried Sleep no more to all the house: Glamis has murdered sleep, and therefore Cawdor shall sleep no more, Macbeth shall sleep no more!'

I really did want a book.

'Why are you muttering?' enquired Cyril. 'Let's walk to the station.'

So we walked nine kilometres along the track to Dete station. Against the smudged white walls of the waiting-room hung a benignly smiling portrait of the president, Robert Mugabe. The waiting-room was cramped and squalid. Barefooted children were gathered in knots, waiting to return to their boarding schools.

In the early hours of the morning the train arrived. The first carriages were fourth class. We peered through the window.

'Oh blast it, Cyril. Let's get a sleeper in second. We'll skip lunch or something.'

But second class was booked solid and so was third. We spent the remainder of the night sitting bolt upright on a metal bench, in a bedlam of pregnant women and very small babies and bulky parcels in plastic-weave holdalls. My bones ached protestingly. The pregnant women would drop off in the most impossible contortions and wake to find me gazing blearily at them. They smiled and resettled their own bottoms and the forms of the children that they had borne already. The children themselves stared back uncomplainingly with their inchoate eyes which gave nothing away.

Then Bulawayo station and the belly-smacking heist. But I did not really mind these kinds of trivial adversities. If they were tiresome, they were also concrete. They prevented the mind from overfilling with its own trauma.

Shop for food, find the campsite, raise the tent, get cleaned up, get some sleep. Life could be stripped of its addenda and reduced to deceptively simple requirements. In the Makadodo market we bought spices, vegetables and fruit from a dusty array of tables. Also on display were the vials of roots and leaves of local medicine, fussy live chickens in cages, empty plastic bottles, packets of peanuts and discarded sections of iron. Several women were vending crude leather sandals made from car tyres.

The Bulawayo streets were wide and tree lined. I asked a red-faced shopkeeper for directions to the campsite.

'Yes, not far. You're on Abercorne Street now. Keep going left and into Crown Street. Not more than five minutes.'

We bore on straight up and presently saw a green lawn behind a hedge. An African man was approaching in our direction.

'Excuse me, is this the municipal campsite?'

'It is. This is Leopold Takawira Street,' advised the man, pointing to the street sign. The sign had been defeated by its own physical length. It read *Leopold Taka* and then the *wira* buckled lop-sidedly towards the asphalt pavement.

'I thought it was *Abercorne* Street,' said Cyril.

'Well, it's *not*. It's Leopold Takawira Street,' said the man, with a frisson of displeasure. Cyril looked as though he might pursue it, so I dragged him away and repressed him.

The camp was pretty and enclosed from the road with a scattering of trees. I had a shower and set about making the fire. Cyril appeared, saw that it was done and pouted. I became schoolmarmish.

'Well, you ought not to have been so long under the shower. It's quite unconscionable.'

There was a harsh drought in the country and notices everywhere implored campers not to be liberal with the water.

He made a face and settled moodily under a tree. But it was a fine evening and I did not care to scrap with him over trifles. We had bought a litre carton of Ndlovu beer – a local brew, *ndlovu* meaning elephant. I poured a finger's width into my tin mug and tasted it.

'Ugh! It's unspeakable!'

It had the stench, taste and texture of human vomit. I gave it away to the camp guard, who was wreathed in smiles.

'Welcome, welcome!' he said.

Now to find a novel. Clutching the Kuki Gallman I made my way from tent to tent. Would you like to swap? Right (growing businesslike). What have you got? Judith Krantz, no thanks. Not Alistair MacLean, thanks. Oh no, not Wilbur Smith.'

'He's dead good on the bush and animals and that. Quite informative.'

'Yes. Have you got anything else?'

'I think me girlfriend does. Stella! Bring that book you finished with out here. She had something, but I think she quit it. Really, you should read Wilbur Smith. He knows what he's writing about – he lives in wildest Africa.'

'He doesn't. He lives in a terribly neat suburb next to mine.'

'Cor, really! Stella! Have you met him then?'

'No, my mother knew him at university. He had a bumper sticker on his car saying "Don't laugh, Madam, your daughter may be inside".'

'What a lark! I'd love to meet him! I thought of writing a letter of introduction or summat.'

Actually my mother was rather reproving on the topic of Wilbur Smith. Once I smuggled one into the house and had just reached the part where a baby is tossed into a flaming house when it was discovered.

'So many good books to read, darling, and you want to read this!'

Stella crawled backwards out of the tent with *The Lord of the Flies*. I pounced on it and gave her my book. She blinked at the new volume through inch-thick spectacles, like the bottoms of water tumblers. Another rump poked out between the flaps and wormed backwards to reveal a second boy, with a guitar. He struck up reedily with 'Yesterday'.

'*Yesterday!*' chorused the guitarist, the Wilbur Reader and the Wilbur Reader's girlfriend, Stella.

All my troubles seemed so far away!
Now it looks as though they're here to stay
Oh, I believe in yesterday!

The Wilbur Reader wallowed his way back into the tent and began summarily to eject debris: a toothmug, a pair of trousers, a lady's brassière. At last he reappeared with a tatty plastic packet and began to roll marijuana cigarettes. Night was gathering and Cyril had come over to see my new friends.

I said something wrong
and now I long
for yesterday – ay – ay – ay.

'We smoke a *lot* here in Africa,' confided the Wilbur Reader. 'Cos it dun't cost nuthing. We smoke too much really. '

'Course,' he amended, 'it's better than acid. In England, I used to wish there was a bit less acid around. Really funny actually, cos now I'm here, I wish there was a bit *more*.'

The camp guard, Felix, was visible, making his way to the toilets. He appeared to be dancing.

'Welcome, welcome!' I called. He flapped his arm with enthusiasm and stumbled over the woodpile.

'*Oh-wow-wow-wow-wow-oh-wow*,' wailed the choir. But the marijuana cigarettes had incapacitated Stella. She flopped forward on her face, burying her spectacles in the grass.

'You all right, love?' queried the Wilbur Reader, poking her in the ribs and struggling to locate the words.

Stella made a muffled throaty gurgle that could have indicated that she was all right, or that she was about to expire.

'The women just can't take the pace,' concluded Cyril, happily.

*

'I am the local nyanga. I treat all ills.'

I took in the apparition of the local nyanga, who was a bony man, slightly taller than me. An array of mangy genet tails hung at his waist, and his anklets seemed to be made from chicken feathers. A lather of plastic beads were laced around his throat, and he wore a necklace made from the metacarpal bones of some animal. His chest had collapsed inward, and the ribcage had become prominent.

'Two Zim dollars to take my photograph, please.'

I gave him two dollars.

'Now you can take my photograph.'

'I haven't a camera,' I pointed out.

He sucked on his yellowing teeth, closed one eyelid and peered at me with the other stained eyeball. Evidently we were mysteries to each other.

'Would you like to see inside my hut? Would you like to see the medicines?'

'Yes, I would.'

I was in a kind of model village behind the Great Zimbabwe Ruins, where Americans, Orientals and Europeans can see Africa as it is reputed to be. A circle of thatched huts, and chicken coops on poles. There were placards too, explaining the various customs and functions.

I followed the nyanga and stooped through the low portal into the gloomy interior of his hut. It was cluttered; a low bier made of cross-lashed wooden poles and sheepskins where I supposed he slept, a scattering of wooden bowls and glass bottles, an array of calabashes against the wall. A terribly obese woman was sitting cross-legged on a blanket in the centre. Her immense cheeks puddled into a smile of welcome.

'Hello,' I said diffidently.

'You come for *muti*?' she asked, meaning African medicine.

'Not really.'

'Love problems?'

'Definitely not,' I answered. When people say that to a young person, they never mean the complex, gruelling attachments one has to one's family. They always mean erotic love. I considered the idea of love at twenty-one to be impertinent. Love was a deeply affecting emotion and must be consigned to one's maturity.

'Health?' enquired the woman, scrabbling amongst the various pots.

'Health is fine, thank you, mama.' The cave-like room had an offensively dank odour, like a mound of wet hockey socks left mouldering overnight in a wicker laundry basket. I re-emerged into the sunlight and blinked at the slabs of ancient stonework visible on the nearby hillock.

The Great Zimbabwe Ruins are a series of mystic edifices. The conical towers and narrow passageways were discovered in the last century by an American who had strayed from his path. Concealed by thick bush, they had survived the centuries remarkably intact. The structures are shaped from granite rock and are renowned for their dry masonry. Neither mortar nor cement was used to bond the walls. The blocks of stone are so precisely hewn that the blade of a penknife cannot be inserted between the joints.

Nobody really knows for certain who built the ruins, but there are two popular schools of thought. One school asserts that the ruins are no more than six hundred years old and were built by the forebears of the present African tribes.

The opposing school contends that the ruins are in fact over two thousand years old and were not built by Africans at all. Instead, they were the handiwork of an altogether different race of people, probably Arabic invaders, who enslaved the Africans, and mined the area for gold. The argument for this turns on the suggestion that Zimbabwe is in a direct line from the ancient port of Sofala, two hundred and fifty miles distant. The implicit assumption is that Africans could not have built the ruins. This assumption was not always implicit. A publicity pamphlet from the first half of the century informs that 'no Bantu people ever possessed the continuity of effort necessary to achieve such masterpieces of architecture, nor can it be claimed that their civilisation was ever so highly cultured as to be capable of such magnificent conception and the power to execute it.'

I had already discovered by a random canvassing of the indigenes, that the view one took hung largely upon which race group one belonged to.

But Zimbabwe, formerly Rhodesia, has always been a nation of contentions. The first recorded civilisation was Monomotapa, which traded with Arab and Swahili merchants. The Monomotapans were conquered by the Portuguese in the early sixteenth century. Later the Rozwi Empire came to prominence and drove off the Portuguese who, in turn, were thwarted by Mzilikazi and his men. This was the same Mzilikazi who caused the Bamangwato chief Khama to appeal to the Queen for protection.

The seeds of Zimbabwe's present divisions were sown when the nation incurred the interest of the eponymous Cecil John Rhodes, the visionary colonist and precious minerals entrepreneur. Amongst whites, Rhodes has retained a legendary stature. When I was a day scholar in Cape Town, I won a place in a local history competition and as a reward was actually allowed to see the great man's bedroom, which had been retained in its original severely manly state. Here was the great man's washbasin, and shaving kit and bed. Which, the tour guide breathed in my ear, had been known, *irrefutably* known, to have been shared by his secretary.

'So what,' I said, screwing up my fifteen-year-old nose in an attempt at sophistication. 'There wasn't a *Mrs* Cecil John Rhodes, was there?'

'Spot on!' hissed the educationalist, pruriently. 'This was the nineteenth century, my girl. The secretary was a *man!*'

Cecil John Rhodes envisaged an imperial corridor, a swathe of British-owned territory from Cape Town to Cairo. In 1889 the British South Africa Company was formed. Rhodes marched his men into the southern territories of Mashonaland and colonised them. In their wake followed a cluster of settlers. They soon found there was no gold, or no mineral gold. But in the harvest time there was plenty, myriad fields of wheat and barley that grew abundantly in the fertile soil. A flood of whites poured into the country known as Southern Rhodesia, to settle and cultivate farms. Jocularly, they referred to it as the 'grain bin of Africa'.

As the numbers of whites multiplied, the Africans were edged out. Fresh legislature concretised their marginalisation; the 1930 land act, the 1934 labour laws. The land to the north and north east had also been opened to white settlement. These areas, Northern Rhodesia and Nyasaland, were federated in 1953. When the federation collapsed a decade later, they became the independent states of Zambia and Malawi.

Flanked by two emerging African nations, the discontent of Southern Rhodesian blacks burgeoned. By now there were two contending parties under African leadership, the Zimbabwe African People's Union (ZAPU) and the Zimbabwe African National Union (ZANU). These two parties orchestrated a campaign of rural guerrilla warfare. Concurrently Britain was pressing sanctions. Many of the whites left for South Africa – 'taking the gap', as it was called.

When the Portuguese regime was overthrown in 1974, Angola and Mozambique also became independent. White Rhodesians accepted that they were facing a continual protraction of the war. The prime minister, Ian Smith, released key political leaders, including the current president, Robert Mugabe. There were some unsuccessful attempts to create a black government with white minority rights guaranteed. Mugabe came to power in April 1980 as the first president of a black majority government.

I walked up the hill and back to the restaurant, where the tourists were taking their tea. Cyril was seated on the grass, pulling at the separate blades with his fingertips. He had been sullen, last night and this morning, because we had been camped next to a pair of female Israeli military personnel. Cyril tried to tell them about Ramtha and the achievement of immortality, but they only stared at him with dry Middle Eastern impassivity and told him he was insane.

I was relieved by this second opinion, but it also made me want to rag him. In the morning, when he got up to shower, I poked my head tauntingly around the corner of the shower room door.

'Take your time, sweetheart. I'm just going to pack away the tent.'

'Nooooo!'

A mad scramble, and then he exploded forth in his underpants, ripped the Kestrel loose from its moorings and galloped away down the track, the sheets of nylon billowing behind him like a full spinnaker. I was helpless with slightly hysterical laughter, but the Israelis were amazed.

'Why does he make like this?'

'It's one of our marriage preparation rituals,' I told them. 'The man bears the home metaphorically upon his shoulders.'

They shook their heads. When he wasn't back half an hour later I felt irritated and went to find him. He was huddled in an empty water chute under the roadway.

'What the hell are you doing in there?' I descanted volubly into the culvert.

'I must be the one who puts it away. It must be me!'

'Something will bite you and then you'll be sick,' I said hopefully, looking at the leafy debris which clogged the chute.

He emerged, damp but defiant, with the bundle of fabric loosely balled against his chest, as Cinderella might have clutched her glass slipper.

With the ruins at my back, I knelt beside him in the grass and touched his thigh gently. I should try to effect a reconciliation with him. After all, he was my lover. But we had nothing in common! It was an abysmally selfish thing to have taken him away from his career, his home, his family. In the beginning, in that headstrong young girl's life I had once lived, I had genuinely imagined we might suit each other. But latterly I had only wanted him as a male, a cipher, because I was afraid to travel on my own. I felt a sting of regret and a wash of guilt.

'Weren't they horribly rude, those Israelis?' I said warmly.

'Shut up.'

'No, really, they wouldn't listen at all about immortality and, after all, you might have a case. There's certainly a precedent for it in literature.'

He looked at me suspiciously.

'Honestly, look at Homer – it's immortality from start to finish. Zeus, Apollo, the whole pantheon, they never do throw in the towel, do they? And Dorian Gray, he managed to delay the whole decay process for ages and ages before he knifed himself accidentally.'

A blank gaze, so I curtailed the potted lecture.

'Come on,' he said finally, restoring what passed for equanimity between us. 'Let's just get on another bus and go somewhere else.'

*

For some hours a fine mist had hung in the air. Now the temperature had dropped, the wind bit at my cheeks and the mist thickened. Individual drops fell from the sky and made tear-shaped furrows in the earth. They gathered on my nose or made a muffled drumming sound through my plastic mackintosh. Rivulets of red mud criss-crossed the path and splashed over my boots. I breathed deeply; the pungent, invigorating scents of mud and rain and the wet, green woods.

This was the Eastern Highlands, Chimanimani, where the rainfall was high and trees and plants grew against the rising mountain slopes in great profusion. On the journey up, women had run to the windows of the bus and held up their produce – oranges and bananas, tomatoes, spinach, spring onions and eggs. I bought everything, and even a couple of the clay pots which the women rubbed up to a silver-grey shine with graphite. I later regretted the pots. They were heavy and it was a five-mile uphill trudge to the base camp.

Night fell, the rain increased, filled my boots and thwarted the plastic mackintosh. Eventually the base camp was visible in the gloom. A high wind had risen and whipped the rain into sideways flurries. We got the tent up, crawled inside and fell asleep in a slop of muddy water.

In the morning the rain held off. All the vegetation was turgid and renewed, sweet with the smell of rain. We began an uphill ascent. I grew weary of the pots and made a little altar with them under an acacia tree, but they seemed to have grown out of the stones and grasses of their own accord.

Kneeling there, the Buddhist chant sounded faintly in my ears.

Om mani padme hum
Om mani padme hum

The jewel in the lotus. The mountains were very beautiful, rising steeply to the skies, a natural barrier between Zimbabwe and Mozambique. Here grew the cycads, the dwarfish precious shrub with its fanlike leaves, which is the oldest tree on earth. Papery everlastings scattered the slopes. The aloes were in flower and made wine-red patches in the valleys.

In the mornings I awoke in the blackness and crept away silently to have these hours, these first few hours, to myself. The first light was white and chill, a taut wind blew the dawn clouds to the west, where the sun was still hiding behind the thickly obscured peaks. Slowly the thick bank dispersed and the sun seemed to send out emissaries of warmth. The dawn touched the dark plains; they became yellow, the flowers yielded themselves up and bobbed playfully on their stalks.

I watched this recurring drama of African awakening from a pile of rocks upholstered with feathery moss, breathing thickly through my balaclava. Every element of nature seemed to have a role and a character. The peaks were old men, venerable but grumpy. The sun was the boldest actor, the pivot, naked, wild and puissant. And all the waking morning things, the unfolding plants, the lilies and proteas and aloes, the fields of thawing grasses, and myself, we were the worshippers.

I took up my diary.

Both of Sarah's feet have broken their subject bondage and entered a numb leaden world of frozen detachment. She kicks them vigorously against the rock to bring them back into submission, to the warm flesh world of motion and pumping blood. At heart, she is a rather parochial and superstitious young girl, and variations from the ordinary

force her to enter a distasteful world of comparative recognition. The
body and feet are mutually dependent – a clear enough precept to all
sensible people, particularly affiliated members of the church. Feet
cannot be allowed to secede themselves to a rebel state of icy catatonia.

I closed the diary and smiled wistfully for the silly nonsense I
had written in it.

'How are you, girl?'

'Fine and dandy, thank you. And how are you, girl?'

An old boarding school trick, dividing yourself in two halves so
that you might have somebody to talk to.

An unbearable sense of loss, of grief, swept through my body.
I could not bear to think that my brother could go so summarily,
so suddenly. I could not bear to think that for ever and ever his
room would stand empty, his place would not be filled, that my
children would never play with his, that I would never again
hear him laugh, would never again chafe at his peremptory
demands. I was growing beyond my girlhood, but he would
never see it, he would never know me as an adult, he would
never read my first novel. He was gone, irrevocably gone.

Year by year, the memories would fade, would grow more
stale, would become sepia-toned. Birthdays would pass and
Christmases, nieces and nephews would be born who did not
know him, they would feel nothing for him, he would be part
of a family legend before their time. I might marry, I might
marry somebody who had no idea of what he had been. I would
travel where he had travelled, I would see what he had seen,
but we could never speak of the things that we had done. My
brother and sisters and I would grow old and feeble, we would
live out our lives, we would watch our bodies sag and collapse.
He would always be with us at the edge of our minds, beyond
what we said and what we thought, in our dreams, in our
recollections, in our regrets. We would grow old, but he would
be for ever young.

Grief is an arid desert, a dry, soundless, wordless, tearless, unrelievedly lonely plain. I sat on a rock with feathery tufts of moss, staring at the mountains, powerless to turn back the clock. The sun had risen, the earth grew brown, the dewdrops dried, the drifting clouds made lazy shadows in the valleys. A lilac breasted roller flashed out of the long grass and flew overhead.

I had lost him and I would have to carry the loss.

*

After Chimanimani Cyril and I headed north to Karoi to stay with a tobacco farmer who was a very old friend of my mother. He had not seen me since I was a schoolgirl and my bobble-headed appearance – with Cyril in tow – was clearly a shock. None the less, he was enormously kind to both of us. But a day or two after we arrived he had to go to the capital, Harare, on business.

'Some people are coming through this afternoon,' the farmer told me. 'Perhaps you can talk to the woman. She's a sort of psycho-babble-whatsit, might help. And Adela will see to anything else you need.'

'All right. Bye-bye.'

I spent the afternoon writing in my diary in a copse of bluegums on the far side of one of the tobacco fields. The farmer's softness and sympathy had unhinged me, had awoken a longing to have somebody to confide in. In addition, my father had sent me a letter asking me to go home and write my brother's biography. In the envelope were a number of colour photographs. The photographs were of children, small, vigorous, sun-tanned children crowded around boats in outsize orange life jackets, mounted on shaggy ponies, splashing in the murky shallows of a farm dam. It was our own childhood, my brothers and sisters and myself. I felt completely unnerved.

I walked back to the farmhouse in the late afternoon, thinking about the farmer. His own life had not been easy. He had been married, happily, to a very beautiful and amiable woman. They had made a home together in the bush and had had four children. But she had died tragically of cancer, leaving him on his own.

Adela, his current girlfriend, was on the veranda and so was Cyril, and another two people who I supposed must be the guests. The servants brought out cocktails, the sun was setting and a reddish light was cast over everything. A zebra grazed on the light aircraft runway and his white stripes became suffused with saffron. They were polo people and had a number of thoroughbred ponies. Some of the mares, who were in foal, had been brought to the bordering paddock. Their graceful silhouettes stood out against the immense circle of fire that the sun had become.

The psychologist guest was called Margaret. Her husband, Jim, was an American. Cyril was speaking as I slipped into one of the easy chairs.

'I think my favourite is Spartacus. No, wait. Maybe it's Don Quixote. Don Quixote's really fun.'

'Oh, lots of fun,' said Margaret, enthralled. 'Oh, I *love* ballet. I think it's *so* brave of you to have taken it up as a young man. Weren't you teased as a boy?'

'Some people thought it was weird,' said Cyril, 'but I never cared. I don't care what people think. If people think something is mad and I want to do it, I'll do it. In this world people always want to tell you what they think you should do. You just have to tell them to get right. You have to know what you want to do, and then you just go and do it.'

I gave him a black look, aware that I was an eminent contender for the role of someone who always wanted to tell him what they thought he should do. But he was not trying to heckle me. He was quite genuinely expounding his life principles. A manservant came out with a glass of lemonade on a silver tray. I thanked him. He was tall and stately in a crisp white uniform and white gloves, with a red fez on his head.

Margaret turned to me.

'What do you do?'

'I did a degree at university,' I told her. 'I'll probably go back and do another one.'

Boring, said her closed lips. Precisely what you would expect from someone of my age and background. She turned back to Cyril.

'How could you bear to leave the stage?'

'Hey, I loved ballet,' explained Cyril. 'Being up there, watching every muscle, seeing the audience. But most of all, I love life. Ballet was one kind of groovy life. But hey, I want to be an entity, I don't want to be stuck in a studio till the day I die. I want to go out and live a crazy, happening, groovy kind of life!'

'That's youth!' laughed Margaret. 'That's *esprit*, that's *joie de vivre*, that's letting it all go! Go out and do it, my boy, go out and be everything you want to be.'

'Yeah, that's just what I'm gonna do!' cried Cyril, his eyes sparkling.

I sank despondently in the easy chair. Cyril had obviously created a deeply favourable impression whilst I had been mourning amongst the eucalyptus, and now we had entered upon a cult of youth. Palpable bonhomie was pulsing between the four of them. I would have to lackey the tide and be jolly and optimistic.

The same manservant appeared and said that the first course was served. We found our places in the dining-room. It was the local delicacy – mopane worms – baked in a small ceramic pot. These hairless black caterpillars eat the leaves of the mopane tree, and have a subtle, nutty flavour.

'What shall we have to wet the old throat, semi-sweet or dry?' asked Adela.

'Oh something light, *n'importante quoi*,' proclaimed Jim, impressively.

Adela disappeared and came back with a Chenin Blanc.

'Here's to art!'

'Here's to being young and carefree!'

'Here's to your journey through life, Cyril,' proposed Margaret, raising her glass.

Cyril smiled charmingly.

We quaffed the wine.

He did look like a sylph or dryad in the evening light, like a glowing river nymph, with his neat, lithe form and his golden curls. One of my elderly relatives had once described him as a little Pan. 'You've brought him to life from a book of fairy legends,' she had croaked, clapping senile hands and leaning over her walking frame.

If Cyril seemed about to alight on the chandeliers like a bright butterfly, I was the lead weight on the end of a fisherman's line. I sat heavily on my chair and said nothing.

A Chardonnay appeared and a Riesling. The manservant brought in the second course of roast chicken. Everyone's voices had grown louder. Jim was beginning a discourse on Reaganomics, directed at Cyril. I wondered briefly what Cyril imagined Reaganomics to be.

'Yes, but the sea is rising and Ramtha says one day it will wash right over our doorsteps,' he interrupted earnestly.

'. . . only too happy to subsist on a welfare state, are arguably people who have never managed to do an honest day's labour in their lives,' concluded Jim.

It was too ridiculous. I rose and went aimlessly into the kitchen. The servants straightened up from their labours and followed me with their eyes.

'What do you need, Madam?'

'Oh, nothing.'

'Would you like to inspect the dessert course, Madam?'

'No,' I said, appalled. 'I'm sure it's very nice.'

But they continued to stand stiffly to attention, so I returned to the dining-room.

Everyone was very garrulous now. Lips were wet. Jim's tie had worked itself loose. The Riesling was finished and they had turned to a red wine, a Nederburg Baronne. Adela lit up a cigarette.

'Oh, let's have a ciggie!' chorused the remaining trio of inebriates.

She passed around the carton and everyone lit up, but the pudding arrived and all the cigarettes dived simultaneously into the ashtray.

Cyril began a long story about some ballerina who fell over and had to have a hip replacement, but lost the thread and it turned into a story about somebody else who had a breast reduction. A noisy argument followed about men who had penis enlarging operations; did it still work as efficiently afterwards, was the million dollar question.

'Dear, dear,' said Adela, holding the Nederburg up to the light. 'Dry as the Salvation Army.'

'Replenishments required!' roared Jim.

Adela went away and returned with two bottles of Cabernet Sauvignon. She uncorked the first one and poured liberally into our glasses.

I had never seen adults of my own social milieu drunk before. These people were house guests. How could they be so unconcernedly raiding their host's liquor cabinet in his absence? These were not table wines; they were fine wines, and costly.

'Adela,' I said uneasily, 'won't he mind about us drinking all of his wine?'

There was a silence. They all stared at me.

The psychologist was the first to speak.

'God, you are Miss Sanctimonious!'

'Miss Sanctimonious,' echoed Cyril.

'*Shut up, you fucking halfwit!*' I blazed at him. 'You don't even know what that damn word means.'

'Oh la la!' exclaimed Margaret. 'Temper! Temper! Do I detect a streak of submerged hostility?'

Something snapped inside me. I began to cry. I had not cried since the funeral. This was a hideously embarrassing place to start, but I could not stop. I sobbed and snivelled and gasped into my Cabernet Sauvignon.

'What's the matter with you?' demanded Margaret, leaning forward on her elbows, trying to focus on my face.

'My father wants me to go ho-ho-home and write a bi-bi-biography of my brother.'

'Tell your brother to write his own biography, if he wants one written. Why can't he do that?'

'Because he's dead,' I wept. 'He died a few weeks ago.'

'Well, that's bad luck, but I don't see what it's got to do with your having to write a biography.'

'My fa-fa-father wants me to go and write this book and he will be miserable if I don't.'

'Well!' exclaimed Margaret, slamming backwards in her chair. 'Of all the drivelling nonsense. Rest assured, your parents can cope fine by themselves. Who ever heard of a girl of your age writing a book? I suspect you're feeling left out of the limelight and you want a bit of flattery.'

She lurched forward again and narrowed her eyes.

'I don't think your father even did write a letter. You're making it all up to get a bit of attention. I tell you what. You're a vainglorious girl, and that brother of yours was quite a hero, wasn't he? Now you're looking to cash in on a bit of emotional capital.'

She turned to the others, who had been blearily watching the developments, and continued, discursively, 'I see this a lot, if the relatives think they can get something out of it, they become ever so tragic.'

'Shtill,' volunteered Adela in a sentimental slur, 'he wash really a *beautiful* boy.'

I pushed back my chair, made for my bedroom and flung myself under the covers. Holding the pillow to my face, I cried and cried and cried. At some point I must have fallen asleep, because I woke to hear Cyril knocking on the locked door.

'What?'

'My toothbrush is in there!'

'Sod off!'

He went away grumbling. I followed the stumbling collision courses of the other guests trying to find their way to their beds. There was a digital alarm clock on the side table. I saw that it was 2. 07 a.m. on Tuesday the 18th of August. It was my birthday. I had turned twenty-two.

*

Cyril and I were hitch-hiking to Harare and had been picked up by a garrulous driver. Now I sat in the front cabin seat of his Ford Bantam bakkie. Cyril was out in the open air, in the rear of the truck behind the glass partition. The driver was a man of liberal proportions, and very affable. Some sanguine warmth flushed his face, or perhaps it was the winter sun. Whatever it was that had possessed him, he became candid and appeared to want to take us into his confidence. He had already made one or two sharp remarks about his former wife.

'Marry in haste, repent at leisure!'

I groped around for an appropriate response, but I couldn't find one, so I smiled in a generalised kind of way.

He returned my smile and resettled himself on the leather seat.

'South African, are you?'

'Yes.'

'You poor buggers.' He whistled out through his lips. 'Writing's on the bloody wall for you lot.'

I looked at him speculatively and didn't respond.

His air of confidentiality increased. He leaned his plump brown forearms on the steering wheel.

'The thing is,' he pursued, 'the thing you've got to realise is that once they're in, they will do anything, *anything* they want. What you have to do, and you can't learn this too soon, my girl, is you've got to manage your life using the African safety

106

mechanisms.'

He lapsed into an expectant silence.

'What are the African safety mechanisms?' I asked, obediently.

'Look at this place,' he remarked. 'You know what they used to call us? The grain bin of Africa! Bloody laugh, isn't it. Bloody begging for international aid we are now.'

We passed a ragged little boy, selling nets of dried mopane worms displayed on a stake driven into the sand.

'In the old days,' he continued, 'we used to keep up grain reserves, of course. Silos and silos of the stuff. Cause you never can tell. One bad harvest and you're down shit alley, aren't you?'

The little boy waved at us and the driver fluttered his own hand.

'Poor bloody little *piccaninny*. Where was I?'

'Bad harvests,' I reminded him.

'Oh, yes. Fag? Lighter's in the cubby-hole there. Ja, well, we had the bloody old war and what not and then this lot came in and gave off a lot of gas about liberation and people's struggle and all their twaddle. And in the due course of time we had a bad crop. No, excuse me, those few farms that hadn't yet been turned into African dust bowls had a bad crop. Well, off goes Mr Minister Of Agriculture to open up the silos and – low and behold – empty as a pocket! Of course, it was all there on paper. But some bloody government cat had shipped the whole lot out to God knows where.'

He opened the window marginally to tip off his ash. The dry countryside continued to slip by outside.

'But listen to this. I sit on the farm and I think what kind of bloody bastards are these guys to let their own people starve to death like this. But they still make like it's the white man's bloody indaba. We've had these field extension people phoning up all year, saying it's racist to grow tobacco on our lands when the people are starving!

'Mind you,' he said suddenly, 'what I say to you here, that's you and me, white people speaking to each other. When you lot go over to an Af dictatorship, if you want to look after yourself, you make damn sure that you don't say a word of protest. Look what happened here. Silly buggers who started creating a huge bloody hullabaloo were the first ones to get their farms taken.'

The cabin was growing stuffy. I opened the window and leaned my head against the frame. Zimbabwe had always been touted by conservatives at home as an example of the lunacy of African government. Since the independence, there had been conflict and corruption, with huge caches of money disappearing. In 1988 a student uprising had been violently suppressed, the universities' funds were partially withdrawn and the students punished.

Robert Mugabe, undeterred by the failed experiments of Zambia and Tanzania, remained a firm socialist and supporter of the one-party system. In 1990 an opposition party was formed to ZANU, but one of the foremost members, Patrick Kamibaye, narrowly escaped an attempted assassination.

Politically, land issues were very much a hot potato, as Mugabe had recently announced that half the lands belonging to white commercial farmers would be redistributed to black subsistence farmers. In itself, this panicked the whites. But there were also murky stories of numerous farms which had been expropriated and were now nepotistically owned by wealthy Africans connected to the Mugabe regime.

But I had also read positive reports about the country. A 1990 report by the Catholic Commission for Justice and Peace had praised the growth in education, health services and agricultural productivity. I found it difficult to discover the mean in this country of polarisations. It was impossible to follow a critical debate because of the restrictions on the press.

But the words 'go over to an Af dictatorship' set my teeth on edge.

'I know what you're thinking,' pressed the man. 'You think I'm a racist bugger, don't you? As a point of fact, my girl, when I was your age I was the first one to run around with a banner in my hand shouting about oppression. Me and Doris bloody Lessing.'

'Oh, you knew Doris Lessing?' I asked with interest.

'Didn't know her,' he admitted. 'What I mean is that I was of the ilk. Belief in the white man's guilt and so on. Well, that was twenty years ago and maybe I've learnt a thing or two. When you lot go over, it won't take you long to figure out who's got their fingers in the till. That's where you use your African safety mechanisms. You want to make a few friends, butter a few palms, look after your own. You don't want to be a soft touch, but you do want to let those munts know it'll be worth their while to leave you alone.'

A goat ran across the road and he swerved to avoid it. The black tarmac panned on and on ahead and the dry fields spread out on either side.

'Grain bin of bloody Africa!' muttered the man drily to himself.

Third World Groupies

The farmer's family were mad about polo and took us to watch a full-length match at the Polo Club. Now it was the end of the fourth chukka and the grooms led out the fresh ponies for the riders to change their mounts. There was a general hum as the stale ponies were walked off. The newcomers stamped their feet and tossed their heads. The three-minute pip sounded, signalling the end of the interval, and the players cantered back on to the pitch.

A polo match has six chukkas of seven minutes each, with a three-minute interval between each chukka to change ponies. A pony can play two chukkas, but not consecutively. The ponies were small thoroughbreds with long necks, sloping shoulders and powerfully sleek loins and quarters. They all had their pasterns bandaged and most were ridden on a martingale, throwing up their beautiful heads against the restriction. They twisted and turned on the pitch as the white wooden ball was propelled by the mallets through their galloping legs. I leaned against the wooden barrier, absorbed in the wild energy of the game.

The ball went flying, the horses whipped past en route for the far end of the pitch. Behind me, the uniformed servants had begun to arrange the lunch dishes. Ranged on the trestle tables were cold meats, green salads and potato salads, curried chickens, breads and cheeses. There was a dessert selection of platters of ice-cream and trifles and strawberries. Each of the several teams in the tournament had a members' tent where the women and children and older men were gathered. People reclined on deck chairs, or stood in groups sipping cocktails and peering at one another through shaded spectacles, speculating on the outcome of the matches. The air was fragrant with horsy sweat and a commingling of delicate perfumes on warm necks.

'There you are!' said the wife of the farmer's son, appearing at my side. 'Will you get yourself something to eat? One of our mares has got a great big cut on her hock! I've got to run and see that something is put on it.'

She was a very handsome woman of remarkable serenity and great managerial powers, in crisp linens and a straw hat against the sun. If a hock needed swabbing, she would swab it; if she dabbled in a garden, great banks of roses would bloom from it. Currently, she was raising ostriches and would walk unconcernedly amongst the hissing birds, admonishing them to be still.

I spooned some salad on to a paper plate and went back to the game. There was a scrimmage of legs and flying soil. I couldn't see where the ball had got to.

'Having a good feed, are you?'

I looked up into the sun. Here was a wizened lady of sixty-odd, in a tailored suit, downy tufts sprouting from her chin. It seemed a rather loaded remark. She was conducting an unflinching appraisal of my person that was clearly not going in my favour. I felt self-conscious. Not wanting to come to the tournament in my old blue sleeveless shirt, I had bought a cotton blouse from an African store. It was made from the material that the African women wear as wraps. I liked its gaudiness, and the row of leaping springbok across the chest. My hair was still knotted up in the array of beads.

'I don't know who let you in here!' enunciated my opponent, coldly. Her acid gaze flicked over to where Cyril was still energetically carving his way through a wholegrain loaf at the trestle tables. He was also in an African cotton blouse, except his had a motif of elephants instead of springboks.

I looked back at the old lady, nonplussed.

'You think you can come in here, you *filthy* third world groupies, sleep with our munts, get them all riled up, revise the world order! Who do you think you are? You can spend your whole life grubbing around with wogs, it's your choice. But I resent, I really *resent* your having the temerity to come here and freeload as and when you like! If you admire them so much, then go and live with them!'

She turned on her heel and disappeared into the interior of the tent. I watched her go, amazed and humiliated. How could I have released such visceral emotion, so unwittingly? Had she confused me with another, I wondered fleetingly.

I had absolutely no idea who she was.

*

I was being retained in Zimbabwe by a pair of boots. My own very elderly boots had given in, and I had bought a local pair which had frayed apart within a week. So I had asked my mother to send me a pair of boots from home. That had been two weeks ago, and I had been awaiting the arrival of a chit from the post office to say I could collect them, but had heard nothing.

'You have sent them?' I asked her on the telephone.

'Yes, of course, darling, the day you asked me to.'

It seemed I should make a personal investigation at the post office. The post office was large and sprawling. The man at 'Parcels Collection' was also large and very jocular. He had a green apron on to protect his suit from the dust and he took down all my particulars. He could not, however, help with my parcel.

'Evidently it has not arrived yet,' he suggested.

'How long does it take from Johannesburg?'

'Three days maximum,' informed the portly postal clerk, filing away my particulars in a drawer.

I calculated. If it took three days from Cape Town to Johannesburg and another three from there, it ought to have been in situ for a week at least.

'It should be here,' I frowned.

The postal clerk lifted his chunky shoulders and dropped them sympathetically.

'What you really need to know,' he said helpfully, 'is when the shipment left Cape Town.'

'Why do I need to know that?'

'Because then we can follow the onward progress.'

I went upstairs to the public phone booths. It took an hour to reach the front of the queue and then another hour whilst I tried to convert the whirrings and buzzings of errant telephonic circuitry into an international call. My mother agreed to phone the post office at home. I guarded the booth sheepishly for twenty minutes, whilst waiting for her response.

'Darling,' she said into my ear eventually and breathlessly, 'I thought I'd never get through! What a horrible roaring noise.'

'Oh, don't worry about that,' I said. 'Nothing seems to work very well here.'

There was a sudden irritated snort in my ear and an abrupt snap. I realised with a start that mysterious telephone operators had been listening to my call and now I had been cut off.

She got through again after another twenty minutes. Meanwhile the groundswell of queuing telephone hopefuls was becoming mutinous.

'Darling, it's so irritating, what's the matter with . . .'

'Shut up, don't say it, Mum! Just give me the date.'

I went downstairs determinedly. The grille of 'Parcels Collection' had been dropped, but the plump clerk was still visibly conducting forays behind it.

'Hi. I've got the date.'

'The Collection is closed.'

'Oh please. I've been waiting all afternoon!'

'No, it's closed. Come back tomorrow.'

I returned as soon as the post office opened the next day. The same clerk in the same green apron was shuffling about in his annexe.

'Can I help?'

He did not seem to recognise me. I looked at him suspiciously. I did think I was fairly conspicuous by dint of being the only white face in the place. But it would not do to be surly, especially as he himself was so unremittingly cheerful. I gave a brief synopsis of the events of the day before and delivered my trump card.

'My boots left Cape Town on the 15th of August, arrived in Johannesburg on the 17th of August, and left Johannesburg on the 20th of August.'

'I see,' answered the clerk. 'And what was the serial number of the parcel containing the boots?'

I looked at him blankly.

He returned my look.

'Is that important?' I said faintly.

'That is the most essential information!' concluded the clerk, pocketing both hands in the depths of his voluminous apron. 'Many, many parcels arrived after the 20th of August!'

'Why didn't you tell me to ask them that in the first place?'

His face became a mask of gentle reproof. I hared upstairs to the phone booth and managed to gallop through the entire proceedings in one hour and twenty-seven minutes.

'Serial number 347A BB6A,' I announced triumphantly on my return.

'Oh, very good,' said the clerk, approvingly. 'And what was the number of the cargo dispatch that the parcel came in?'

'I don't know,' I said.

Each word seemed to drop out of my mouth separately like

a little stone and bounce along the dusty counter to bury itself in the bundles of packages that filled up the poky annexe.

The man's face twisted in regret. 'I see. Well, I'll do what I can to trace it.'

'But I need it now!'

'Excuse me,' he said, very patiently. 'The cargo of that particular day may perhaps still be in storage. It might be in storage in the Parcel Storage Room. In the Parcel Storage Room there are many dispatches. You do not know which dispatch your parcel came in. The Parcel Storage Room is a very big place. The post office itself is a very big place.'

I retired to a bench to think. The man was perfectly right. The post office was a very big place. There were also a great many people milling about in it. After a while I made a decision. I picked up the bench and moved it directly in front of the Parcel Collection Office. The tips of my worn away boots rested on the bottom supports of the Parcel Collection Counter.

The clerk looked at me enquiringly.

'I'm going to sit here,' I told him, 'I'm going to sit here until Parcel Number 347A BB6A is processed through the Parcel Storage Room and appears at the Parcel Collection Counter.'

He blinked. 'But that might not even be today.'

'Well then, I will sit here tonight,' I said. 'And tomorrow. And tomorrow night. I will sit here for as long as I have to until I have my boots.'

The man grew thoughtful. He seemed to dip gracefully under the counter and stir one fleshy arm amongst the midden of objects which reposed there. A moment passed. He resurfaced. In the grip of one fist he now held a brown paper package.

'Miss Sarah Alexandra Penny,' he said, reading the label. His eyes searched generally through the lofty hall, and came to rest on me. 'That is you,' he supplied, almost as an afterthought.

'That is me,' I agreed graciously.

'Miss Penny,' announced the clerk with an air of happy

coincidence, 'I have a parcel for you.'

'Thank you very much,' I said.

*

The Harare Show is an important event in the agricultural year, being the venue where all the prize cows and goats and pigs are displayed. Recent innovations are also marketed there: fuel-saving stoves, portable toilets that do not require chemicals and naturopathic ointments and preparations. This year there was an exhibition of gleaming tractors and tractor parts. The main tent had a government display of advances and improvements in farming methods.

Droves of people massed around the tents or milled their way through the alleys between the stalls. There were a number of whites, but they kept to their own groups, and away from the crowd. The Africans were more dispersed and numerous. As it grew dark, hordes of revellers congregated at the beer stalls. The beer was being sold in plastic litre buckets which by now were randomly strewn about. Drunks lay sprawled on the patchy grass or tussled with each other. I kept side-stepping to avoid being pinched. Hands seemed to shoot out of nowhere and grab at my breasts or thighs. I slapped them away sullenly.

I found Cyril and hurried up to him.

'Don't leave me.'

He looked at me, surprised. I did not usually cling. But I felt exposed in that crowd, a solitary white and a girl. And I did not want to be felt up by drunks. The other white women were closeted in the ranks of their men, and peered out on to the world from within those closed circles.

The high point of the evening was a fireworks display. We wormed our way into the crowd and sat down on the grass. People had gathered in family groups and were dispensing pieces of chicken to their children. The fireworks display was preceded by policemen leaping over one another on motor cycles.

I was diverted by the sight of a man making his way through the crowd. He was clearly in his cups and, worse, he seemed to be bearing down on us. Two friends were propping him up as he propelled himself through the crowd. Mothers grumbled and gathered in their children. I looked around for an escape route, but there was none.

The man halted directly in front of us and launched into a rambling monologue, pointing first at me and then at Cyril. The crowd laughed. I could not understand a thing. He was speaking in Shona.

'Cyril, let's go, please!'

'Huh? No, I'm watching the bikes.'

The man's finger remained on Cyril. He made several gyrations with his hips and thrust out his pelvis. The flow of dialogue reached some kind of culmination. The crowd guffawed.

Cyril finally noticed that he was being lampooned.

'Hey man!' he said genially to the perpetrator.

This was evidently very funny. The joker and his two props dissolved into laughter. But I was feeling excruciatingly embarrassed. We were the only whites in the crowd. All the others had paid for tickets in the grandstands. I could not understand the mockery, but I could understand the intent and it was not good natured.

They moved on as the sky began to explode with bursts of coloured light and the attention of their audience shifted. The crowd had come to be diverted and fireworks were a greater diversion than the baiting of whites.

But the feeling of being singled out remained. I walked silently back to the place where we were staying, the farmer's town house in Harare, and ran a bath. Tender blue smudges were rising on my thighs and chest.

A new feeling was fomenting in my heart as I watched the water spurting into the bathtub. I resented being groped by faceless men that I did not know. I resented being mocked. I resented that the predilections of the white camp were being borne out, that you will not be accepted, that you must keep with your own. I resented that things were this way because I was white and they were black, and I resented that I had tried to dispense with these barriers only to have them resurrected. This black/white thing, this man/woman thing – I wanted these divisions to be myths only, but they would not become myths. I am mocked because I am a white, I am molested because I am a girl. If I pretend not to see the divisions, they will still exist and others will insist on them. Africa is a continent of polarisations.

To the black mass I am the enemy.

For the first time in my life, I was essentially aware of myself not as a young woman, but as a young white woman.

A member of the white race.

Because an element of my resentment was clearly racial hostility.

I had become conscious of racism fairly early. At our prep school my best friend and I would exempt ourselves from singing the national anthem. I missed singing the national anthem because all the other children would sing it and it had a nice emotionally rousing tune, but on the other hand I was determined to be aware.

At boarding school it was a simple issue. Racism was a propensity of the fascists, those who would crush, who had no art in their souls, the polyester-clad headmaster and his coterie of refugees from already independent African countries.

'Sir, could I speak to you?'

'What is it?'

'Well, I've noticed, sir, that our housemistress won't allow the African parents over the doorstep. Which is out of keeping I think, sir, because we are multiracial now, after all.'

'Can you ask a leopard to change its spots, Sarah?'

'No, sir.'

'You can go now.'

'Yes, sir.'

'Oh, Sarah.'

'Yes, sir?'

'Don't get beyond yourself.'

'No, sir. I'm sorry.'

In the mid-eighties South Africa exploded into violent unrest, following the 1984 introduction of P W Botha's tricameral parliament, a divisive and convoluted 'new dispensation' which offered all non-white racial groups some marginal political representation, with the solid exception of Africans.

This was the era of the mass riots, the school boycotts, political funerals and police death squads. In July 1985 a State of Emergency was temporarily declared in the East Rand and the Eastern Cape, allowing for immediate arrest and detention, banning political meetings and imposing severe press censorship.

My whole adolescence was pock-marked by States of Emergency settling and lifting around the country like giant ideological rain squalls. When the eight o'clock news demarcated the current boundaries of the 'hot spots' I thought of the other obvious insidious meaning of a 'State of Emergency'; of the spirit of the South African people, wrapped up and obscured in a chrysalis of state laws, but slowly pupating, gradually evolving towards a transformed future.

My school did its bit to impart an understanding of the stirring times we were living through. The police were invited to show propaganda videos about the country. Aged sixteen, I was learning population development and algebra and the proclivities of blacks. Youthful cineastes – we watched tyre necklacings and African mobs dancing on the body. An image remains of a charred corpse, one supplicating hand still partially held aloft.

I did believe that these things were happening. But I could not accept that they sprang a priori from African atavism. And I had doubts about those who were offered to me as heroes. I did not believe in the police or the headman as saviours. I did not believe in them as innocents.

At university I found left-wing politics. In the time left over from my Beautiful People activities, I joined the newspaper and various protest movements. I also became a march marshal. The job of marshalling a march was terribly gratifying for a youngest child, particularly one whose mother still required her to be in bed by eleven on week nights. A march marshal gets to wear a red handkerchief around her upper arm. All the march marshals join hands in a great circle around the march itself.

As the march surges forward, the march marshals say keep together, guys, and viva comrade to all the other students, who are hopping from one foot to the other and bellowing freedom songs. Eventually the police will arrive and the march marshals scurry around the group telling everybody to stand still. A student leader detaches himself from the group, walks up to the police and shakes hands. If the student leader is white, he will have untidy sandy hair and be gorgeously beautiful. If he is black, he will be tall, prepossessing and just a little bit cynical. Whatever his colour, he will be unfailingly polite to the cops. But the cops always say the same thing.

The cops say: 'Three minutes to disperse!'

The student leader relays this information to the march marshals and the march marshals pass it on to the marchers themselves. Everyone shifts their feet and squints into the sun. The students are wearing sloganised T-shirts or tie-dyed blouses and have the university at their backs. The police are dressed in their blue uniforms and stand against the squat hollow trucks called casspirs. Over their shoulders, they hold the teargas firers. All of us, police and students, are the same age, about nineteen-odd, except for a few senior policemen.

One two three minutes tick slowly by. A very faint smell of sweat permeates the air. Nobody says anything. People glance at their shoelaces. We marshals shoulder against one another on the front line. We are so close we can see the pit of a fading acne pustule on a policeman's jawline.

'Ready fire!' call the police.

'Run!' shout the marshals.

We duck and sprint, weaving over the lawns and fences, racing up the tarred driveway. Overhead the plumes of teargas whizz, before drifting down. It gets in your throat and nose, which are bursting anyway with the effort of running, and makes you cough and splutter. In your pocket you have a vial of Vaseline to rub in your nostrils and at the corners of your eyes.

Invariably the march makes you late for your next lecture or tutorial and you have to try and slip to the back unnoticed. The teaching staff could not always be counted upon to show the proper reverence for the red handkerchief around the upper arm. I suspected them of not being entirely sympathetic to the Struggle, or at least that sector of it played out on the university plaza during the lunch hour.

Still, it did not matter, nothing superficial mattered – least of all black and white. Either you were for the people or you weren't. Non-racism, non-sexism and democracy – that was the creed of the left. I had spoken it, chanted it, written it, thought it. I had sat drowsily through numerous prolonged speeches whose entire structure was hinged on the periodic surfacing of that phrase.

I touched the smudgy bruises bleakly with my fingertips. Non-racism and non-sexism. These two forums of oppression were hitherto inseparable concepts in my mind. Now I was beginning to suspect that they did not make easy bedfellows.

I had always perceived the imminent dismantling of apartheid as a pure attainment of liberties. Freedom for all. But for me, as a white girl, there might be a curtailment of past freedoms. If white Calvinism had bundled up and stultified its womanhood, it had also protected them. Black Africa clearly was not a nirvana for women.

A repository of charitable inclinations, I had formerly had a slogan for everything and a rehearsed ideology to back it.

I had gone to the outside of my slogans, and was looking in

on them. They no longer seemed to cover the whole of my experience.

*

A strand of tarmac connects the capital cities of Harare and Lusaka. Tar roads can dominate and destroy, but not in this case. Elephants still browse freely alongside and the road is subordinated to Lake Kariba on the one side, and the Mana Pools National Park on the other.

I adore roads, because a road is like a promise, a pathway into the unknown. I had become obsessed: a village or town rapidly grows stale, only the road seizes my imagination, and the quest to keep moving onwards. To see what is around the next corner, and the next, and the next.

I abhor roads for the same reason. A road beckons indiscriminately. A road doesn't question the motives of those who pass along it. A road can too easily spell the end of its destination.

Sometimes a road will fancy you and suck you relentlessly into its bosom. After an hour or two a car will pass. The face of the driver becomes distinct, he sees you through his sunshades, he chews on his moustache, his apologetic hands tumble over each other, a rush of warm wind through your hair and the rear of the vehicle is already waning in the distance. Enraged, you shake your fist, you stamp your boots in the dust. But the driver is only recognising a recondite philosophy which you suspect yourself; that you do, for the moment, belong to the road.

I had this bondage on that part of the road which runs between Makuti and Chirundi. It was alleviated by *The Lord of the Flies*. When you have read a book several times, over a number of years, it becomes a benchmark of your own progress. The same book at twelve, at seventeen, at twenty-two, seems to develop a different text. Extraordinary that you could have missed so much, that you had never known this or that, you try to feel your way back into the growing awareness of that child or adolescent, you can surmise it, but the gates are closed.

It was a very still midday, of tolerable heat. The landscape was attractive here; the road was on a rise and the valley fell away beneath, thick with msasa trees and flat umbrella thorns. A francolin was scrabbling in the nearby bush, detectable from her frequent hoarse call. Apart from us, everything was hidden from the sun. Only the swallowtail butterflies fluttered in the air, and darting sand lizards scuttled from rock to rock.

Cyril located a tick on his leg and squashed it.

I looked at him critically. We had not said very much to each other since the drinking session a fortnight ago.

He seemed to be absorbed in the tick or the blood or the dust or something.

What does he think about? How did we ever manage even to have a conversation with each other?

'Cyril,' I asked him, 'how do you feel about me?'

Such a woman's question, that one. How ridiculous for it to have spurted up out of my mouth.

He looked up, his brow creased. He considered it.

'Hey man. You exist. I exist.'

Horrendous. I would never probe the sources of those Delphic abstractions that comprised his world.

A sand lizard exploded into the open, recoiled from one of my new boots and vanished into a crevice.

'How do you feel about me?' he said, unexpectedly.

I thought about it.

'Weariness,' I conceded eventually. 'Weariness is a sort of constant foundation. Apart from weariness, there's confusion, amazement, horror, disbelief, scorn, anger. At times – loathing. At other times – neutrality.'

'And sometimes you like me,' he said comfortably.

'Occasionally,' I admitted. 'Occasionally I manage to reconcile myself. But it doesn't last.'

He laughed. I watched him closely. Another man might have found this little exchange distressing. But not Cyril. The obvious attacks never budged him an inch. He continued to squat equably on the roadside and search his thigh for further ticks.

'I cannot bear travelling with you, Cyril!' I said tremulously.

He lay down on his back in the sand and covered his face with his hat.

'I can't bear it, I really can't! It's madness, Cyril. You're probably a terribly nice boy, but we're the most wildly unsuitable people for each other.'

'We were fine when we met,' he said indistinctly from beneath his hat.

'Yes. No! Everything's changed thoroughly since then. I've changed thoroughly. Sit up, for God's sake, Cyril!'

He did sit up, and peered at me from under his hat. He had not changed a bit, I realised. He was the one constant factor.

'Cyril, try to understand what I'm saying to you,' I continued, more calmly.

He looked at me non-committally.

I drew a breath. What I wanted to say had something to do with the jumbled chaos in my head that was the last few weeks.

'This thing with my brother, Cyril, it's really affected me. I know you don't believe in death, but I have to believe in it. It's happened to me.'

'You never try and go beyond,' he mumbled.

'Cyril, I'm falling apart. I can't try and muddle through this with New Age sententiousness. I have to stop being near you. I have to stop with all this right now. When we get to Lusaka, I want to get a bus to Malawi and sit on a beach and be by myself and think about everything.'

'I don't want to go to Malawi,' he said stubbornly. 'We're going north.'

'I don't want you to go,' I said.

He saw the light. His brow contracted.

'Where will I go?' he asked.

'I don't mind where you go,' I told him, 'as long as it's somewhere where I am not.'

'Fine,' he shrugged, blowing out his cheeks.

The afternoon continued to while away. I looked speculatively at him from time to time, wondering if he minded. Perhaps away from my fussing he would get himself to a place where he could use his bush survival skills.

A vague throbbing arose on the warm air. Far in the distance the ribbon track was birthing some emerging object. The hum grew louder and more resonant, the object increased in size. It became an orange blob. The blob swelled and refined itself into a truck. I saw it was a maize conveying transport lorry, from the Wheels For Africa company. The door panel bore the distinctive logo of the shape of the African continent, divided by a swathe of tyre marks. The truck drew alongside our waving arms and braked. We scurried to the driver's side and squinted up at him. He was black, not young, his tight curls were streaked with grey and his mouth encircled by lines.

He looked down at us.

'Good afternoon. Where are you going?'

'Where are *you* going?'

'Lubumbashi.'

Cyril and I looked at each other.

'Where is that?' I asked.

'It's in Zaire.'

Zaire. I hesitated. I had heard so much about that country. Pygmies and equatorial rain forest. Joseph Conrad's *Heart of Darkness*. Dian Fossey and her mountain gorillas. Zaire was where Nicholas had hidden in the jungle during the revolution. The country with the vilest and bloodiest colonial history in Africa. The country whose president was so unprincipled, so single-mindedly avaricious that he made our apartheid führers look like philanthropists by comparison.

I knew I would not go to Zaire on my own.

'What do you think?' I said to Cyril.

'Hey, sounds like a trip.'

'How far is it?' I asked the driver.

'About two days.'

I glanced at Cyril to see if he thought I was losing face, but he was as inscrutable as always. We crossed to the opposite side of the truck, hoisted our bags inside, and settled ourselves into the front cabin.

The One Who Leaves Fire In His Wake

Evening fell on a laager of colossal orange trucks. We had reached the town of Kitwe in the copper belt of Northern Zambia and were parked in the depot of the Wheels for Africa trucking company. The unprepossessing edifice of the administration office sat squarely in the centre of the lot, surrounded by warehouses. Fringed around them were the trucks themselves in various stages of readiness, or disrepair. Some were being overhauled, and had their bonnets gaping. The burr of gunning engines rankled on the cooling night. Detached from their vast cargoes, the cabin sections looked puny and effete. It seemed impossible that they could drag these myriad heaps of goods all over the subcontinent.

Men tinkered and delved in the automotive stomachs, or stood about in groups relaying words to one another. They bunched their hammy fists in pockets or wiped greasy spanners on overalls. A high brick surround with a jagged glass edging kept the market urchins away, but a vague stink of shit permeated from the sewer spills. The predominating scent was the bland floury flavour of putu boiling on coal braziers. A half dozen truckers squatted separately on footstools over the embers of their own braziers, doughty forearms evenly stirring the sallow powder to a thickening pulp.

They stirred with half their attention, because an astonishing spectacle was unfolding in the midst of the unvarying routines of the Kitwe truck depot.

Here was a white man, backlit by the remains of the sun, ringlets afire, damp with perspiration, one hand resting on the furthest extremity of our truck. *Grand plié* in first position, *grand plié* in second position, *grand plié* in fifth. His slender thighs bent parallel to the dust and then straightened. His arm extended and curved and extended again.

The putu stirrers were rapt, circling wooden spoons in thick iron pots, their own broad chins rising and falling with the young man's movements. They murmured amongst themselves, they pressed closer to see better, foreheads crumpled, heads shaking in muted amusement.

Our driver's name was Girison. Girison had already been exposed to two evenings of *barre*-work. Initially mystified, he seemed to have reached an inner, unfavourable conclusion. His back was turned; we huddled together at the far end of the truck in disassociation, chopping up tomatoes and spinach for the putu sauce.

My skin gave off the pungent odour of chlorine. When we had arrived in the late afternoon, scurfy with dirt and sweat, a white man had been at the depot, a manager, hale and plump, and replicated almost exactly in youth by a teenage son. The son lost his tongue at the sight of me, smiling bashfully into the puddles of grainy dirt at his feet.

Well, well, said the manager, and where were you going to sleep? Under the truck, sir. Over my dead body, lordy, lordy, you lot, is that any way for white people to pass a night, and you a young lady as well. I'll give you the office keys and you can bunk in there. It's not the Ritz but you can make yourself tea and coffee. Keen for a swim?

Twenty minutes later I was splashing in the shallows as the Zambian national swimming team ploughed up and down the lanes. From my rucksack I had dug out a streaky blue bikini with *Sensation* in saucy black lettering across the halter. I felt quite self-conscious, virtually naked, stropping my armpits hurriedly under the spurting shower head. The bikini seemed to stem from a sunny late adolescence that had vanished for ever. But the swimmers were an earnest body of boys, ruddy, sunburnt and bristly blond. One of them offered me a towel afterwards and quavered on alternating feet, making light conversation.

The truck depot and its environs were staunchly masculine. The men were intrigued by Cyril, but my intrusion into their world embarrassed them. To me, the relations between uneducated African men and women frequently seemed hostile and remote. Moreover, these men had a minimal family life. They subsisted in their own world, toiling up and down the byways of the continent.

Earlier in the evening I had gone to the pump to draw water, but they could not wash down their hot, spent bodies while I was there. I left it to Cyril and sat at the office desk in the administration building writing poetry.

I took out my diary and wrote some silly verse.

While Cyril drew water with the men
I meditated upon zen
I said to Krishna, 'Will I ascend?
In khali yoga it's the trend.'

He said 'Little Woman – in all fairness
you're better off to grow a penis.
Look at Buddha, Jesus and Jah
and even Srila Prapupadah.

I offer the truth without disguise.
Remember I am old and wise.
Don't imagine that I'm balmy
or some insane old crackpot swami.

*The path to spiritual perfection
begins at the end of one's erection.'*

Meanwhile the prostitutes had converged in a little knot outside
the entry gates. They remained there, giggling and gossiping
softly among themselves. The custom having completed its brief
toilette at the pump, they swung open the barrier. There was a
terse appraisal of the girls. They shuffled and flattened their
blouses against their breasts. Some were picked out and a
muttered discussion followed, an exclamation, an annoyed
waving of hands. A winsome young thing who had made a
spirited declaration was replaced after some dithering by a
saggier, gap-toothed harridan, which I assumed must have been
a budget decision.

The rejected ones settled themselves in the scrappy grass to
await any further lusts the night might rouse.

Those men who had not bought women had Cyril and his
grands battements as a diversion. Up soared a lissom leg, muscles
tautly linear, a pointing toe raised to the sky. I spooned the
quartered tomatoes into our own aluminium billy which was
heating on a vacant corner of Girison's brazier.

If I was an odd figment in the camp, Girison was another.
With his grizzly hair and his air of venerability he seemed oddly
professorial and apart from the other men. I had already learnt
that he came from the South African homeland of Venda and
that he was sixty-seven. It seemed an unlikely age to be hauling
those megalithic machines across the continent.

'Why does he do these things?' Girison had asked, of the
grands battements, the first night.

'I don't know why he does anything,' I replied. 'He's just
one crazy bwana.'

The tomatoes began to steam and bubble.

'Girison, do you ever do that?'

'What?'

'Take a woman.' I indicated the random trucks, now

130

converted into boudoirs.

'Uh uh.' He shook his head, paused in his rhythmic stirring of the putu. 'I've got a wife and six children. These women make you sick. How will I explain to my children if I get too sick to work? And my wife – I could make her sick too.'

'Don't they think they'll die?' I asked, looking at the truck cabins.

'They don't believe it. They think they're men, they're big and strong. They think Slim is a sickness for women and small children.'

Slim is a Central and East African term for Aids, because of the loss of weight that the disease inevitably causes.

The following morning we rose before dawn and began the trek to the border post at Chililabombwe.

Progress along the national road was arduously slow. The road itself was the old British one, unfurbished since independence. Wide dusty depressions pock-marked the randomly adhering tarmac. Alongside, telephone wires looped sadly along the ground, like a series of children's skipping ropes caught up on poles. The smashed street lamps trailed wires and shards of glass.

We reached the border at midday. Urchins hawked warm bottles of Coca-Cola and freelance money changers jostled each other to get to us. I made an exchange of two hundred dollars. One American dollar at that point was worth about 2 350 000 zaires. The money changer paid us out in 500 000 zaire notes. Never having been much good with figures and calculations, I made him wait in the cabin whilst I laboriously counted through the vast cache of notes. When they were interred in the money belt I wore on my waist, I looked as if I was well into my second trimester of pregnancy.

In the border office my visa was examined and stamped. I entered all my details into the record book. At that moment a florid white man appeared at my elbow.

'Excuse me, Miss. We has a problems here. Does Miss speak

French?' asked the man anxiously in a tremendously guttural Afrikaner patois.

When I said that I spoke both French and Afrikaans, his flushed face bulged with relief and he dragged me after him into an office. Another two burly whites in shirt-sleeves were there, and behind a desk sat a small black man in a suit. A contretemps of considerable bellicosity was clearly under way.

Everybody began to present their side to me. The Afrikaners bellowed in Afrikaans. The Zairean made neat little ripostes in French. I tried to process it into English and represent the different points of view.

After a few minutes I had garnered the basic thrust of the argument. Everyone who travels in Zaire has to have a yellow fever jab, valid for ten years, and a cholera jab, valid for six months. The Afrikaners, who were transport drivers, had had both vaccinations in 1990. They had renewed their cholera vaccinations periodically since then. The official wanted to see the yellow fever renewal. He could not loose them upon the nation without it, he implied.

'But we don't need one for another eight years!' protested my countrymen, when I communicated this.

The official was unmoved. Did they have South African rands, he wondered. If they had South African rands, he could arrange to minister the inoculation in his own office.

'Over my dead body!' voiced the florid one stoutly. 'I'm not having a kaffir needle in my arm, to get me a HIV.'

'An inoculation for twenty-five rands,' repeated the official.

'But they don't need it,' I argued.

'Twenty-five rands,' he reiterated softly.

I got it.

The Afrikaners gave up their money with a bad grace. The insistent official tucked the notes behind a ballpoint pen in his breast pocket and smiled politely, seeming content to stand corrected on the issue now.

By mid-afternoon some twenty or thirty trucks had

assembled at the border. This vast convoy rumbled slowly through the border post. We crossed into the opposite lane as the Zaireans drive on the other side of the road.

The huts here were square and built of bricks, rather than mud and poles. Dilapidated official buildings bore the remaining stains of ancient letters and anachronistic functions. *Dispensaire* said one. *Laboratoire* read another. Presently we left the town. Little boys ran out from the trees, waving and dancing in the air to catch the fluttering notes that the drivers threw.

'Why do you give them money, Girison?'

'They pack the holes in the tar with mud.'

After a while the road gave out altogether and was replaced by a belt of loose ferruginous dust. One of the trucks had come to a halt and the driver waved urgently.

'Why doesn't anybody stop, Girison?'

'You can't be left behind from the convoy.' He crouched over the wheel, guiding the vehicle over the uneven surface, his forehead damp with sweat. 'If you get left behind or stop, the bandits will come for your cargo. They might cut your throat.'

Behind us the figure of the luckless driver grew smaller and fainter. A fire of dust rose up from the truck in front. It filtered in through every gap and cranny, turning the interior of the truck into a haze of rufous particles. We tied cloths around our mouths and noses to filter the grit, and crooked our forearms over our heads to cushion the frequent connection with the roof.

We passed the poor and desperate, the human oxen, dragging immense wagons of manioc behind them by thongs around their foreheads. Black and wet, their straining bodies were sculptures of contorted muscle. They barely seemed to notice our passage, not even recoiling from the billowing dust we raised.

In the early evening we came to the low hills of Lubumbashi and the truck pulled into the main drag. A putrid stench rose from the open channels of shit which paralleled the street, flowing a metre wide on either side. On the banks of the channels grew terraced market gardens. Here and there the sewage overflowed and puddled into the road. Carcasses of dead dogs littered the pavement, the flies buzzing in their mouths. Silent townspeople came out and stood in their doorways, watching the convoy pass.

Here, then, was Zaire.

*

When Stanley made his historic journey down the Congo river in 1874, white men realised for the first time that that vast swollen waterway was navigable. King Leopold the Second of Belgium evinced great interest in this fact. The monarch hired Stanley to open up a network of road and river communications and claimed the territories for his own.

The Zairean people were not newcomers to exploitation and foreign interests. Eastern Zaire had been invaded by the Arabs from their stronghold on the Eastern seaboard of Africa. And the Portuguese had conducted a slave trade on the west coast almost four centuries earlier. Countless thousands of human beings were abducted from their villages and fields and sandwiched vertically in layers between the narrow boards of the Portuguese galleys, bound for the Americas and the Caribbean.

King Leopold was no more humane than his predecessors. He summarily granted land and mining rights to companies who would assist him in his opening-up of the interior, and gave them his imprimatur to conduct their transactions as they wished. The companies, many of whom were profiting from the rubber boom, became increasingly savage and brutal. The Africans were forced to slave on the plantations. If they could not fulfil their quotas, draconian punishments were exacted. Old photographs show expressionless black men holding out baskets of severed human hands. The hands were presented to the plantation bosses to illustrate that discipline was strong.

Joseph Conrad's *Heart of Darkness* was written about this period. The anti-hero, Kurtz, raises his head in his dying moments and cries, 'The horror! The horror!'

By the early twentieth century news of the infamy in the Congo had spread and Leopold was obliged to cede his estate to the Belgian nation. Belgium had to absorb the debts which the king had acquired through prodigal squandering on his European palaces. The greater abuses were curbed, but little was done to develop the Congo. Education was left to the efforts of the Catholic missionaries.

The Belgian government did not allow any political activity amongst Africans. Tribal divisions were supported in order to reinforce Belgian policy. But in 1955, after an African insurrection in Leopoldville (now Kinshasa), the irritated coloniser made the mercurial decision to discard her colony. Africans were told that they had six months in which to prepare for elections and self-government. At that point, the Belgian Congo had precisely six African university graduates.

Patrice Lumumba became the first prime minister. His arch enemy Joseph Kasavuba became president. Within a fortnight the army had mutinied and Katanga, the richest province, had ceded. The country erupted in civil war. Of the white missionaries caught in the crossfire, many were raped and killed. Lumumba himself was murdered and Kasavuba came to power. He was backed by the army, led by General Joseph Mobuto.

In 1963 Mobuto came to government in a coup, according himself the title Mobutu Sese Seko Koko Ngebendu wa za Banga, meaning 'the all powerful warrior who because of his endurance and inflexible will to win, will go from conquest to conquest leaving fire in his wake'. He remained in power until his deposition by Laurent Kabila in May 1997.

There were still a few Belgians in Lubumbashi (formerly Elisabethville). A gaggle of young men who worked under the auspices of the trucking company allowed us to stay with them for a few days. Like all white Africans, they talked nostalgically about the old days, about the quality of life and the beauty of the country. But their attitude was very clinical. They had left as young boys, babies almost, and come back into the carnage with the sole aim of making money. The house was hung with tribal masks and artwork, but it was an unsympathetic assimilation. They clearly detested Africans.

Oddly, the main householder was a former male model. His recurring image sprouted in spruce black and white stills amongst the feral carvings. In some, blue jeans hugged his bare waist – the zip divided to reveal a promising column of pubic hair. In others, he rested a granite chin in a waifish girl's clavicle – arms locked around her naked back to throw the taut muscles into shadowy relief. He remained attentive to his upkeep, marking his passage in billowing drifts of aftershave. Each morning we woke to the regular whine of his blow drier. The hair itself sighed and dipped in obedient blond wafts, in rhythm with his incontrovertible stridings.

His subordinate was genial and asked us to stay, but the model twitched and looked me over as if he might have wanted to make love to a white woman. I was a gaunt, filthy, dust-festooned scrap. He turned away without concealing his disgust.

I did not like to impose on them, but when the night drew in I recoiled in fright from the world beyond the mastiffs and the steel gates.

By day the city teemed with life. The crumbled pavements were massed with moving people and fringed with pedlars hawking foodstuffs or small goods like writing paper and pens. The men laughed and pointed after us.

'*Touristes Americaines!*' they called.

As dusk fell the streets cleared. In a matter of minutes the city centre emptied and a brooding illusion of calm settled on the place. On the first evening we were in a chemist's shop. The man behind the counter began to scratch at his beard and shift on his feet. When we had paid he thrust the money into the till and began rapidly to calculate the day's takings, keeping one dark eye on the doorway.

We emerged from the shop. Gone were the pressing crowds, the vendors and their carts, the sweating human crush. The cool air sighed heavily against our cheekbones. On the opposite side of the road a solitary woman trotted past, her floral bottom turgid with hurry. Our chemist was clawing down the protesting metal window blinds.

The smell of the night came upon us, distinct and dangerous, overpowering even the sickening sewer vapours. We began to run through the streets, away from that deserted, waiting place.

Lying in bed at night, the disembodied cracks of gunfire bit into that cold silence.

One morning we were woken not by the ritual thrum of the blow drier, but by a different sound, a beating throb, a drumming of insane proportions. I lay in bed tensely; the throb acquired volume and seeped into the very windows of the bedroom until even the walls seemed to shudder and jolt. I heard now that it was a song – a chant – and the slap, slap, slap of thudding boots. I climbed from my bed and moved to the window sill.

In the vestiges of the death silence of the night Mobutu's troops were in training. They ran ten men abreast, in full uniform, with their automatic rifles held against their shoulders. They came in waves, as far as I could see, a regimented expanse of songs and boots and guns, the tightly packed ranks of men as volatile and dangerous as mercury.

The army which had brought Mobutu to power had remained his backbone. Mobutu was not a popular leader. He maintained an attitude of breathtaking disregard for the lives of those he governed. At this time, the per capita income of the nation was about one hundred and eighty American dollars per month. The common people might earn thirty dollars a month – the price of two sacks of the cassava vegetable that formed their staple diet. Whatever else they might need had to be eked out of the soil, or forgone. Their lives were an unmitigated hell, a daily raw grappling to remain alive. They led a lifestyle unthinkable to a Westerner. For many there were no hospitals for the sick and no schools for their children. Where these did exist, the doctors, nurses and teachers frequently went on strike because of the conditions they had to work in and the long hiatuses in the payment of their salaries.

The country's foreign debt stood at 12,5 billion US dollars. In the mean time, Mobutu had amassed a personal fortune of six billion dollars. He lived removed from the chaos, in his European palaces and his African mansions, wilfully blind to the degradation and suffering that was his legacy to the nation.

Mobutu was merciless in the execution of his will. When the students of Lubumbashi University demonstrated in 1990, he dispatched his troops who promptly slaughtered a hundred of them inside their own dormitories. He shored up his own invulnerability by using his wealth to win over his enemies, and to make sycophantic millionaires of his friends.

Mobutu would not have remained in power as long as he did, had it not been for the unequivocal support that he garnered from the West. The president endeared himself, despite his iniquities, by announcing frequently that he was committed to thwarting the spread of Soviet influence in Africa. His regime was strongly underpinned by that traditional champion of human rights, the United States of America. In 1989 President George Bush bestowed sixty million dollars in aid upon Mobutu who, incidentally, was the first African head of state to visit him. There was also support from Belgium, France, China, Germany and Israel. Obviously much of this support took the form of weaponry.

With the collapse of the Soviet Union and the cessation of the Cold War, Mobutu's funding was abruptly halted. Realising his now precarious position, the president made belated mutterings about possible democratic reforms. Meanwhile, several months elapsed during which the army went unpaid. In

September 1991 bedlam broke loose in Zaire. Mobutu's troops mutinied and there was wave upon wave of looting and rioting in Kinshasa and Lubumbashi. Shops and international investments were entirely razed. Vast numbers of the weapons that had flooded into Zaire were now in the hands of the rioting soldiers. In fact, no precise records had been kept of how the weapons were deployed in the first place. I have frequently heard a theory that many of the arms used by UNITA in the Angolan civil war were in fact second-hand American weapons sold off by Mobutu Sese Seko.

Fourteen thousand foreigners had to be evacuated from Zaire during the riots. This was the period during which my brother Nicholas had abandoned his art collecting and gone into hiding in the jungle.

I watched the final platoon jog past – a fleet of damp men, steaming against the rising morning, the cadence of their uneasy chant fading on the first light – and leaned back meditatively against the window frame. Ostensibly they were loyal again, but nothing in this country could be taken for granted. If soldiers found tourists alone, they frequently held them at gunpoint and stripped them of everything.

'What ought I to do if I am confronted by a soldier with an automatic rifle?' I asked the Belgians.

'Call him Sir,' they replied.

*

My arrival in Zaire coincided with the onset of a physical malaise that was to surface intermittently in one form or another for the rest of my peregrinations in Africa.

At this point it was vomiting. Everything I ate would sit undigested and leaden in the pit of my stomach for a matter of hours whilst I grew queasier and queasier. The attack would be heralded by a sudden clarion grumble in my midriff, before dinner spewed itself upward and outward. I would have to crouch greenly on the grassy kerb, or the pavement or wherever I happened to be. Passing Africans stared and chuckled at the spectacle. Eventually I barely ate at all. I never felt hungry. Eating was simply a mechanical refuelling of the body. The vomiting became commonplace – a series of pauses in the mish-mash fabric of the days.

It was difficult to avoid eating things that were not suffused with filth. The whites spent disproportionate amounts of their expatriate salaries buying imported foodstuffs from the grocery shops. Before independence Zaire had been self-sufficient in food. But at this point the Mobutu regime was importing most of its requirements. The shops were filled with South African products for which they charged exorbitant prices.

I tried to eat what the people ate, and almost everything made me ill. At first we bought papaws and vegetables, until we saw that the market gardens were all carved out of the side of the shit sewers and the shit was periodically churned into the surrounding soil as fertiliser. We ate ice-creams which were delicious and cold, but were made from the river waters into which the shit sewers emptied themselves.

For a while I ate *baignés*, small sweet balls of dough with a neutral insipid taste, which the street vendors hawked. I reasoned that their immersion in hot oil must burn the bacteria off them. But one morning as I was waiting for my *baigné*, I saw the vendor calmly tip a can of motor oil into her vat.

'Madame! Where did you find this? You can't use it! It's for cars!' I exclaimed, horrified.

'Oil is oil,' she declaimed toothlessly, sagging back into her bosom.

I suppose it had been purloined from some garage during the lootings.

I found the Zairois French a hard and grating patois, with none of the lyrical grace associated with the language. It wore me down to have to communicate constantly in my third language. Besides that, I speak French appallingly. I had studied it at my day school as a young girl and my parents had even sent me to summer school in France at fifteen, which was a tremendous privilege in those isolated apartheid years when travel in Europe was beyond the means of most adults. But at boarding school it was the headman's class and I shut down mentally against the slaughter of Antoine de Saint-Exupéry and Guy de Maupassant.

I also had to decide what we were going to do with ourselves now that we were actually in Zaire. What I really wanted to do was travel on the legendary Zaire river boat, upstream from Kinshasa to Kisangani (formerly Stanleyville). I had read a *National Geographic* article about this boat which described the way in which it had actually become part of the social fabric of the tribes living along the river bank. Apparently a manhood ritual had evolved which entailed young boys leaping from the highest point on the boat. I was fascinated and wanted to see it for myself.

Whatever path of action we were to take, it would need to be quickly initiated. Cyril was giving out dangerous signs of mutiny. He was not dealing with the country well at all. The echoing gunshots in the night would startle him into wakefulness, clutching at the sheets. And then, disastrously, we went to the Hotel Macris one afternoon for a Coca-Cola, and met a pop-eyed and egregious Belgian miner of advancing years.

Cyril outlined the game plan for the old man's benefit, more or less accurately.

The man stared at us.

'*Mais vous etes folles!*' cried the withered Belgian, spilling his gin and tonic on the table cloth in his excitement. 'You're crazy! Ze gel! Bootiful blonde hair! Bootiful blue eyes! *Mon dieu!* She will be rupped! Rupped! Rupped!'

He glowered at me.

'Do you want to be rupped?'

I glowered back.

Cyril looked at me appraisingly.

'And you!' resumed the man, turning to Cyril. 'While she is being rupped, you will be keeled!'

Cyril jumped.

All afternoon he twittered on about raping and killing. To shut him up I concocted an entirely fictional yarn. According to the *National Geographic*, I told him, the river boat was practically a floating palace. In first class you could take your meals in a restaurant. The toilets flushed and were cleaned daily. First class was quite cheap really, but only the best-behaved locals could afford it because everybody was so ravenously poor here. We would take first class and we would eat like princes and in the evenings we would sit on the deck with frosted drinks and watch the verdant jungle fringes slip by.

'That man didn't think it was like that,' argued Cyril.

'Yes, but a horrible smelly man like that!' I interjected. 'Obviously not a *National Geographic* reader.'

Yet this was not the only stumbling block. The Belgians had built 50 000 kilometres of road in the country, but after independence the roadways had been subsumed back into the jungle or fallen apart with neglect. The big cities were like islands in a sea of impenetrable jungle. The only feasible way to get to Kinshasa was to fly. The flight money would have to be summoned out of our dwindling resources.

*

On the appointed morning of the flight I woke up feeling as if every gastric complaint known to medical science had decided to manifest itself in my body. But there was nothing to be done. I packed my rucksack in a dogged and sullen silence and we walked the mile down to the ticket office to reconnoitre with the air service bus.

The air ticket salesman, who had described said bus with breezy enthusiasm on the previous morn, seemed to have forgotten its existence entirely.

'There is no bus! To go to the airport one needs to hire a private vehicle.'

I looked at him bleakly through a haze of nausea.

'But great good fortune! I have ordered a private vehicle which will come here shortly and carry you to the airport.'

I moved to the side of the office and sat tightly on the floor, burying my face in the cordura sides of my rucksack, for the reassuring smell of it, and the rough texture against my face.

A medley of screams filtered through the door and now two women exploded through the opening and fell on to the floor, tearing at each other's floral dresses, scratching and biting scarlet welts in their dark skin.

'It's for a man,' supplied the passers-by who had followed the onset of acrimony from the street, and the man himself stood in the doorframe, half heroic and half sheepish. Meanwhile, the shrieking women slid back and forth against the tiled floor, disarranging the layers of their African dresses, the vertical spikes of the Zairois hairstyle bent and crumpled in the battle.

'Excuse me,' said a soft voice at my side, a man I'd never seen before. 'The vehicle is waiting.'

Outside stood a dapper little bus, already full of waiting Africans.

'This is the private vehicle?' I asked confusedly.

'Oh no. Special free delivery service.'

I crawled to one of the back seats and pressed my forehead to the window glass. The engine gunned and came to life. Dimly, I saw the ticket vendor running behind us. Who will watch the office? I wondered. He fought his way to the back of the car and sat down immediately in front of us, from which vantage point he kept up a running prattle about the magnificence of the private car.

We duly arrived at the airport and we all dismounted.

'A wonderfully smooth and comfortable ride has been had on this private vehicle,' announced the ticket vendor, 'and now to pay fifteen American dollars.'

I lurched to the left to be sick.

'Hurry up!' said Cyril with nervous rancour.

We staggered into the airport building with the man trotting behind us. I slouched down against a wall, extracted my rain mac and wrapped it round my head so that I couldn't see him.

'What about me? A present for me!' penetrated the crackling darkness, but after a few minutes he went away.

The airport was a low-slung hall, streaked with dirt and dotted with people and their listless baggage. The room I had chosen to slump in must have been a restaurant in the former era – it had counters and trailing electric sockets and squarish shadows of damp on the walls where a battery of refrigerators had once stood. Now there were only teetering wooden benches and on the wall the ubiquitous photograph of the One Who Leaves Fire In his Wake.

Beyond the clouded windows threadbare flags with the Zairois emblem – a hand clutching a flaming torch – fluttered in the tepid breeze.

To pass the slow feverish hours I studied the Mobutu lineaments, remembering a wickedly funny sketch of the country I had recently read by the comedy science fiction writer Douglas Adams, who made a world tour writing about endangered species. In Zaire, said Adams, he understood the attitude to endangered species when he first saw a leopard. Or rather, a part of a leopard – the piece which had been fashioned into 'a rather natty leopardskin pillbox hat' worn upon Mobutu's head.

Beneath the hat nestled the well-cropped wings of hair. In truth, the paucity of the Mobutu coiffure belies the very draining expenses necessary to its proper maintenance. A European hairstylist was flown out twice a month at a cost of five thousand American dollars per trip to groom the presidential head.

I shifted my gaze to the heat-flickering outside. Although runways did feature in the landscape, the airport seemed otherwise innocent of its purpose. It was already several hours past the time nominally provided for departure.

In the mid-afternoon a paunchy woman in her middle years arrived with a trestle table under her arm and announced that the plane was due in a half hour. Settling herself behind the trestle table, she began to deliver boarding passes.

We queued. To no avail. The woman had never heard of us. To obtain a boarding pass, she explained, it was first necessary to go into town to purchase an air ticket.

I was about to explain that we had an air ticket, when I realised with sudden clarity that she was perfectly aware of this.

Under the Mobutu regime minor officials might go for months without receiving their pay packets. The only way to make ends meet was through corruption and the tourist was the natural target. To every single official you meet, you are nothing more than a repository of American dollars. The one thing that stands between your American dollars being their American dollars, is your breaking point. Once your breaking point has been surpassed, you will be handed on to the next official and the whole procedure will start anew.

My breaking point was immeasurably shored up by a rapid mental calculation of our paltry stash of American dollars.

No point in arguing with this woman, I might as well go for the top dog. I whizzed outside to pre-empt the next hour's illnesses and made my way to the office marked *Le Directeur*. Cyril was still in the grip of bubbling neurosis, but fortuitously had been asleep on a bench for several hours and gave no sign of waking.

The *directeur* was holding court from behind small Everests of paper, in a magic circle of subordinates. I shouldered my way through.

'Why is my *billet* not sufficient?' I demanded, waving the offending ticket in his face.

He looked at me as one might look at a small child, and waved his hands wearily in expanding circles.

'It is not my fault,' disparaged the *directeur*. 'It is the fault of

145

the ticket office of Air Zaire. You will have to return to the town and take it up with them.'

'But then it is your fault too! You are the *directeur* of Air Zaire!' He looked offended.

'Excuse me!' he said icily. 'It is not my fault. I have never seen you before in my life. It has nothing to do with me and I cannot help. Leave my office now and go to town.'

'But my flight is leaving in half an hour!' I screamed, in a magnificent jumble of mispronunciation and two left-legged grammar. We were speaking French at great velocity. Whenever I could not think of a word, I threw in another which seemed pertinent. My fluttering hands mimed the actions in accompaniment.

'Half an hour!' I repeated wildly.

In truth, this last premise was entirely fanciful, but I didn't know that at the time.

The *directeur* became quite stern, and his face puckered into a veneer of remonstration.

'*Regarde*,' he said sharply, removing his spectacles and inserting them neatly betwixt the Everests. 'I work here at the airport. The people who made the mistake work in the ticket office. We have nothing to do with each other.'

'Nothing to do!' I discharged explosively, losing my rag altogether. 'You listen to me! A company has many parts, *n'est ce pas, Monsieur le Directeur*, and in this company you are a part and the pilot is a part and the ticket office is a part and you all work together, godammit, you aren't blasted solipsists.'

'Perhaps,' sniffed the *directeur*, disdainfully and he turned his back on me, as if to indicate that the conversation was terminated. He resumed talking to the ring of subordinates, who shuffled attentively and gave me baleful stares.

A minute passed. The *directeur* looked at me again, enquiringly, as if to say – what, still here?

I slammed both fists on the table, and snatched up the abandoned spectacles.

'Look here!' I admonished. 'These spectacles are one unit, as your company is one unit. Here are the two round lenses through which one looks. Here are the two legs by which the entire article adheres to the ears. But the spectacles are not about lenses and legs. The spectacles are about serving your eyes. Do you see that?'

The *directeur* was intrigued and agreed that he did see that.

'Now I am going to detach one leg and then you will see that when the composite of the parts do not work together, the unit is no longer functional.'

My didactic purposes were restrained by calmer hands.

Many, many hours later the aeroplane actually arrived. There was a whip-round amongst the passengers, ostensibly so that the pilot could run into town and buy some fuel for the journey. And at last we took off into the black night with a great rumbling and shaking of loose parts. Terrified, I seized upon my seat belt, which came cleanly away in my hand. Presently the hostess arrived with a bucket of grey meatballs. She seemed blithely undisturbed by the fact that she made her living by tearing over the jungle, a mile into the sky, in the confines of a loose connection of spare parts.

By the time we arrived at Kinshasa airport, an air of survival camaraderie had arisen amongst the passengers. The man across the aisle had a car waiting and gave us a lift into town, to the Hotel Estoril. I tried to run a hot bath and couldn't and crouched shivering in the cold brown water.

Numb and exhausted, I crept between the sheets in the first pale streaks of daylight. I had an overwhelming sense of having interred myself, and Cyril, in an extraordinary mess.

*

When I awoke things did not improve. Within a few hours we had located the Bureau Centrale de Navigation de la Rivière Zaire. The desk clerk informed us that the river boat had not been operational since the revolution. No fuel, you see, he laughed, spreading his hands wide in a gesture which conveyed the hopelessness of the situation, *absolument rien*, everything was stolen or broken, but who knows, one day, perhaps a month, perhaps a year.

I sat on the steps outside the building, sick with disappointment, running my fingers over my plaited scalp. A thorough botch, a thorough, thorough botch. There was no other way to see it. And at twenty-six dollars a night, we could not continue to stay at the Hotel Estoril. There were cheaper hotels in the outlying areas, used exclusively by Africans, but I could not risk staying there, not in this city. There were no provisions for shoestringers here, because they never came this way.

Oh God, how can I manage? Oh God, I wish there were some adult to whom I could turn, who would hold the reins whilst I re-ignited my waning lights. White South Africans of my circle grew up slowly, particularly the girls. Not very much was demanded of young women, beyond the prerogative of safeguarding their physical purity until marriage. All my life, my family had cloistered me within the soft, terrible boundaries of love, until in my early twenties I saw an endless, stunted childhood stretching away before me, and decided to shatter all the rules. But this first foray into adulthood was too sudden and too wild.

I made a decision. This was a capital city. We must have an ambassador. I would have to find him.

We began to walk through the streets of Kinshasa, to the riverside neighbourhoods, the Avenue des Ambassades, where all the dignitaries resided.

In speaking of Leopoldville, Graham Greene said, 'Europe in Leo weighs down on the African soil in the form of skyscrapers.' With the expulsion of Europe, the monstrous architectures seemed to sag and spill slovenly into the earth. Europe claimed Kinshasa from the wilderness, but the jungle persists and wins. Not a jungle of foliage, but one of flowering junkyards, meandering trickles of human excrement, rotting motor cars and rubberised strips of tyres, a profusion of spaza shops, and sporadic bursts of cultivated corn plants, the lasting ruralism of the urban peasants. Over everything hangs that singularly Zairean smell, of decay, of danger, of faeces baking under a putrefying sun.

In the Avenue des Ambassades the reaching baobabs sprawled overhead, and technicoloured lizards as thick as my wrists flicked along the wide branches. The houses themselves recoiled from the road behind steel barricades. At last we came to the great river itself. My anxieties, for the moment, were engulfed.

The Zaire river is 2 900 miles long, the sixth longest in the world, second only in volume to the Amazon.

'A mighty big river,' wrote Joseph Conrad, 'resembling an immense snake uncoiled, with its head in the sea, its body at rest curving afar over a vast country, and its tail lost in the depths of the land.'

We were standing at the neck of the snake. Further than I could see, further than I could feel, spread the torpid blue waters. A diaphanous mist suffused everything, drew a bride's veil of vapour over the trawling fishermen and their precarious canoes. In that weird opaque shroud, the river itself seemed a god, and the men who battled the swallowing tides were as priests, their frank dusky skins the canvas of a chiaroscura.

Down the banks plunged the stinking squatter houses and the children played in the black mud. I stood silently for a long time, watching that immensity of water pass by, almost at the finale of its long, long journey out to sea.

Not two hundred yards from the great river stood the ambassador's house. In response to our tentative knock, a small flap in the steel gates opened, and a face peered cautiously out.

'*Monsieur*, I am a South African citizen. I want to speak to my ambassador, please.'

'*Monsieur l'ambassadeur* is out.'

'But is he coming back?'

'Of course!'

'Can we come in?' I begged him, crouching on a level with the flap so that he could examine my features.

He dragged back the steel gates a yard and we slipped through the orifice.

I gawked, feeling like Queen Susan in the Narnia books.

I had stepped into a kingdom of clipped lawns and groomed garden beds, delphiniums, gardenias and crisp, white roses. The sunlight winked on the surface of a limpid swimming pool. In the little gazebo the morning papers lay spread carelessly over a deck chair and a small wooden table. The main house was fronted with bullet-proof glass which slightly magnified the interior. I saw a neat settee, a coffee table, and coffee table books.

Coffee table books. I could have cried. I sat on the tiled steps in this sanctuary of the gods, scented with blossoms, and waited for *Monsieur l'ambassadeur*.

Presently the steel gates slid back once more to admit an olive green jeep, driven by a chauffeur. Both rear doors swung open symmetrically. On the near side emerged a tall, moustached man who I supposed must be the ambassador. On the far side a petite, neat, fetching woman – his wife.

The ambassadorial couple stared at us in amazement. I suppose we must have been quite a sight – dishevelled and waiflike, in that dislocated city, still struggling in the aftermath of revolution.

The ambassador recovered himself first.

'*Hemel en aarde!*' he exclaimed, lapsing into Afrikaans idiom in his surprise. 'Where on earth have you come from?'

Over coffee, I recounted our story.

'Penny,' mused the ambassador, weighing up the word as if it were yielding up some hidden image. 'Penny. It couldn't be . . . You don't have a brother, do you?'

'Yes.'

'Nicholas?'

'Yes.'

'Well, my heavens. Well, of all the extraordinary . . . Why, he was here for a few weeks, he was up here last year. Man, I can't believe it. We tried to get him to fly out when everyone else was evacuated, but he wouldn't do it. He went and buried himself in this great big old backyard jungle we've got growing outside. Well, well, well' – shaking his head – 'so you're the sister.'

'Yes, sir.'

'When's he coming back? He's still got things holed up all over the place here, you know, all that art stuff, I don't know, it might have all been stolen. I've been wanting to follow him up, but I didn't have a contact address.'

They were still puffed up with the coincidence.

'He's dead,' I said.

An abrupt silence. They looked at me as if what I had said had been crass or vulgar. I dropped my head and picked at a stray thread on the sofa.

When at last somebody spoke, it was the ambassador's wife. She leaned forward and looked into my face.

'Why don't you send a radio message to your mother and tell her you're here with us?' said the ambassador's wife, very gently.

*

We were invited to stay on at the embassy for the next few days, to my incalculable relief and gratitude. At first I went down to the waterfront every day, to the junkyard of old boats that lay there, to see if there was any chance of finding a private boat that was going up river.

But the boats were not making the journey. There had been too much piracy by the starving, disturbed tribespeople upriver. I realised I would have to scotch my plans. Besides, Cyril flatly refused.

'*Monsieur the ambassador has proclaimed himself appalled, as the minister of internal security called our impending plan of action lunatic,'* I wrote sadly in my diary.

There was nothing I could do except arrange a flight back to Lubumbashi. We booked the passage on a private airline, as I had had enough of Air Zaire or *Air Peut-être* – 'Air Perhaps' – as it is more jocularly known.

Behind the heavy steel gates lay a world quietly flavoured with Afrikaner culture and wealth. We might have been at the home of any of the old Huguenot-descended families of South Africa. Only the exotica betrayed the real setting – the stark jungle carvings, and the scarlet and grey parrot that dwelt on the veranda. At the end of his working day the ambassador would remove the bird from its cage. With huge self-possession, the little bundle of feathers and fluff marched up and down the ambassadorial arm, or pecked affectionately at the hairy upper lip. If any one else tried to touch him he would shriek in furious rebuff.

I was aware that the ambassador and his wife must have represented South Africa during the apartheid era but, in the current period of political quicksand, I had no idea if they were *verlig* or *verkramp*, as we call the distinction between those Afrikaners who supported the De Klerk initiatives and those who despised them. I steered clear of the subject of politics but, surprisingly, the ambassador brought it up himself.

'People think that the Afrikaners are like concrete blocks,' he said over breakfast one morning. 'I read these learned treatises about our *laager* mentality. Whatever we did in the past, we did because we thought it was the right way,' he added, pausing and touching his fingertips to his forehead. 'Now we see that that way is bad, that it will not work for the country. In the end, what we want is for the country to function. We are not tied rigidly to keeping to the one path, when we can see that the path is wrong.'

I toyed with the sugar spoon. Zaire is not a country which easily engenders a natural empathy between black and white.

Reduced to the personal, political theory flies out of the window. I wondered fleetingly how he reconciled his new-found liberalism with the volatile chaos beyond the steel gates. I had spent years soaked in anti-colonialist, historically revisionist sympathies, but I still responded viscerally to the ceaseless wheedling and bribery.

On the other hand, there could be no better example than Zaire of what happens when white and black can find no meeting point.

The embassy was where the handful of South Africans who lived and worked in the city congregated. In the tepid evenings they gathered around the *braaivleis* for drinks and conversation. They spoke in Afrikaans or French – the language of the hearth or the lingo of the workplace – there was little need for English in the country. I did not try to interpret for Cyril. I was in retreat from him.

I was also in retreat from a flickering identity that no longer seemed to fit me. I loosened my hair from the braided, gaudy beadwork. The swathes fell about my shoulders, lank and waxy from their long confinement.

One afternoon after I had been swimming in the pool, I unexpectedly came face to face with my own image in the reflective silver of the sliding doors. I gazed in disbelief at this apparition of a body that could only be my own. The sun had streaked my hair into a fey halo of light and burned my skin to a deep and even ochre, a dusky layer at which the points of hips and clavicles poked. A visible bracket of ribs rose and fell with each breath. As I moved I became a network of barely submerged muscle. It was a ludicrous moment of discovery. If I felt as though the sane world had vanished, as if dementia lay only a moment's lapse away, my body would not betray it. For the first time in my life, I looked like a girl in a suncream advertisement.

On our last day in Kinshasa, we went down to the market to buy a gift for the ambassador's wife.

Vegetables in Zaire seem to grow to outrageous sizes; the

trestle tables groaned under the accumulative weight of the enormous melons and pumpkins. A gap-toothed woman ground out peanut oil in an antediluvian press and a vendor sold single shoes from a blanket on the ground.

The rank smell of the meat section permeated everything. Buckets of goat's heads lay shorn off at the neck, trailing bleeding strings of flesh, the open mouths seemed still to transmit their final bleat of panic. Dead fish boggled in smelly lifelessness, eyes clouding rotten by midday.

Beyond the entrance lay the tourist art – malachite bead necklaces and raffish chess sets – and the monkeys roped to stakes in the ground, circling in endless mournful protest at their fate. From an adjacent cage a double score of shrieking parrots screamed their anguish at the free world, flapping their wings in a fruitless effort to be free of the crush of one another's bodies and pecking, bewildered beaks.

And in the interstices of all this lay the endless spoils of the recent looting. Bell's whisky, Moët et Chandon, Cointreau, all lay higgledy piggledy in the sunlight. The best French wines turned slowly en masse to vinegar.

Clutters of compact discs, fur coats, lycra gym leotards, Nike sneakers, stereo equipment, crystal decanters, a cashmere cardigan from Paris with the label still attached, a set of bath salts, a hoard of English novels. I paused to buy *A Tale of Two Cities.*

'Buy a television! A very good television, madame!'

'No, thanks.'

'Madame, a typewriter then. Completely new.'

Turning my head, I saw the man was trying to hawk a computer keyboard and monitor. Someone had kicked the mystery of the hard drive into the dust.

That evening we went for drinks at the Kinshasa Club. That ancient relic of colonial times – the club – remains alive and well in the hearts of English white Africans. My childhood was deeply stamped by the nearby satellite of the Club, where one met to play croquet and tennis, for Sunday night meals or for the spate of Christmas festivities. The Club was a forum for weddings and twenty-first birthday parties, and a venue for visiting luminaries like pianists or boys' choirs. In my mother's generation one met all the right sort of young men at the Club. My generation, sniffing at the winds of change, found this contrived.

The greatest virtue of the Club, of course, was its absolute intransigence, from year to year. Even now, I can recite the menu, precisely as it will appear tonight, as it appeared throughout my childhood and adolescence, throughout the life of my father, and my grandfather, and his father. There will be a rump steak in a monkey gland sauce, a fresh sole in butter, a side of pork, sliced, and, to follow, the same sturdy old timeless puddings of Empire, caramel custard, strawberry trifle, and chocolate éclair. The same liverish old gentleman will half-rise in arthritic greeting from his chair, snuffling away the sunset hours of life in a mouldering smoking jacket. 'Cambridge '33' says the stoop of his imploded shoulders, angled uncertainly at the birth of a new and incomprehensible Africa.

But the Kinshasa Club wasn't like that. Drawing on the tiny reserves of the wealthy, the Kinshasa Club was rather more nouveau in its approach. Years later, I saw the Tom Stoppard play *Indian Ink* in London, and it made me think fleetingly of the Kinshasa Club. To misquote horribly, one protagonist announces that the Club is very much more mixed nowadays. Oh, English and Indians, you mean, says the heroine. Oh no! protests the protagonist, shocked, you know, civil chaps, business chaps, clerical chaps.

The Kinshasa Club housed all sorts of chaps, markedly rather more white chaps than black chaps, and seemed to run in particular to sporty young Americans in ankle socks and gym shoes. Somehow, they got wind of the fact that 'Nick's sister' had arrived and they crowded in on me, lobbing the punchy slaps at one another that seem such an indivisible element of

American etiquette. I had to tell them, again and again, that 'Nick' would not be coming to see a car, to play scrum-half, to retrieve a belonging, not now, not ever. They fell away, embarrassed and disturbed, their eyes disbelieving and suspicious, as if a weird inner mania had compelled me to invent my story. But even to me, the words, too blithely delivered, sounded false and hollow; I could not really believe what I told.

When I went to bed that night I lay for many hours brooding over a bitter sense of failure. We had very little money left. Soon we would have to return home.

In the morning I woke and packed my rucksack.

'I suppose the rest of the family will be taking a package holiday to Kinshasa,' said the ambassador genially in farewell. He had offered us his chauffeur to drive us to the airport. We wound slowly down the Avenue des Ambassades and into the heart of the city, stopping at the market so that I could buy a trinket for my mother.

The obscene cage of parrots was still squawking in noisy, incessant terror. I remembered a story that the ambassador had told about when the foreigners were evacuated during the revolution. Many of them had not had time to organise their entry papers to South Africa, and the usual severities were waived in the face of the crisis. But what had been seized had been the illegally transported parrots, quite a number of them.

'Parrots?' I said, surprised.

'Oh, yes. They're sold for quite a bit of money in South Africa, but there are all sorts of regulations and paperwork that have to be observed.'

I looked at the cage and its pinioned inmates.

'Cyril.'

'What?'

'Do you see those birds?'

'Yeah?'

'You can sell them for a lot of money at home.'

'Yeah?'

156

'We could do that.'

'Could we?'

'Sure. We could buy a few, sell them at home, make some more money, and carry on travelling.'

'Don't you need, like, a licence or something?'

'Oh, that's all just worldly stuff,' I said, coercing him with his own stock phrase.

Within fifteen minutes, between our rucksacks in the front of the jeep, stood the cage of six birds, all extending their cramped wings and haunches cautiously in the sudden relative freedom. When I put down water and nuts for them they fell feverishly to nibbling and dribbling the liquid down their parched crops.

I find it difficult now to try and remember what my thoughts were when I decided to take the parrots. A few months before I had been almost neurotically concerned with the environment. I argued in support of Greenpeace and opposed the multinational corporations. I read treatises on Gaia, bought dolphin-friendly tuna and biodegradable detergents. I called myself 'green' and disparaged those who did not.

But for months I had been living in a contorted cycle of grief, fear, stress, and bewildering loneliness. Strangers had crossed my path and for a moment their warmth had fallen across my face, like the flame from a candle – Nessie, Marius, Katie, Girison, the ambassador and his wife. But one after the other they fell away, and I was left alone to resume my obscure, acrimonious relations with Cyril.

At this point I was occupying a remote plane of isolation where the outside world had receded beyond my grasp. My yearning to succumb to the comfort of another human being had passed; for the moment, I walled myself within the numb interiors. Dimly, I felt I must continue, the only anchor in my rootless world was what I did, and what I did was travel.

I read my diaries to see if I felt a remorse or even an under-standing of the fact that my actions contributed to a horrifyingly careless pillaging of the jungle life, but there is nothing.

In the same wave of desolate self-containment, I boarded the aeroplane with the parrots under my arm and returned to Lubumbashi. The aircraft seemed to be awash with the plundered birds, being spirited to God knows where. In the morning we left once again on one of the massive trucks, this time southward bound to my home country.

The Graveyard of Dreams

'What frightens you the most about marriage?' they used to ask at girlish slumber parties, when the havoc of puberty first made us think about these things. The requisite answer was 'sex', followed by a spate of giggles and grimaces. I said sex too, but I lied. The thing that frightened me the most about marriage was that it seemed to herald the end of a private life.

In the elegant suburban homes of Cape Town, the parental bedroom always seemed to be a place where individualism fused into a monotonous blandness, a blandness of double bed, built-in cupboards, the smiling pictures of my classmates and their siblings on the walls. More rousing by far was the inevitable temple of Daddy's study, a place of books, of groaning shelves, suffused with the sensual scent of leather. But where was Mommy's study? The mother's life, I realised, was expressed in children, and in communal living spaces.

So in girlhood, I would lock my bedroom door, to the merriment of my sisters who demanded to know what I did within those four prohibited walls. Homework, I said stiffly, but that was another lie. I spent the time reading, or writing long treatises on my family life.

Living cheek by jowl with Cyril, I had to lock him out with subtler devices. Eventually he began to do it too, and then he usurped me at it, until now he could live alongside me, eat, sleep, exist a yard away, and yet be as cold and remote as a star.

On our downward journey to South Africa, he began to live apart in this way. As I began to thaw, he congealed into an ungiving spike of ice. Therefore, on another suffocating African night spent in a truck cabin in Lusaka, Zambia, I snivelled and sobbed and hiccuped my way back into the sensate world of human feeling, whilst Cyril's back remained turned in resolute rebuttal.

Disconsolate and vengeful, I picked up the diary that he had left carelessly on the dashboard.

'*Thought is : is thought! WOW!*' he had inscribed earlier in the week.

I perused another page and another, but it was all the same. A disembodied noise of vocal disgust rose in the back of my throat and I extricated myself from the smothering cabin.

I was promptly accosted by what I thought was an albino black, but the passage of clouds revealed a true white man in a moment's moonlight, a pallid stale creature doused in drink.

'You listen to me, my little girl,' said the thing, lurching towards me. In a spate of 'darlings' and 'sweethearts', half-cajoling, half-threatening, he gave me to understand that he knew about 'my little secret', that unless I gave him a substantial sum of money he would make sure I spent the better part of the next decade suppurating in an African jail.

I retreated back to the cabin in blank terror. Two days ago I had been just a girl, perhaps confused, perhaps grieving, but just an ordinary girl. Now a moment's madness in an African market-place had converted me into an underworld criminal.

At first light I woke and began systematically to scour the trucks, to see if I could locate one that was leaving for the border with Botswana. But no one had stirred yet. Only the prostitutes sat upright in the passenger seats, looking at me with expressionless faces and combing the night's work from their wiry hair, while the man lay spread-eagled and unconscious in the bunk.

Defeated, I walked to the bakery across the road, and there I met Mohammed.

Mohammed was avuncular.

'Don't bother with a truck,' he said. 'Take a train to the border.'

I went back to the depot to rouse Cyril, and to tell him to hurry.

If Mohammed was kind, he was also seasoned with his own brand of crusading insanity. He was a Palestinian, a member of the PLO, but he had been exiled from his homeland. Whilst he gave us coffee and white breadrolls, whilst he changed currency for us, whilst he drove us to the station, he betrayed the driving demons that possessed him. In his terse quiet convictions, I felt the indignity of the tent camps, the dispossession of his people, the careless racism that had turned this principled zealot into an outlaw.

'What are your family names?' enquired the Arab, at one juncture.

I mentioned mine. Cyril began to say his, the nomenclature of one of the twelve tribes of Israel. I dug my fingernails into the back of his hand and smothered his words with an Anglo-Saxon alternative.

'That is *not* my name!' he whispered furiously.

When the Palestinian had left, I turned on him.

'How can you be so stupid! Do you think he would have helped us if he knew you were a Jew? What the hell is the matter with you? You're Jewish, dammit! Don't you have some kind of interest in what's happening in the Middle East?'

'I don't care about the Middle East! I don't care about worldly politics! I don't care about worldly knowledge! That is not the kind of entity I am. I am an entity who lives in the world of emotion.'

But not my emotion, I thought drily, recalling the barren solitude of the previous night. The fragile link had snapped.

For the next fortnight our communications reverted to expedient monosyllables.

We spent the rest of the day loitering at the station, until the train arrived in the late evening. We managed to get a first class cabin, which was offered in partnership by the only other white on the station, an ancient and hairless Irishman whose skin had the texture of paper and the smell of dust.

I had hoped that the first class would encompass running water and faeces-free toilets, but I was disappointed. The mattress, once yellow, had turned a dun brown with filth. And the corridor, which served as an unofficial extension of the economy class, was a bedlam of mothers and babies.

I realised, while I waited for the train, that these impoverished people did not buy nappies for their babies. The baby, needing to urinate, whimpers at the mother's back. She expertly whips up the lower fold of the bundling cloth and leans forward so that the urine sprays backwards from the child's naked loins, like the release of an elephant, spattering any unfortunates who do not remove themselves in time.

The Irishman had lost his mind, from a lifetime of living alone in the squalid outbacks of Africa. He raged on about plots and conspiracies of mystic origin.

In turn, Cyril explained to him, with apparent authority, that 'our government liked the Xhosas, but didn't like the Zulus'.

I was impressed. If he had muddled the alignments rather, he had at least gone so far as to garner an impression of tribal favouritism. South Africans at that time had just learnt of the surreptitious fundings of Inkatha rallies by the National Party government – a huge embarrassment to both the government and Mangosuthu Buthelezi's faction of the Zulu. These revelations had put Buthelezi himself in a rather delicate position, as for many years he had claimed to stand in opposition to the apartheid government.

I fell asleep thinking about Codesa – our negotiating process – which at that point was experiencing a near fatal rupture, and dreamed a fervent dream in which Cyril, the Irishman, Buthelezi and the parrots all vanished for ever into a fathomless abyss.

*

The train pulled into Livingstone at midday on Sunday. We soon established that the border was closed, and there would be no trucks running. Disconsolately, we sat in the dust on the road-side, beside the shelter we had made for the parrots. As they had begun to fatten, the birds had become livelier and noisier. A constant undercurrent of clucking and chirruping issued from their cage.

The sun burned and burned overhead until, at last, the evening winds began to eddy about us. As the sky started to turn pink, a white Suzuki appeared on the road before us, and sloughed off in the dust just ahead of us. I saw a woman, a white woman, of indeterminate age. She wanted to know what we were about.

'Come along,' she said authoritatively when we told her. 'You can't sit by the road all night. Get into my car.'

In this way I met Honore de Romanof. This is not her real name, but it is not my business to breach the privacy of some-one who, for over thirty years, had concealed herself in pride and solitude in the ferocious secrecy of the African bush.

We drove out along the tar road, and at last turned on to a dust track. At first we moved through agricultural lands, ploughed in readiness for the spring rains, and then into the bush proper where the sparse acacias rose up on either side of the track and bushbuck bounded away at the sound of the engine. At last we came to a gate and I saw a sprawling old bush homestead – a gaggle of white-plastered buildings slung together on a ridge of land. Behind the homestead, a taggle of wild land fell away to the banks of the Zambezi and the wide sluggish river itself predominated.

A half dozen African dogs came to nose and lick and whip

their mangy tails from side to side.

'*Allez!*' said Honore tetchily, kicking at the nearest cur with the tip of her boot. She glanced at us with her keen small eyes. 'These terrible dogs. I used to have such beautiful animals, a spaniel I had, and a Weimaraner – but that damned crocodile ate every one of them. Now I keep such ugly things, I don't even notice when they go.'

We took tea on the veranda, closed in with mesh netting against the mosquitoes. From the river bank came the grunts of the hippos, rousing themselves for an evening's lovemaking.

Over the days that followed, I pieced together the puzzle of Honore's life. Honore's story did not begin in Africa, but far, far to the north. Her parents were white Russians who had fled for refuge to Belgium. But the restrictions of Europe chafed the young Honore, and she chose instead to work in the colonies of West and Central Africa, first as a schoolteacher and then in the diplomatic services of the Belgian government, until at last she holed herself away in this stray corner of land to battle the lapsing decades.

At one time there had been a husband and a child. But Honore's life seemed to have been an ineluctable collision course with tragedy. The husband absconded early, leaving her alone with the infant. Twenty years later he telephoned, asking to speak to his little girl and wanting to know if he could send her a parcel of schoolbooks.

'Schoolbooks!' spat the former wife. 'She's a married woman, with a child of her own.'

Honore's daughter married a grim, bald, cadaverous man who stared out of the old photographs. There were only old photographs. Honore battled with her daughter's choice; the couple went back to Europe, and sent cards at Christmas. Seven years had passed since the last visit.

So the world the old woman now inhabited was the graveyard of the dreams of her youth. Once the whole homestead had been surrounded by a menagerie. There had been peacocks and white doves, humming birds and parakeets; tame buck had grazed on the lawns and the fruit trees had grown in orderly rows.

But as she grew old and frail alone, the Africans preyed on her. They stole her birds and chopped down for firewood the trees that she could not keep watered. Her pump disappeared and her patio chairs, and the wire mesh and poles were stripped from her cages. So now when she said here was this and here was that, I saw only a gaping cavity surrounded by strings of rusted wire; I saw an old lady who bathed daily in a bucket of cold water brought up from the river by her one black retainer, and who fed all her animals on the putu that boiled incessantly on an ancient Aga. Because she still had a few of her animals – the African dogs and silky cats, half-tame monkeys who clattered playfully over the roof, and a trio of African Grey parrots that she kept in wall-to-wall cages on the patio.

Honore didn't like Africans, but she wasn't mad about whites either. The brunt of her acrimony was reserved for her immediate neighbours, a riverside resort that had wanted to syndicate with her at one point. But the plans had gone awry and now nothing could cause that embattled brow to contract as much as the mention of next door.

I spent what time I could at the river, in the branches of an overhanging tree, trying to spot the log back of her bugbear crocodile. She preferred Cyril's company to mine, yielding up her reserves of dourness to his prettiness and gaiety. He could chatter and charm, could fill the house with his dancing steps, as winsome and ephemeral as the crystal vases she still kept polished on her mantelpiece. But I was sunk by the old lady's privations of the heart – by that dark, hard loneliness written into the lines of her face.

It was to Honore de Romanof that we sold the parrots, except for two that we wanted to keep as house pets. In a past re-created by her memories, the forests hereabout had been punctuated by the flash of their scarlet wings, but the Africans had killed and eaten them. Her dream was to start a breeding scheme, to reintroduce them gradually to the woody growth that fringed the river.

In the morning we moved on, hitching a ride in an open-backed van. Eventually we came to the ferry crossing at Kazungula – the border between Zambia and Botswana. Here the van was meticulously searched – the young soldier even opened up our backpacks and sorted through the contents. I showed him everything guilelessly, while sitting on the cage of birds in the back of the open van. By some divine providence they made no noise, but only continued to peck in silence at the handful of nuts I had scattered on the floor. A few yards further on, men came with metal detectors and discovered the cage.

'What is this?' asked the first border guard.

'Chickens?' enquired the second doubtfully. They were not supposed to allow livestock over the border.

'Yes, chickens,' I answered. 'They've already had a look at it.' I waved back to the first set of guards, who returned my gesture. The second guard shrugged, and let us pass.

On we drove, through the forests and sandy pans of Botswana, spending the night at the South African border. In the morning we passed through without incident.

Before lunch we had reached the sprawl of Johannesburg and were let out upon the pavement. All this time my head had been filled with an overwhelming emptiness, as if nothing mattered, as if I was nothing but the passage of air. For a moment lucidity returned, and I saw that it was my home country and Cyril walked beside me.

I snarled and struck out at him, despising him, despising him entirely, and he sank his neatly kept fingernails into my arm, gibbering in mockery and excitement.

A day later we took the train to Cape Town, and then the suburban train to the leafy suburb where my mother had taken a day job in an antiques shop to keep her mind occupied.

I watched her for a moment through the window, moving amongst the precious old things that she loved, still resonant with the demure reticence that had lingered on from a girlhood spent in the farming towns of the interior.

At last, I tapped gently on the window.

She looked up, and her eyes widened hugely.

'Hey there, Mom,' I said.

The Vain Citadels

I lay on my bunk in the grimy old Zambian train, this time
travelling the reverse route, from Livingstone up. This
compartment seemed even filthier than the one we had had
before. The window glass was obscured with muck and legs of
solid dirt hung on the walls like two-dimensional stalactites.
On top of that, it was insufferably hot and the crevice of the
jammed-up window was not wide enough for me to hang my
head out of it. A sour human stink rose from the mattress. I
wore as little as possible, and tried not to think of the thousands
of bacteria that were in all likelihood navigating my body, which
was covered in dust and soot.

I thought instead of the past two weeks. We had stayed in
South Africa for a fortnight in order to attend my niece's
christening. It was reassuring to see my family and realise that
they, like me, were slowly beginning to grope their way towards
a renewed existence.

But I found the quiet order of our home suburbs harrowing.
The river which cut through our property coursed as it had
before, the spring limbs of the old oaks blossomed with new
life as they had in the past, the mountain rose up behind our
house, magnificent and eternal. But I was still wild with
restlessness and the wilderness inside me had to correspond to

a wilderness beyond.

So Cyril and I vanished on a random, reckless trek that took us through the Orange Free State and into the silent, brooding mountain ranges of Lesotho, returning briefly for the christening and then heading north immediately afterwards.

I had thought of ending my journey, or parting company with Cyril. But Cyril – for better or for worse – was an established part of my travelling life. I resisted the idea of separating from him. Besides, during the fortnight I had sat an interview at Rhodes University and had been accepted into a postgraduate course. However gruelling or chaotic the next few months might prove, university waited at the end of them – solid, formal and benign.

My ruminations were interrupted by a sustained rattling of the door. I sat upright and wriggled into my clothes. Cyril had gone to what would have been called the dining car in the past. There was the sound of two hard objects scraping against each other, and then the groan of yielding metal. Finally the lock contraption shattered. The door slid back to reveal an African man. He took a step inside and looked covetously at the nearest backpack, before he noticed me on the top bunk.

'Get out!' I said tersely, holding up my boot in defence.

He got out and I repaired the broken lock as best I could.

We had come up to Livingstone on a truck. En route, we had been obliged to participate in a very unfortunate washing ceremony which was part of a drive to limit the spread of foot and mouth disease from Botswana to Zambia. A policeman had hailed us and indicated a bucket of glaucous liquid. The driver stuck his hands in it. It was quite apparent, from the floating film of grease, that this selfsame bucket had been applied as a curative measure to every peasant and trucker who had passed this way during the last few days. However, there was nothing to be done about it. I held my hands out in front of me for the next few hours until I found a place to wash them, as if they were some peculiarly unattractive part of somebody else.

In Livingstone we met up with Honore again, and learnt that of the four parrots we had sold to her, the two younger ones had died already. By this time I had begun to realise the ramifications of what we had done and I was feeling very ashamed of myself. I told her that I ought not to have done it, and that on my return to South Africa I would make reparations by returning her money. I also promised that I would try to persuade Cyril to do the same thing.

We were headed for Mpulungu, at the base of Lake Tanganyika. After two days' train ride, we reached the end of the line at Kapiri Mposhi and spent the night at the United Motel. In the morning we transferred to an antiquated bus.

The African bus is a singular form of transport. In general, with their steel bodies and upright seats of hard plastic, they give the impression of having been originally designed for the convenience of inter-suburban shoppers in the 1970s. In the latter day, however, these petrol-belching beasts are used for ferrying huge numbers of people across vast tracts of terrain in forty-eight-hour odysseys. As the ageing suspension fails to thwart the potholed African roads, those selfsame plastic seats hammer away endlessly at the luckless spine.

Yet it's rather good luck to get a seat at all. The aisle is regarded as the legitimate home of at least one quarter of the vehicle's passengers, with a complete disregard for those effete little signs which announce, in English, that this bus is authorised to take no more than twenty-two standing passengers.

Humanity crushes together – withered old grandmothers with blackened teeth, young women holding stoic little newborns boiled with heat and with gaping fish mouths, charm amulets slung around their soft necks to ward off diseases and curses. And drilling away constantly at the mind is the tinny, distorted shriek of *soukous*, the Zairean music that is wildly popular throughout the subcontinent.

Of course there's no room left for baggage. That all goes on top: chickens, plastic-weave holdalls, sacks of cassava, bicycles.

I would not part with my backpack and consequently had to sit on top of it in the confines of my seat, a ridiculous jumble of aching immobile limbs.

At around midnight we reached some kind of station and everybody promptly spilled out of the bus and fell asleep on the concrete veranda, without further ceremony. At dawn I wandered away and found a bed of wild mint which I crushed and rubbed all over myself. For the rest of the day the fragrant scent of mint lingered, dissipating the discomfort of the cramped stewing hours.

At last we reached Mpulungu. From here we would board the *MV Liemba*, bound for Bujumbura, the capital city of Burundi.

*

In Europe, a ferry is nothing more nor less than a ferry – a bland method of getting from A to B. But in Africa a ferry is something entirely different. For the peasant people who live along the strung-out eastern shore of Lake Tanganyika, in alcoves hewn out of the brachystegia forests and served only by a barely passable dust track, the ferry is a magic beast.

Twice weekly the mystical shape intrudes on the horizon, on the upward and the downward bound. The village galvanises into action as the loaded canoes are dragged down to the water's edge. The ferry is a commercial opportunity, but also much more than that. It is a conveyor of news, a respite from the tedium of village life, a carrier of mysteries, of suited business-men from Dar es Salaam, and of those curious phenomena – the *msungu*, the Swahili word for a white person.

The *MV Liemba* began life as the *Graf von Goetzn*, in the days when Tanzania was a German colony. The ferry was transported in sections by rail from Dar es Salaam, and then assembled on the lake shore. After World War One the Germans scuttled her, to prevent her from getting into British hands.

But in 1922 the British dredged her up from the bottom of the lake, gave her a lick and spit, and rechristened her the *MV Liemba*. In a Western country, the *MV Liemba* would be a museum piece, but in Africa she's a work horse, and still serves the lake districts as irreproachably as she did when she first went into service almost a century ago.

From my vantage point on the deck, I watched mesmerised as the flotilla of canoes drew near. Foremost were those who could afford outboard engines, and in the vanguard followed the paddlers. The boats were stacked with sacks of cassava and sugar cane, which the captain hoisted on board with a crane. One canoe held nothing but the skinned carcass of a cow, a scarlet slush of meat which trailed a wake of blood as it flew through the air, dangling on the end of a metal hook, presumably the raw stuff of our dinners. I had given up on vegetarianism by this stage as I was the hell in with subsisting on putu, the maize flour porridge, and beans.

I bought a shaft of sugar cane for fifty shillings and stripped the bark with my teeth, which were set to tingling from the sweetness. Meanwhile, a great clamour of voices arose from the third class in the bowels of the boat, where most of the bartering was conducted. Down below, the floor was a mess of blood and salt water. Fights erupted amongst the slickly wet, swarming bodies, divided from the sanctity of second class by a metal barrier. Stowaways, announced the ferry captain, and in horror I watched a half dozen chained men being bundled into a tiny cavity in the recesses of below deck, the whites of their inchoate eyes rolling.

The lake waters surrounding the boat were littered with sugar cane bark. Passengers from the canoes attempted to embark, and a noisy correspondence proliferated between the canoes and the third class over the levering of fearfully obese mothers into the ferry. A white dove escaped from the neck of a sack, and the owner extricated the rest of his booty one by one and ripped out their tailfeathers. The children had sparrows to play with which they tied by the leg to a piece of string, and then flung into the air like a yo-yo, until the little birds died of exhaustion. I rescued a couple at first, but Africans think the white man's sentimentality for animals ridiculous.

The young boys shouted and whistled whilst they clambered like monkeys from the sterns to the bows, or dived beneath the canoes, now illuminated with tilley lamps. It was like a carnival, a huge rambunctious, rowdy, instant carnival, that only ended with the reluctant withdrawal of the ferry into the concealing night.

In the night the stench that pervaded from the third class was of sickening strength. Even from the open-air bunks on the top deck, I could not help but lean over the ship's rail, as the foul reek settled. Cyril giggled at my antics; he had the constitution of a billy goat.

Each morning I woke at dawn and crept to the ship's stern with my diary. Now the lake was perfectly still, a winking blue-silver plate of water, and the rosy cumulus billowed into fantastic dream shapes. The lake fishermen worked in pairs, the net spread between their crafts, weighty with the shoals of small *nshembe* they had gathered up during the night. In the east, the shore rose and fell in an undulating line, covered in forest, and to the west was the limitless water, and the faint, faint trace of the Zairean shore.

Cyril and I were having a difference of opinion about where we should go. He had been seduced by the sphinx promises of that westerly smudge.

'I've got this really deep feeling we should go west,' said Cyril.

'I've got this even deeper feeling we should go east!'

But he leaned on the boat rail, staring out at that unplumbed streak of land and in the end I capitulated, for I was also interested.

My private storms were abating. I had begun to dream about the future once more. Sometimes in the solitary quiet dawns, watching the trailing wake of the ship, I would feel, for a moment, almost serene. At other times, I would be filled with an immense sadness that tinged every raw element of my soul with longing and regret, but I did not try to fight it. I cloaked myself within the comfort of my own silent thoughts until the spell had passed.

It seemed to me that I had passed through some rite of passage, obscure but crucial, and now I was taking up my arms on the far side. It was as if a new being was growing within, still tender, still in bud, but stronger than anything I had ever been before.

I read voraciously now and during this time I found a verse in an Elspeth Huxley novel, that she recalled at the death of somebody she loved.

Courage was mine and I had mystery
Wisdom was mine and I had mastery
To miss the march of this retreating world into
*   the vain citadels of cities that are not walled.*

The words said nothing and everything, they lingered on in my mind and seemed to walk with me throughout the days, until they became my own mantra.

One morning, when the clouds swelled heavily with the dark, tantalising promise of rain, we came to the somnolent old colonial town of Kigoma and disembarked for a shore visit. Here monstrous mango trees soldiered the one main street, and the rich, red mud ran in rivulets at our feet. The air was sweet and full with the incipient rain, which infected everyone with good spirits; the giddy children skipped and sang, and old women mumbled and creaked with well-worn laughter.

In the market-place we found a restaurant – Hassan's, four sets of tables and chairs secluded behind a gingham curtain – and watched the townspeople scurry through the deluge as it broke. Hassan brought sweet spiced tea, flavoured with cardamom, and beans and chapatis and kaokaos, a pastry which twists in upon itself in crackling folds.

Afterwards we went to the market for soap and mangoes, and all the time I breathed in with all my senses that distinctly different influence on East Africa that is the legacy of the Arabs.

For a moment there was a lull in the storm, and we raced back to the ship. From the canopy I watched the renewed drumming of the rain until it drew out my spirit entirely and I stood out upon the stern and lifted up my face to the resounding thunder until the ceaseless flurry made my sodden clothes cling to my body and my heart race with a rain-fever of delight. All night the rain continued to fall, and I lay below deck in the stifling cubicle of the women's cabin, listening, until I slipped into rain-dreams of my own making.

The following day we reached Bujumbura and everyone filed into an interminable queue for the Customs. While I was standing there I saw a little huddle of Africans surrounded by parcels, all waiting on the beach. I wandered down there, to see what they were about, leaving Cyril in the queue. It transpired that they were all Zaireans who had come to Burundi to shop, and they were waiting for a pirogue which would take them back to Uvira in Zaire.

That's a bit of luck, I thought. We can go directly from here; it will save time and we won't need to buy the visa for Burundi. I retrieved Cyril from the queue and we huddled down amongst the waiting Africans. Presently the pirogue captain arrived. He was quite amenable and said we would reach Uvira in less than two hours. Bujumbura and Uvira face each other directly, separated only by the narrow head of the lake. Will we be able to report to Customs when we reach Uvira, I asked him in French. Oh yes, he said merrily, but of course, that is what everybody else will do. When we arrive, I will show you the place.

By mid-afternoon the whole contingent of passengers had arrived. We all squashed into the pirogue in a lather of shopping and bodies, the captain started up his engine and we ploughed off across the lake. Presently the sky grew dark with rain and then the heavy drops began to spatter. A thick tarpaulin was drawn up and we all crouched beneath it, while streaks of lightning fired into the rippled surface of the lake.

When the rain held off, I poked my head out of the tarpaulin. Night was encroaching in shadow fingers of grey that stole across the new-washed skies. On and on we motored, across the head of water, until the sky had dulled through all the nuances of grey to a raven black. To starboard, the close lights of Uvira began to twinkle and an upwelling of distant fires burned along the shore.

'When do we turn, *Monsieur*?'

'Ah, *non, non, non*.'

'But this is Uvira.'

'Ah, *oui*.'

'But this is where we are headed.'

'Too late, too late, too late.'

'Why is it too late?'

'Trouble with the police now. We are going to Mboko village where my brother is a policeman, a *gendarme*. Very good *gendarme*.'

'But we need to go to Customs!'

'In Mboko is Customs.'

'But what about all these people? Don't they think they're going to Uvira?'

'Ah, like sparrows. They don't mind where they go.'

The sparrows, who didn't speak a word of French or English, nodded their heads peaceably. I looked daggers at Cyril. Were it not for his interventions, I would now be comfortably ensconced in a rest house in Kigoma.

Much later we bumped up against the shore. By the faint beam of my torch, I saw it was a little inlet, fringed with rushes. The captain killed the engine.

'This is the village?'

'This is where we sleep.'

Everyone was stretching and shaking out their limbs before bedding themselves down for the night. I sighed and squeezed into a vacant corner. All night I lay on top of what I was convinced was the curve of a gardening spade, although in the morning it proved to be a kitchen pot, cast in iron.

My immediate neighbours, who had not addressed a word to each other all day, suddenly discovered a heartfelt camaraderie and proceeded to confer in the vernacular throughout the night, in their velvety, resounding voices. No one protested. The peasant Africans, accustomed to sleeping in a confined and communal hut, can tolerate conditions that make me rage with insomnia.

At one point, I gave up on the theory of sleep, and scrambled out of the boat to sit on the bank. The captain opened one sleepy eyelid.

'Don't do that! There are crocodiles!'

I got back in the boat.

In the morning after everyone had washed, an odd little ceremony got under way. Everybody in the party hoisted up their bundles and disappeared into the thicket of reeds, emerging empty handed some minutes later.

'*Monsieur*, why are they doing this?'

'The customs tax,' explained the boatman.

When we set off again the boat was considerably lighter. Gone were the iron pots, the Western items like oil and sugar, the bundles of second-hand clothes. Every last one of the passengers carried in his or her fist a ridiculous little plastic packet containing a loaf of white bread, wrapped in brown paper. It seemed to me that it would have to be a fairly odd sort of customs official who could truly believe that all these people would endure a two-day return trip to a foreign country, which included dossing in a swamp surrounded by crocodiles, all for the sake of a loaf of bread.

A short while later, the pirogue began to nose in to shore again, until its prow rested in the grainy white sand. I caught my breath. Spread before us was a picturesque little village. Square mud brick houses, topped with reed thatch, looked out on to the lake, separated from one another by neat dust tracks which led off into the distance. Plump little black babies giggled in the sand, their fists in their mouths, while fussy roosters strutted amongst them. The beach was dotted with giant palm trees, dancing gaily in the morning breezes.

I stood up and waved to the children. Astonishment rooted them to the spot; their mouths fell open and their eyes grew immense. At this point, I noticed that the departing peasants with whom we had spent the night were all giving us a rather peculiar look over their shoulders. It was the sort of look one gives the crustaceans in one of those restaurant display tanks, when lobster stands clearly written on the menu.

A curious figure dressed in a blue suit had appeared on the nearest dusty track. As he drew closer I made out the tie knotted around his neck, and the unmistakable flavour of officialdom that infused his stride across the burning sands. He stopped in front of us, and his small porcine eyes took the measure.

'*Monsieur, le gendarme*,' announced the captain of the pirogue.

∗

'As I say, investigations must be made into the suspicious movements of those who enter the minerals zone.'

'But I didn't know it was a minerals zone! And I keep telling you, we didn't even want to come here. We wanted to go to Uvira. Besides, we haven't made any suspicious movements. When could we have possibly managed to make a suspicious movement? You nabbed us the minute we set foot on shore.'

'But intent must be established. It is not for me to establish intent. A higher authority must establish intent.'

'But honestly, sir, it's all a horrendous mistake. There wasn't any intent.'

'Don't betray the boat captain,' hissed Cyril. 'He's our friend.'

I broke off my line of argument and looked at Cyril.

For three hours I had been struggling in French with this nasty policeman, and for three hours Cyril had been a shifty-eyed conspirator in a spy thriller of his own imagining.

'Excuse me, Cyril,' I said coldly.

The *gendarme* fiddled his pencil on the convex arc of his paunch and looked at each corner of the roof by turns. He made an impatient gesture at the twenty small children whose clustered heads were competing for space in the cavity of the glassless window. The heads withdrew momentarily and then regrouped.

'The captain of the boat will explain that we requested to go to Uvira.'

'Yes, but now you are in the minerals zone, and you do not have any permission to be here.'

'Yes, but surely you see that . . .'

'Don't betray the boat captain! Don't say where we spent the night! We're honour bound not to tell!'

'One moment, *monsieur*,' I requested the *gendarme*.

He acquiesced.

'*Shut the fuck up, Cyril, before I kill you.* How am I supposed to think, dammit! Do you suppose your damn boat friend thought for one moment he was taking us to Uvira? We're going to have to pay a massive bribe and he'll get a huge bloody cut. All that shopping will be to hell and gone by now, they hid it only about fifteen minutes' walk from here. If you can't manage to say something sensible then just keep your mouth shut.'

I quit yelling and subsided. The *gendarme*'s small eyes had distended in surprise. He withdrew for a moment to the outer office. The gaggle of children took the opportunity, as they had in every other absence of his, to hoist themselves on to the window ledge and blow farts from their ragged buttocks, to hilarious encouragement from one another.

Towards late afternoon the *gendarme* decided on a game plan of sorts, which was that we should go to Uvira in the morning

179

and report to the *Bureau d'Immigration*.

'Well, that's all right,' I said limply. I was dog-tired from the heat and the arguments, the sleepless night on the boat, and the antics of the taunting children.

'Of course, you cannot go unsupervised. You must be accompanied by an *agent de police*, who will bring your confiscated passports.'

'Right.'

'And naturally you are expected to put him up at a hotel and to pay for his food and transport. To be paid in advance.'

'How much?'

'An amount could be, *par exemple*, forty million zaires.'

'Forty million zaires! Where is this man going to stay – at the Savoy?'

'These things can take quite a bit of time,' said the *gendarme* softly.

'All right, all right, we'll pay.'

Once outside, the twenty children increased to sixty who gambolled and scrimmaged in our wake. I put my arm around Cyril, contritely, and thirty imitative couples formed behind us, in a spate of giggles.

'I tell you what, I'm jolly hungry. How about you?'

'But we've hardly got any zaires left,' he said sadly.

In one of the coastal huts we found a plump mama who shooed away all the children and swapped a bowl of bananas for my comb and deodorant stick. We left the woman and her sisters smearing the deodorant in slimy lines along their fore-arms, helpless with mirth, and booked into another hut which served as the village hotel.

In the morning the agent arrived to begin his supervisory duties and we dutifully tagged along behind him to wait for the transport under a palm tree. Our arrival intersected the daily march of the village children to elementary school. On and on and on they came, barefooted squadrons of learning, each clutching a pen and exercise book, two, three, four, five hundred.

'But surely, *Monsieur*, all these children cannot come from this area alone?'

'Oh yes!' replied the agent modestly. 'We Zairois are very accomplished in the making of children.'

And then the transport lorry arrived, from which human bodies sprouted like needles in a pincushion, jammed one against the other. The lorry itself was so severely rusted that the bonnet and cabin roof had gone altogether, and the engine was semi-covered by planks of wood. It seemed barely possible that it could tolerate even one more body, but somehow they squeezed us in and lashed our backpacks to the sides.

All along the road to Uvira were the same pretty little villages. The road itself was scoured by gullies, and the gullies were bridged by tree trunks. Whenever we came to one of these makeshift bridges a murmur of anticipation would rise up from the human herd accommodated in the rear of the lorry. The vehicle itself seemed to paw at the earth like a Pamplona bull, before making a headlong rush at the obstacle. Somehow, miraculously, we bounced and lurched over the cavity each time, and another murmur arose, a mumbled litany of thanksgiving, in which I joined fervently.

We arrived in Uvira at two in the afternoon. It seemed to me a pedestrian town, like any other unremarkable African town, the main road in disrepair, the square single-storey buildings slung out along its perimeters.

I had been told to report to the *Bureau d'Immigration* at four, so it seemed politic to book into a hotel and get something to eat before submitting to the next bout of harassment. The hotel nearest to the Bureau was called, with an inappropriate grandeur, Le Guest House. Nevertheless, the proprietor was genial and concocted a meal of rice, chips and salad. We fell on it savagely, having eaten nothing but bananas for three days.

The agent eyed our meal wistfully and turned his head away to look at the vista of the lake, only a hundred yards from the hotel.

'*Monsieur*, why don't you get yourself something to eat?'

'I don't have any money.'

'What do you mean? I gave the *gendarme* forty million zaires for you.'

'Ah yes, the *gendarme*,' he sighed, and his eyes followed the passage of a passing pirogue.

I relented and passed him a plate of rice and salad. With luck, one day he too would be a *gendarme*. But for the moment he was just a lowly agent who couldn't buy himself lunch.

The *Bureau d'Immigration* was an unlovely building fronted by a square patch of sand. The Zairois emblem of the torch in the hand fluttered on a solitary pole. The front door opened on to an office and a desk, with another door leading off to the right. Behind the desk sat an official, and on the desk itself a bulky two-way radio buzzed out a muted roar of static.

'*Je m'excuse*, are you the *chef*?' I asked. I hadn't asked Cyril to wait with me. He would not understand the questions and would only grow restless.

The official stopped fiddling with the controls of the radio and waved carelessly at the right-hand door. I started towards it, but he held up an admonitory finger so I took a seat on one of the classroom chairs that flanked the wall. After an hour the forbidden door opened and the *chef* emerged. He was an enormous man, with the big-boned rotundity that the Zairois tend toward. I followed him into his inner sanctum and repeated my little story, which now had the familiarity of a mantra, that I had come with my friend as a tourist, that I had no interest in minerals, that I had been tricked.

'No one comes to this country for tourism. Business only.'

'It's the truth, sir. I was interested in the history and culture of your country.'

'I don't believe you.'

I could only tell him the facts. After an hour I began to falter and to rub my eyes with fatigue, my nerves worn thin by the constant babbling of white noise from the adjacent room.

'Tourism in this country is only allowed with special permission.'

'But sir, I've been here before, on an ordinary visa.'

'Are you telling me how the country is run?' he shouted vitriolically.

'No, no.'

'Would you like to run the country? Do you want to sit behind this desk?'

'No. I'm sorry. I . . . look, give me permission to leave and I'll go tomorrow.'

'Yes, you'll go and take your secrets with you.'

'No! I don't have secrets,' I pleaded, despairingly.

His eyes were hard and relentless, his mouth set in a tight little line. As I became worn out, he seemed to feed off my waning strength. His triple chin swelled with power. At last the subordinate tapped on the door and called him outside. After a moment both of them reappeared.

'Come here and explain this!'

They were both staring unpleasantly at something in the yard.

I looked.

Arms extended, legs neatly split in the air, they were *grand jetés*, a series of *grand jetés*, followed by a *temps de poisson*.

'What is he doing?' demanded the *chef* with deep suspicion.

'*Cyril*! Stop that! Stop doing that right now.'

'Jesus, Sarah. Stop this. Stop that. Shut up. You're like a stuck record. When are you coming back? It's time to eat.'

'Please, *Monsieur*, let me go. I'll come back first thing in the morning.'

He shrugged and I left rapidly before he changed his mind.

The hotel in the mean while had received a new influx of visitors, schoolchildren in late adolescence, a little younger than Cyril and myself.

'*Bonjour*,' I said to the first one I met.

'No, no, speak English. We are here for writing examination

in English. Please the English for practice.'

'Oh, I see. Well, break a leg.'

'Uh?'

'*Bonne chance.*'

'No, please. To speak English!'

Cyril was in good spirits. Before arriving for the performance in the yard, he had made friends with a Hutu woman and her children and they had invited him to participate in a meal at their home.

There were a good many Hutu living in and around Uvira, who had fled from neighbouring Burundi during the 1970s. The Belgians were granted a mandate over Rwanda and Burundi after the First World War, these two closely related territories having formerly been German possessions. The Belgians practised the divide and rule policy which was so commonly used by the European colonisers to aid in the administration of their colonies.

In this case, they reinforced a feudal system which had been in place since the sixteenth century, the subjugation of the Hutu by the Watutsi. Under the Belgians, the Watutsi were allowed to acquire education, wealth, and administrative powers, while the Hutu essentially remained peasants. The extreme hatred fomented between these two groups is evident today in the carnage of modern Rwanda.

As darkness fell we went down to the little strip of beach that abutted the hotel lawns. I picked at the sandy grains with my fingers and stared wistfully at the bank of distant lights that was Bujumbura. So near, so ridiculously near, yet so impossible to reach.

The passing night honed the interrogating skills of the *chef*. His opening gambit completely threw me.

'People,' said the *chef* obscurely, 'could spend many years in jail. People who have been caught scouting in the minerals zone.'

I stared out of the window at the infestation of black-bellied bustards that had nested in the mango trees during the night.

'And don't think you'd go to jail with the little man of jumpings. For you – the women's prison. For him, the men's.'

'Please, *Monsieur*, I know the ambassador of my country in Kinshasa. Can you not radio him?'

'We have no radio here,' replied the *chef* with magnificent insouciance.

I gaped, grimaced, and rubbed both eyes. He continued to sit implacably in his chair.

'Is this about money, *Monsieur*?' I asked him at last.

But he would not say how much, not yet, not until he had completely worn me down.

Cyril was with the Hutu family, showing the fascinated children how to do the different positions of the foot. I slumped against the low wall of their house, feeling that I couldn't deal with much more. The Hutu woman was pounding grain in her iron basin. She stopped what she was doing, crossed her yard and pulled gently on my sleeve.

'Don't be sad. This morning the *chef* is making life bad, but this afternoon you can go to the Mission Catholique.'

'There's a mission?'

'Oh yes, come with me, I will show you.'

In the interior of the humble little mission I found the man of God. He was a white man, an Italian, bent over a two-way radio of his own. I approached him in a surge of gladness and spilled the details of my trials. The surge was short lived.

'You are mad to come here, you silly girl, mad, mad, mad. This is no place for white people.'

'But, Father . . .'

'Do you see white people here? Hmmm? Do you?'

'No, I don't,' I said, very cowed.

'*Exactement*! So you better get out,' he exclaimed, the blood colouring his sun-lined face.

'Yes, well, I would very much like to, Father, that's why I need your help!'

'Go away, go away, you crazy child, and I'll see what I can

185

do.'

Back at the hotel, the last vestiges of my resolve cracked and I descended into an abysmal riot of sobbing, perched on the edge of an old bath whose plumbing had rotted away completely.

Cyril, entering the bathroom, offered words of encouragement.

'Sarah, you can't deny the is-ness. Whatever the is-ness happens to be, you've just got to open up and say to yourself I am a great wondrous living entity, full of joy.'

'Oh, Cyril, it's not the is-ness that's getting me down, it's the police.'

'Ah man, that's crap. Levitate on your own plane. Know yourself as a sovereign entity. You are *your* entity. You're not *his* entity.'

'And you're an entity that's going to be facing sodomy-buggery in a men's jail if I can't get you out of this, my little man of jumpings,' I said bitterly.

In the mid-afternoon the priest returned and together we made the journey to the Bureau. Their French was too rapid for me to follow, but somehow he swung it. The *chef* turned to me charmingly and pronounced, as if there had never been the least doubt about it, that I might be escorted from the country on the morrow, together with my friend.

I rushed back to the hotel whooping, and relayed the good news to Cyril. His face fell.

'No,' he said stubbornly.

'No? What do you mean, no?'

'I want to stay. It's Paradise here. You could definitely settle down here and live in oneness with nature for ever.'

I looked at him, blew out my cheeks and then deflated them slowly.

'Well, I guess you can stay, Cyril, but I'm leaving.'

'But I want you to stay in Paradise with me,' he said mournfully.

But by morning he had decided to leave after all. Our

186

passports lay on the table next to the radio that didn't exist. I opened mine and saw that my photograph was smudged with fingerprints and a sticky viscous smear of unmistakable origin trailed across the picture. My image had clearly been part of some onanistic ritual.

The last commandment of the thwarted *chef* was that we had to pay for a private car and another agent to take us to the border. We returned briefly to Le Guest House to pick up our rucksacks. All the schoolchildren were sitting in huddles on the lawn. Some were laughing carelessly, but others were subdued and sombre.

'So how did it go?' I asked the nearest boy.

'We did not write.'

'Why not?'

'Our teacher ran away with our examination fees.'

'Good Lord! How terrible.'

'Yes,' said the boy darkly. 'If I find him, I'm going to cut his throat.'

The private car drove us to the border. As I passed into Burundi, I felt a surge of euphoria, of release. I knelt down and picked up a handful of earth to reassure myself that the last four days were really over, that I had not been hurt, that I had not even had to pay very much in bribes.

A few weeks later Mobutu issued a new five-million zaire note, and used the tender to pay his military forces. Mobutu's rival for power, the prime minister Etienne Tshisedeki, promptly had this note declared illegal. In consequence, it was not accepted by any of the shopkeepers. Once again the country erupted into an orgy of fighting and looting, as the desperate soldiers realised that their pay packet was worthless. Over a thousand people died in this bout of violence, including the French ambassador.

Emissaries of Angels

In Bujumbura we pitched our tent at the yacht club, the *Cercle Nautique*. It was a peaceful place, a spread of green lawns bordering on the lake, and I fell asleep that night to the familiar grunts of the hippos who wallowed beside the pierhead.

During the evening an overland truck arrived. I woke up in the morning to find that twenty identical blue and yellow tents had sprung up around our Kestrel. Forty young people were in various stages of waking. Some were showering, some had been relegated to breakfast detail, whilst others were trying to lie in. The breakfast team were scrambling eggs and heating coffee. The late-night drinkers, po-faced and sickish, were dousing their groggy heads in buckets of water.

I wandered amongst their operations, intrigued. I had never seen an overland truck before. It seemed to my *gendarme*- wearied senses like a kind of liberal boarding school on wheels.

After a few minutes of watching, a thickset young chap caught my arm and said, ''Ere, get your kit together, you lot are going to the ferry in a few minutes.'

I pointed out that I was not one of his charges and that I was trying to get to Kigoma.

'Oh,' he said. 'Well, our lot are all getting on the ferry from here. Me and the lads are going to pick 'em up at Mpulungu, and you can bung in with us if you want.'

The lads turned out to be the driver and a doughty passenger whose hair was shaved in chequered patches all over his head. The doughty passenger was sick to his stomach. Every now and then we stopped for him to vomit into the foliage.

'Are you not feeling very well?' I asked sympathetically.

'Too much beer and too much rooting,' he replied, swivelling bloodshot eyes.

'Mooting?' I asked uncertainly.

'ROOTING!' repeated the chequer-head sarcastically, with a little pelvic mime to illustrate what rooting was.

Two of the lads were Londoners and two were Liverpudlians. During the forty-eight hours we spent in their truck, I watched them in endless fascination. I had met quite a lot of Englishmen during my childhood, schoolfriends of my brothers out on their gap years between school and university, and relatives with whom we retained familial links, but this was my first real encounter with the working classes. Wanting to fit in with them, I tried to learn their expressions and follow their jokes. But, clearly, they thought I was a hopelessly antiquated colonial product.

We spent the days travelling through the steep hill country of Burundi. Verdant green mountains rising up to bury their apexes in the low-lying cloud, purple jacaranda trees, the dust road winding on and on through the gullies and the valleys between the ochre cliffsides. The slow passage on the truck through the mountains was soporific; Cyril and all the English apart from the driver fell into a rhythm of slumber.

What are clouds
but emissaries of angels?
The shades of the deities
are the purpling of the blossoms
of the jacaranda trees
in spring, I wrote in my diary.

My gauche poetry and the passage of the magnificent green terrain moved me, and I slid into a quiet, reflective frame of mind.

Spring had settled over Africa like a mantle of renewal. Every bush was speckled with buds, and the rains had bolstered up the sap strength of a landscape of trees. All these months at the back of my mind had lingered the thought that perhaps the annual rebirth of the world would restore my brother. Like some animal of the earth he would come out of his hibernation, as he had always come and gone, in accordance with his own raw instincts. But here was the spring and here were the rains, and still there was no respite for me.

At last we reached Kigoma. The driver and his assistants made off for the market-place, leaving the chequer-headed passenger to guard the truck. Cyril and I began to gather our things together. At this point the chequer-head turned nasty. He cornered Cyril with all the ferocity of a rabid bull mastiff and touched him for ten American dollars. Afterwards he came for me, but after the terrors of the Zairois *chef*, I was feeling fairly menace-proof.

'What shocking manners you have,' I said. 'Why do you pick on someone who's half your size? Give him back his money.'

His face creased up. I thought he might hit me and retreated, but he broke into laughter.

'What a toff little madam you are,' said the partial skinhead, with a skewered smile. 'I wouldn't half mind a go on yer. But sorry, matey, your boyfriend's fair game.'

Because we had come into the country at one of the more obscure border posts, we had to go to the customs house in Kigoma to have our stamps verified. On the way we passed a public witchcraft ceremony – an elaborate affair involving a posse of terrified chickens which kept trying to escape headlong into the crowd. I asked one of the bystanders what the ceremony was for. To cure a husband's infidelity, he said, but someone else thought it was to chase the HIV virus out of a child. We

190

walked on.

As an outsider, the practice of witchcraft seems an alien and primitive thing, a vicious stranglehold on the lives of the people. But to many Africans the ancestors are as real as if they visibly walked the earth, and infinitely capable of interfering for both good and bad.

The customs house official obligingly stamped my passport. As I was leaving the building I had a strange sensation that at first did not make sense. Once outside, I realised what it was. I've lived since birth in the old guest house of Lord Charles Somerset, governor of the Cape Colony in the early nineteenth century. The Georgian facade to the house had been grafted on to the existing structure of an eighteenth-century Dutch farmhouse. I sensed in the customs house the same dusty breath of history that was my cradle legacy. From the outside I realised that it was an old colonial house. Beyond the decades of accumulated dirt, the chronic disrepair and the crumbling decay of brickwork, lay the remains of a magnificent piece of architecture.

I raised my camera to take a picture, but my arm was jostled down by a passing guard.

'It is forbidden to photograph government offices.'

'But it's so beautiful,' I said artlessly.

The guard drew down the corners of his mouth sceptically, and I saw it through his eyes: an ugly old place, gone to pieces, behind whose smashed-out windows the customs officials yawned in boredom. In a few decades it would collapse altogether, a rubble of bricks which would be stolen overnight to fortify the hut walls of the peasants.

In Africa, the capital cities created by the whites, like Lusaka and Nairobi, have become frenzied and dangerous, a throbbing hub of burgeoning human life. But these isolated old towns mutate more subtly and in their mutations make nostalgic mockeries out of the grandeurs of the past. For eventually the ghost edifices of the white people will melt back into the dust, as if disclaiming that they ever existed. And beside them the mud huts and the banana trees will thrive and at last they will grow into the old buildings, so that dance halls become maize plots and reception rooms bear a yearly crop of groundnuts.

From Kigoma we caught a sleeper train to Tabora, from where we hoped to make the journey north to Lake Victoria. Apart from us, the cabin held three African women, each with a child at her breast. The women were cassava traders and the cabin was stocked with huge piles of the malodorous root. I had tried it once – it had the taste and texture of chalk. And wedged into the furthest corner was an East German girl called Bianca.

The cassava women hummed and suckled their babies. Bianca sat up and began an oration. Apparently she had been out from Europe on a work camp to introduce a revolutionary new fuel-saving device to some remote village in Tanzania. For our benefit, she whipped a pen and notepad out of her leather bag and drew diagrammatic representations of the fuel-saving device. Absorbed in her drawing, she forgot about us temporarily and scribbled in a number of little labels which she underlined. Then she made two columns on either side of the drawing – one was headed Mechanics and the other Pragmatics.

'It looks like the Starship Enterprise,' observed Cyril, who had the upside-down view of the fuel-saving device.

Bianca came out of her trance and remembered that she had an audience. Collaring Cyril, she led him through Pragmatics and Mechanics. I didn't take to her very much. Biancas proliferate in Africa – well-meaning outsiders from Europe who bustle in, brimming with political correctness, but they nevertheless manage to reduce the villager's own experience to nought, and traduce accumulated lifetimes of experience. To the village people themselves these young invaders are exotic oddities. Girls like Bianca are treated with clucking sympathy for their childlessness, for in African terms they are almost overripe.

For a fortnight the Biancas descend and build their stoves, and the villagers stand by and watch, a little amused, a little intrigued, always distant. In another fortnight the novelty wears thin and the villagers resume their old ways, leaving the revolutionary new device to rot into oblivion.

As darkness fell the cassava women sealed up the window against the African distrust of night breezes and the cabin quickly became a stifling, airless coffin. The top bunk had no guard rail, and every time the train came to one of its numerous jerky halts I had to grab at the edges to keep from tumbling to the ground. Just before dawn we reached Tabora and disembarked. Over the minarets the haunting cadence of the muezzin dispelled the monopoly of night.

At daybreak we boarded the bus to Shinyanga. This bus was so ramshackle that the covering had been completely stripped away from the seats leaving only the iron framework intact. En route we had two flat tyres and two engine failures, punctuating the day with lengthy roadside siestas.

Each time this happened we seemed to be in the middle of nowhere but, as surely as sunrise, within a few minutes small children would come running from the bush fringe with woven baskets of eggs and salt, or buckets of ripe mangoes. The passengers spread themselves out in the sunlight, cracking the shells from the rangy, flavoursome eggs and dozing off in the heat until the driver managed once more to draw a reluctant splutter of life from the old engine. The children roared, we gingerly arranged bundles of soft things between the iron rim and our bottoms and winced away the bouncing hours until the next breakdown.

In the twilight we reached Shinyanga and spent the night there, rising at dawn to catch the train to Mwanza and Lake Victoria.

*

Mwanza is Tanzania's most important port on Lake Victoria. It is a pleasant little town, nestling amongst hills. Grey-white boulders break the surface of the lake water. Most of the townspeople are Wasakuma, members of the largest tribe in the country.

To us, Mwanza was a sanctuary of gods. In the middle of town there was, impossibly, an ice-cream parlour. The ice-cream parlour had gaudy representations of sundaes painted all over its outer wall. This first impression was confirmed by the sight of actual ice-cream eaters, clearly visible through the glass apertures.

We stood outside for a moment or two, fever whipped with anticipation, the slavering wet of longing gathering in our mouths. At last we went inside. We watched the waitress as, with agonising sloth, she spooned the stuff into a glass and caught a trailing bead of it with the tip of her little finger. At last we had it before us. Shivering, we dipped the tiny spoons and gathered up a hillock of snow, travelling the distance from glass to mouth, until it lay upon our febrile tongues, cold and sweet, a nectared ice delight. Eyes closed, breath suspended, there was nothing in the world but this frozen ecstasy that we had somehow stolen down from heaven.

Mostly, I tried not to think about food, about food as a prelude, about food as a masterpiece. But sometimes at night, lying on my back and following the loose-limbed tracks of spiders across a mud roof, I might say:

'Cyril.'

'Uh huh?'

'Remember cheese?'

'Oh . . . God,' he would breathe softly, and I felt the same vision form in his head, as remote as a star, as close as torture.

'Melted cheese.'

'No, stop it.'

'Melted cheese on toast.'

'Sarah.'

'With a milkshake.'

'Sarah!'

I would wait until he was almost asleep and then add, just above a whisper.

'A great big creamy chocolate milkshake.'

'Shut up! Shut up or I'll leave this room right now.'

From Mwanza we caught the *MV Victoria* to Nansio island. The islands of Lake Victoria are timeless pockets of earth, untrammelled by modernity. Here the yams and cassavas sprout their rising branches in uneven lines that stretch between the mango trees. The landscape seems bright and unreal, as if the mind is touched with a permanent hallucination of tropical vapours. Everywhere the yellow butterflies dance between the palms and banana trees, the bushes are scattered with a profusion of multicoloured flowers, and the tethered goats blink back the secrets of their yellow eyes.

We walked for hours across the island, stopping to touch the glistening coats of the pretty little cows with curved horns, to eat fire-blackened lakefish in the peasant huts, to pick off the savage siafu ants that collected on our ankles. At night, as the great red sun dropped over the rim of the lake, we warmed our hands on bowls of *mazive na ndogo*, the milk of goats, spiced and sweet.

At last we moved on and slowly made our way up the eastern littoral of the lake. We were marooned for a day in a village so small that nobody spoke English, but the children whispered in breathless delight when they dared to paddle their stubby fingers in the unfamiliar straightness of my hair.

The next town we stopped at was Musoma. It was full moon and the dhow boats sailed out across the lake in ghostly shadows.

From Musoma there was a bus bound for the Kenyan border. We had almost reached the border when a tyre blew out with a thundering bang. Outside the bus the air was cool and moist from the perpetual spring rains. The dirt road had a hale, earthy scent and we were surrounded by a landscape of green hills, flourishing in rain-sprung fertility. Overhead the late afternoon clouds made an ethereal ceiling from which the faint precipitation settled on our cheeks like a misty caress.

I skipped up a small hillock and looked at the distant rain-sweetened country, about which I had read so much.

'Kenya,' I whispered, and drew a long breath of gladness into my lungs.

The Essence of a Continent

'This is River Road?'

'River Road,' confirmed the matatu driver impatiently, already engaged in the mathematical precisions of sandwiching the highest possible quantity of human flesh into his vehicle. A matatu is an African taxi – of the same variety used for institutional hockey teams in richer countries.

I took stock. The area seemed to be a Stygian bedlam of human residue. A number of horribly disfigured polio victims were crawling in the muck. One of them walked on his knees, which were strapped with a rubber binding, balanced on steadying hands encased in rough sandals. Behind him the two poles of his wasted legs stuck out like boat rudders. A little boy watched us with one bright eye. The other was sealed up in a wasteland of pink scar tissue. On all sides fruit vendors flicked away the flies, matatu horns bawled their electronic anthems, sharp young men in rubber ankle boots loafed against walls. A couple of obvious hookers made their way into an insalubrious-looking cavity from which discordant music bawled. *Modern Green Bar* read the overhead sign.

It was my first glimpse of Nairobi.

We had crossed the border at Kisumu and spent the night there. In the morning we were offered a lift to the capital by a deputation of government ministers in the agricultural sector. The ministers were friendly enough. Encouraged, I began to ask them questions about what they did and about the issue of land provision for the different tribes, but they neatly circumvented each enquiry in turn. In fact, they had an air of marginally menacing sloganised groupthink that made them seem ludicrously like overgrown school prefects.

After a while I shut up and stared out of the window to the north. As a South African, this part of the country was of particular interest to me, because it was the destination of the very last Afrikaner trek. Three hundred boers, men, women and children, made a journey over sea and land, arriving in Nakuru on 18 July 1908. From Nakuru a scouting party rode out to Timboroa, beyond the Eldama Ravine. Here they found a level, treeless landscape. In the rare, pure air, with the abundance of game and the distance from other human settlement, the boers saw their chance to recapture their past in an environment very similar to their abandoned highveld homes.

As they had done in South Africa in the previous century, they travelled in tented ox wagons. The women and children rode inside the wagons. The men walked alongside, quickening the pace of the oxen with their sjamboks, or rode on the outskirts with rifles at the ready. At night they formed the wagons into a protective laager, in the midst of which they would eat and sleep. In this way they reached the Eldama Ravine and cut back the forest escarpment until they had struggled to the top, to the camp they called Brugspruit. Moving on, they dragged their wagons across the treacherous Sugar Vlei and across the Sosiani river, staking out their farms on the Uasin Gishu plateau.

It was a monumentally arduous trek. Only the Afrikaner, with his indomitable desire to be left alone, his stalwart religious convictions and his unbreachable stubbornness, could have done it. When there was nowhere left to trek in Africa, this selfsame inventory of traits would become a towering conviction, making South Africa into the last colonial power.

Incidentally, the grandchildren of the Kenyan Afrikaners were to trek back again when Kenyan independence became imminent in the early 1960s.

The road to Nairobi was dotted with game. Animals grazed incongruously beside the infrequent billboards and road signs – frisky little Thomson's gazelles with screwdriver horns and flicking black tails, the odd hartebeest, dozens of zebra browsing on the lush spring grass. As we climbed up the far side of the Rift Valley towards Nairobi the temperature dropped, the air became cool and fresh and human settlements spawned along the road's edge. The ministers dropped us off on the outskirts of the city and we took a matatu into the centre.

Nairobi is a new city. One hundred years ago there was nothing there but a boggy swamp, a plain of unremarkable flat land at the base of the sudden ascent to the highlands. The soggy earth infused the windswept air with noxious swamp odours. Of humans there were none, but the animals proliferated in tens of thousands of every species.

Legend has it that the first white man to camp on the site was Sergeant Ellis of the Royal Engineers. Nairobi, through no distinction of its own, became the capital by virtue of being situated almost exactly half way between Mombasa and Uganda. For this was the turn of the century – the heyday of the scramble for colonial territory – and the British were building their railway with an eye to establishing a British East Africa which would repudiate further German claims to the land.

Now Nairobi became a city of tents. An Indian workforce of thirty-two thousand from Gujarat and the Punjab was imported to work on the railway. Africans began to move to the urban area, and of course the colonists themselves came out from England – the provincial and district commissioners, agriculturalists, police, bureaucrats, doctors, railway administration and pioneering farmers. Almost ritually, these young Englishmen returned home to find a bride. Once a home had been established in advance, the woman would be sent for and the couple would be reunited, terai-hatted, bashful and largely unfamiliar to each other, on the dockside at Mombasa.

Gradually Nairobi acquired a distinctive character. Up rose the genteel columns of the Muthaiga Club. Nairobi became a city of flowers – everyone was planting roses and bougainvillaea – which bloomed almost perpetually in the warm climate. The governor had a pet cheetah, polo tournaments were organised, Race Week drew the smart set away from their stamping grounds at Wanjohi, and a statue was raised to the pioneering farmer, Lord Delamere.

'In the few days I had spent in Nairobi, I found myself falling in love with Kenya,' mused Evelyn Waugh in the 1930s, recounting comically how the affable Englishmen who plied him with champagne, pink gin and cigars incessantly implored him 'not to think Kenya is always like this'.

'Nairobi has become one of the most attractive and certainly the most flowery of capitals,' wrote Elspeth Huxley in 1963, the year in which the country won its independence.

I came to Kenya for the first time almost thirty years after independence. Nairobi is still an attractive city – if you happen to be able to afford to reside in the right parts of it. Because I was a shoestringer, the parts of the city that I saw the most of were gripped with poverty and plight, and a high incidence of crime. The rueful nickname which many luckless tourists have bestowed on the city is 'Nairobbery'.

I could not but suppose that the deprivation that now spilled openly on to these streets had been breeding throughout the past century, a diametrical opposition in black suffering to the opulence and grandeur of the whites.

But Uhuru was no panacea for the destitute. Whilst the first black president, Jomo Kenyatta, is still held in a generally favourable light, he was undoubtedly biased towards his own tribal group, the Kikuyu. Less popular was his successor, Daniel arap Moi, a Tugen with close links to the Kikuyu. Dissenting Kenyans argue that their combined excesses have led the nation to become what one disillusioned Mau Mau fighter described as a country of ten millionaires and ten million beggars. Kenya became a one-party state in 1964. Young blacks who were brave enough to speak out were systematically picked off, either through assassination (Tom Mboya, J M Kariuki), imprisonment (Oginga Odinga), or exile (Ngugi wa Thiong'o).

Nevertheless, with the collapse of communism and the consequent alteration in the balance of power across Africa, Moi was having to concede to the international pressure for multiparty elections. Kenya in late 1992 was in the grip of election fever. Posters and promotional flags were everywhere. Burbling loudspeaker trucks crawled up and down the main drag of all the towns, dark rumours circulated about arson attacks on opposition homes, and sporadic knife fights erupted between partisans.

Every day the newspapers carried photographs of smiling *wananchi* (peasants) receiving a handout and a sloganised T-shirt from the government. Apparently Moi had printed billions and billions of Kenyan shillings with which to buy off *wananchi* votes. Certainly, immediately after the elections the Kenyan economy suffered a severe collapse.

All this aside, the opposition did not seem to be making a very co-ordinated effort. At one stage there had been only one opposition party, but the various members had fallen out and now there were a half dozen or more. They seemed to spend more time heaping recriminations on each other's heads than they did on defeating the government. In the mean time Moi could make full use of the country's resources.

One afternoon I went to the cinema. I had arranged to meet Cyril there. We were improving our relationship by having significant time apart. Both of us still possessed the dapper boy scout hats that we had bought in Cape Town, although now – drooping, dirty and rain-soaked – they had acquired the appearance of outsized mussel shells.

By the time the show was ready to begin Cyril still had not

appeared. I walked inside and slid into my seat.

The cinema attendant hurried up the aisle and tapped at my elbow. He was a small man in a wine-red uniform with thick contracting eyebrows.

'When the national anthem is played you must take your hat off.'

'Right.'

I settled back in the seat. The cinema was warm and comfortable. Another wine-red uniform was making his way along the front seats with a tray of ice-creams and chocolates.

'Excuse me.'

The cinema attendant was back again. I looked at him politely.

'To remind you about the hat.'

'Why don't I just take it off now, shall I? That'll save a lot of trouble.'

He looked mollified. At that moment the cinema darkened and the first chords of the national anthem sounded. Everybody stood up very straight and seemed to quiver to a motionless attention. On screen, three flags fluttered in a portentous breeze.

'Sarah! Hey! Shit, it's dark. Ow! Where are you?'

'Here, I'm here. Don't sit down. Quick, hat off!'

'What?'

At that moment the cinema attendant pounced, each eyebrow a caterpillar of down-plunging fury.

'*You are wearing a hat!*'

'Yes,' agreed Cyril, flummoxed.

'It is forbidden.'

'Forbidden to wear a *hat*?'

'Do you want to make trouble,' hissed the cinema attendant murderously. 'I'll call the police.'

'Oh God, no,' I intervened. 'Look here. Off with the hat. I'll bung it under the seat and we won't touch it for the duration of the show, I promise. Promise, Cyril.'

'I promise,' he said, mystified.

The cinema attendant reluctantly accepted this modus

vivendi and retreated with a threatening backward glance over his shoulder. We settled down to watch a twenty-minute short on His Excellency arriving in the presidential cavalcade, His Excellency visiting the *wananchi*, His Excellency inspecting the *wananchi*'s hospital.

After the film we walked back to River Road in the twilight, through the hustlers, beggars and prostitutes, stopping at a Somali food stall to buy the triangular curried pastries called sambusas and the flat doughnuts known as mandazi.

The striking good looks of the Somali women have ensured their desirability in the West as supermodels. Here in East Africa these beautiful Cushitic girls were as poor as churchmice; many of them still bore the savage wounds of their pubescent clitoridectomies, but they were as aloof and proud as eagles.

At the intersection of Latema Road and River Road was the New Kenya Lodge where we were staying. A narrow passageway led off the street and up to a metal grille. Behind that huddled a dozen dormitories and scores of young people, a cheerful congregation of travellers only yards away from the grim miseries of the street. It put me in mind of Anne Frank's secret annexe.

It was the first time I had been in the environment of a youth hostel. After my long period of spiritual and physical isolation, I plunged into the atmosphere of conviviality. At night all the inmates would crowd on to the roof amongst the flapping washing, smoking cigarettes and exchanging nuggets of information about where they had been.

Growing up in apartheid South Africa, I had been isolated from the rest of the world. Now I sat on the corner of a dilapidated sofa and savoured their national quirks. If they discovered that I was a South African, they would pepper me with questions. South Africa was generally still considered too unstable to be a part of the traveller's route. In part, I found their hesitation a relief, because I wanted to keep secret the sequestered gullies and inlets of my youth, those sylvan arcadias where I had first played with my brothers and sisters, where I had danced under the moon with the Purple Bubble, where I had hidden in private and ecstatic collusion with my pens and notebooks.

The River Road district is the centre of Nairobi. To the north is the Asian community of Parklands, to the east the African districts of Eastleigh and Pangani, and to the south the extensive Nairobi National Park. The western stretch contains the affluent suburbs ranging out to the Ngong Hills and the semi-rural smallholdings of Karen, named for Karen Blixen.

'Africa distilled up through six thousand feet, like the strong and refined essence of a continent' is how Karen Blixen described the foothills of Ngong. In the past, the coffee plants would have flowered at this time of year in the aftermath of the rains – 'a radiant sight, like a cloud of chalk, in the mist and the drizzling rain, over six hundred acres of land.'

Now her old homestead is a little shabby. An antiquated tractor and wagon in the grounds set the tone, and vanloads of Americans descend on the driveway.

'Gee whiz – so close to the road! Did you think it was so close to the road, huh? Don't get it in the picture, honey, let's take it from this angle, then we can get that hill in the back.'

'Hell, it looks kinda different from the movie.'

In fact it *is* different from the movie. They thought shooting it in the original house might damage the delicate wooden interiors. Besides, the farmhouse is part of town now.

The Americans nevertheless took turns to strike literary poses at Karen Blixen's escritoire, ignoring the guide's explanation that the current furniture is all replacements. Karen Blixen sold every scrap when she returned to Denmark in virtual penury after her seventeen years in Africa. Coffee, they subsequently discovered, simply will not grow on the highlands. Dairy would have been a better thing, and in point of fact it would have been the Blixens' thing, had not the cheerful, personable, but essentially incapable Baron Blixen bulldozed over his wife's intentions.

Because of the Hollywood movie, Karen Blixen, incarnated in the delicate accents of Meryl Streep, has become the most celebrated of Kenya's writers.

But Kenya bred a number of remarkable daughters. As an African child who wanted to be a writer, I used to devour the stories of their lives. My favourite is Elspeth Huxley, author of *The Flame Trees of Thika* and *The Mottled Lizard*, who had almost total recall from early childhood.

Nicholas stimulated this interest; one birthday present was *West With The Night* – the autobiography of Beryl Markham. Born Beryl Clutterbuck, she was a motherless child raised in the outbacks of Kenya with only the roughest education. But she learnt to hunt with a spear and to break in horses. Headstrong, wild and beautiful, she had married and divorced by eighteen and had a passionate liaison with the Duke of Gloucester, brother to the Prince of Wales. She became a famous horse breeder and aviatrix, defying the strictures on her gender by flying safari parties around East Africa. In 1936 she made a famous solo flight from England to North America – the first person to attempt the difficult route from east to west.

But apart from the writers there were many other Kenyan women who became infamous in the early part of the century: Lady Idina who married six times; Alice de Janzé who shot her lover in a fit of pique on a Paris station; Diana Broughton whose dashing lover, Josslyn Hay, twenty-second Earl of Erroll, was felled by gunshot.

By now these were old legends, and most of my generation was not interested, or they thought these figures of the past despicable.

'Elderly colonials have become period pieces in their own lifetimes,' lamented Elspeth Huxley in the foreword to *Out in the Midday Sun*. But they were not period pieces in my framework, because I came from a country which had been resolutely stuck in the past for almost half a century.

All the time I was in Kenya I could not help but feel my way through the thoughtscapes of two Kenyas, present and past. They never really reconciled and at times they seemed to cancel each other out. Sometimes I thought my preoccupations were nothing but fanciful syllogisms. But at other times I would look into my soul and realise that I was uncertain because I, too, was a white African on the threshold of change, and I would also face a future which could not be predicted by anything that had gone before.

*

After a few days in Nairobi I felt suffocated. We decided to take the bus out to Lake Naivasha. After boarding I checked the fee with several of the other passengers. I always did this because usually there was a unofficially different and larger fee for *wasungu.* On the whole I thought that was fair enough as we had so much more access to money. But sometimes the price hikes would be outrageous.

The bus wound its way down into the Rift Valley towards the small agricultural town of Naivasha. From Naivasha we hailed another matatu to the lake itself. Once vast tracts of this land had belonged to Lord Delamere. In the 1930s Naivasha was one of the playgrounds of the Happy Valley crowd. In those days there was no airport at Nairobi. The flying boats from Southampton would land at Naivasha at the end of their four-day journey and the passengers would continue to Nairobi by bus.

On the southern side of the lake stands the Moorish mansion known as Oserian, meaning a place of peace. The exotic beauty of its minaret and crenellated exterior led to the nickname, the 'Djinn Palace'. It was built by Cyril Ramsay Hill as a present for his wife Molly. In the event, Molly ran away with Josslyn Erroll, whom she subsequently married. Unable to keep pace with his profligate lifestyle and careless squandering of her fortune, she later died of drug and alcohol abuse. For these reasons, Ramsay

Hill came under some suspicion for Erroll's murder, as did Sir Delves Broughton (Jock), Diana Broughton's husband. Broughton underwent a lengthy murder trial in Nairobi but was eventually acquitted. Despite his acquittal, he lost both his wife and his social cachet in Kenya. He returned to England where he later committed suicide.

We stayed at a place called Fisherman's Camp, not far from Oserian. It was a beautiful campsite – a sheet of vivid green grass interspersed with acacia and fever trees which threw out puddles of shade in the noon heat. At night the primal grunt of the hippos reached through the stillness. By morning the place was a symphony of birdsong. Wild ducks and geese flew overhead. In the green papyrus thickets I saw coots and herons, cormorants, dabchicks and spoonbills.

The lake was bordered with pink and blue water lilies whereon the long-legged lily trotters picked their way in delicate and considered hops, depending for support on their impossibly long and widespread toes. As I lay on my stomach in the grass a pair of miniature malachite sunbirds sidled along a twig to investigate me. I even saw a fish eagle, who flung her piercing call down from the treetops.

Cyril came to lie alongside me in the grass to watch the bright-eyed sunbirds. We had been getting along more successfully with each other in Kenya, in this safe, Westernised country where I did not continually have to arraign him. Sometimes I managed to recapture the moods of giddy foppishness that had enabled us to communicate in the beginning. Now that we were in periodic contact with other *wasungu*, my draining solitude was diminished. And in another couple of months I would be back at university. I would go to pubs with other students and be told off for late submissions. My life would be deliciously ordinary and pedestrian. And Cyril would be away communing with oneness in nature.

We walked up through the Hell's Gate National Park to the summit of the cliffs. It was a misty and bracing morning. The slopes were covered with browsing zebra and antelope. Shrouded by the fog, they did not detect us until we were almost upon them, so that at times I felt as if I could have touched their rich pelts. The fog would reveal for an instant a flank of black and white striping, a nosing muzzle whipped towards us, and then the animal withdrew in a indolent canter to resume on the cud a little way off.

We also visited Elsamere, the lakeside home of Joy Adamson who wrote *Born Free* and its sequels, the story of Elsa the lioness. She lived there for seven years before moving to the Shaba Reserve near Isiolo, where she was murdered in 1980 by her servant, Paul Ekai. George Adamson never spent much time at Elsamere. During the latter part of his life he was based in the northerly Kora Reserve until his death at the hands of Somali poachers in 1989.

Joy was an Austrian. She was born Friederike Gessner and had studied metalwork, painting, sculpture and piano in Vienna. George was born in India under the British Raj, and spent his schoolboy years at Dean Close in Cheltenham. He moved to Kenya with his parents at the age of eighteen and worked as a gold prospector and safari operator before he was taken on by the Game Department.

Joy had come to Kenya with her second husband, Peter Bally, who was a botanist. The couple were attending a Christmas function by the Tana river, hosted by the District Commissioner of Garissa. George arrived at the party in a camel train and was prevailed upon to take the Ballys on safari, which he did. But before the safari was over he became alarmed by the growing attraction between Joy and himself and fled. Subsequently, however, they knocked into each other in Nairobi, and as George put it with gruff and endearing succinctness in one television interview, 'that was that'.

These two extraordinary people endured a difficult and tempestuous marriage that lasted over thirty-five years. I had heard and read enough about Joy Adamson to realise that not very many people took to her. George, on the other hand, was perceived as a self-sufficient and serene man to whom one was naturally drawn.

The main charges levelled at Joy were that she was capricious, that she had a surging temper, that she indulged in indiscriminate affairs, and that she was jealous of every area of George's life that excluded herself. The word that peppered most descriptions, even the generous ones, was 'mercurial'. But then consistency, as they say, is the hobgoblin of small minds.

Nevertheless, in the form of her books, her conservation efforts, her magnificent flower paintings and tribal portraits, Joy left a clear imprint of her powerful personality on Kenya. Elsamere has been well conserved and it is clearly still Joy's kingdom. The interior of the house has been converted into a museum. Here is the ballgown Joy wore to meet the Queen, here a photograph of Elsa, here a page of diary script. It is moribund in the way that all museums are, because they countenance the plundered privacy of the dead.

I preferred the front lawn, where a tangle of growth reached down to the lake. The colony of black and white colobus monkeys that Joy nurtured still inhabits the garden. The monkeys are handsome creatures with capes and bottlebrush tails of pure white. When the stream of visitors poured on to the lawn for tea at three o'clock the troop swarmed up to the roof and sat upon it, chattering and jibing at the intruders.

The other species which is famously connected to Elsamere is the Verreux eagle owl – the largest owl in Africa – which Joy used to raise on chicken heads. Although I did not see any, I heard that there were still quite a few about.

Before we left Naivasha, we hired bicycles and rode to the village of Kongoni, on the western side of the lake. Some distance beyond the village lay a natural lake formed out of a volcanic crater. It was an arduous ride of several hours. The heavy old iron bikes had to be wheeled uphill and on the downhills the wheels slid about alarmingly in the loose dust. At last we came to the reserve, paid the fee and walked inside. It was another couple of hours' trek to the lake itself. En route we startled several giraffes, who bunched themselves up and galloped away in their slow-motion gait.

The lake itself was a green emerald of water. We glimpsed it from the rise above it – a lush oasis of vegetation in the midst of the hot, listless midday bush. Finding the path, we slithered down to the glistening circle and plunged in. The red volcanic mud came up to our knees and the thick algae-rich water left us smelling like a pair of wet dogs.

Back at the gate, we met a young warden's assistant in an open-backed van who offered to give us a lift back to the campsite. We hoisted the bikes into the back and climbed into the front. The warden's assistant was about our age and dressed in khaki bush clothes. He had soft sandy hair which had slightly outgrown its superimposed style. He told me in due course that he had lived his whole life around Naivasha, apart from boarding school in Nairobi.

'Really? Did you know Joy Adamson then?'

'I didn't really know her. I used to see her around when I was little.'

'What was she like?'

'Bossy,' said the boy, meditatively, leaning his body against an arm propped in the cavity of the open window. He grinned and drew his forehead together in a mock grimace. His skin was the colour of ripe wheat and he gave off the faint familiar scent that I had always connected with boys – of sweat and exertion, part mischief, part diffidence, the lingering odour of long days spent in a fragrant countryside.

'How long have you been a warden's assistant?'

'Oh, not long. I've done bits and pieces since finishing A-levels. My parents are trying to persuade me to leave for England or South Africa.'

'Why?'

'They don't think there's much future for whites here. Most

of my family pushed off after Mau Mau or since Uhuru.'

He blew a breath of air upwards so that it lifted his blond forelock and gazed gloomily along his freckled nose at the bonnet of the car, beneath which our earlier bicycle tracks were disappearing.

After a while he spoke again.

'Which part of South Africa are you from?'

'Cape Town.'

'Oh, *Cape Town*,' he said disparagingly. 'That's where my parents want me to study. Either Cape Town or England. But I couldn't live in Cape Town. I spent a winter there once and I thought I'd die of cold.'

'Well, England's worse,' I said, laughing.

'Oh, England,' said the boy dismissively. He blew at his forelock again and then his cerulean eyes slid sideways to meet mine, collusive, merry and insouciant.

'Africa would have to be in a whole lot more trouble before I'd go and live in England.'

*

There was one last thing that I wanted to do in the Highlands, and that was to climb Mount Kenya. I had seen quite a few sepia-coloured photographs of figures like Delamere and Finch Hatton standing atop the various summits in masterful poses. Some of Joy Adamson's flower paintings preserved in the Nairobi museum had been executed during a four-month retreat on the lower slopes, whilst she waited for her divorce from Bally to come through. The Maasai and the Kikuyu believed that Mount Kenya was the seat of God. My imagination was fired. Besides, although I had done quite a lot of trekking and hiking, I had never done a high altitude climb. Mount Kenya is Africa's second highest mountain at 5 199 metres.

We hadn't any equipment, but we found a tailor shop in Biashara Street near River Road that ran a camping hire outlet as a sideline. We settled on two threadbare and malodorous parkas, a gas stove and an ordinance survey map of the mountain with a description of the route. Then we boarded a matatu for Chogoria.

The inn at Chogoria was called inappropriately 'Chogoria Sunshine'. It was still the middle of the rainy season and the weather was conspicuously sunless. In fact, it was not a very good time for the ascent as the terrain would be boggy and damp, but I thought if I did not do it now I might not have another chance for years. Cyril was also keen.

We settled down with a plate of chips and mugs of coffee. During this repast three different deputations drew up the adjacent chair and struck up a general conversation about the dangers of the mountains. They cited the yearly death toll, invoked the dreadful weather, advised us how slim our chances of survival were. After a while their remarks switched to the subject of porters, how efficient porters were, how well versed in mountain lore, how crucial to an expedition. And then, incidentally, they would confess that they themselves were porters, in fact, the very best porters.

I demurred. It seemed a bit wet to have a porter.

The next visitor was a short, wolfish-looking man who wanted to know what we thought of multiparty.

'Very multi,' I mumbled through the chips. An additional pair of opposition parties seemed to have sprung whilst we had been in Naivasha and the street arguments and loudspeaker upbraidings had grown ever more ferocious.

'No doubt you have had the happiness to live since birth with the freedom of multiparty,' pressed the lupine man.

'Not really, actually.'

'Where are you from?'

'South Africa,' I said sheepishly.

'Excellent! Excellent!' He pumped my hand and then Cyril's. 'Never before have I met a citizen from your country. Now tell me, how is my friend Mr Nelson Mandela?'

'He's very well,' I replied, smiling. I was often reluctant to tell Africans where we were from, but invariably we met with a warm reception.

We woke up at five and started the trek to base camp, a twenty-eight kilometre uphill haul that could have been done in a truck. The first part of the walk was through thick tropical forest, vibrating with birds and wildlife, reputedly even buck and elephant, although we did not see any – only bright-eyed little quail that hopped from leafy branch to branch twittering indignantly at our intrusion, and hornbills which formed silhouettes against the sky. The road was lined with soaring acacia and euphorbia trees.

The soil underfoot was rich, red, loamy and pungent, and the vegetation grew lushly along the verges of the path. Once a little rat dashed into the road, gawped at us in bug-eyed horror and made a headlong flight back into the undergrowth.

We stopped at noon under a dense euphorbia tree and chewed on the wild mint that flourished in its shade. Everything had gone sluggish in the heat, even the birds and insects were silent and the air was thick and warm.

By early afternoon we had reached the bamboo belt and now traipsed through a thicket of tall swaying poles cut through in places by buffalo paths. One could see where their huge bodies had crashed, leaving wide scars in the even formations of bamboo.

By evening the thicket had turned to green grassland studded with pretty little flowers. It rolled away in inviting undulations on either side of the road.

By this time my mouth and throat had closed up with dust and thirst. We had stupidly brought no water, thinking there would be streams intersecting the road because of the rains. In the event, it was bone dry. We stumbled the last few kilometres to the Meru Mount Kenya Lodge base camp under a brilliant and incandescent red-orange sunset.

The base camp was full of teenage girls from one of Nairobi's swanky public schools who had come up in a landcruiser. A

213

harassed-looking teacher was presiding over them.

'Cathy, buck up with the fire.'

'But I can't remember where I put the methylated spirits, sir!'

The girls were all very chummy and vigorous. They had just completed an eight-kilometre circular on the grassland and were now seized with the intention to consume massive quantities of bread, jam and tea.

In the morning we set off again. The walk from the base camp to the Mintos hut on the Chogoria route is only about thirteen kilometres but it is an arduous trek on a steep uphill gradient. The problem is not so much the physical exertion involved in scaling the slope, but the effects produced by the rapidity with which one ascends. Hoping to avoid altitude sickness we walked slowly and rested often, gulping down quantities of water at every spring, since altitude sickness is supposed to be related to dehydration.

The day's walk was exceptionally pretty. We climbed up the face of the north side of the mountain over a series of ridges like the bumps on a dinosaur's back. The slopes were festooned with reeds and grasses and rivulets of pure icy water. Little delicate purple and yellow flowers with satiny petals grew amongst the heather.

As we rounded the face a bank of cloud lay beneath which cleared slowly to reveal that we were walking on the edge of an immense precipice. Below us lay a long narrow valley studded with tarns. The air was much thinner now, although it still was not cold enough to wear the parkas.

The vegetation was slowly changing. The grasses became shorter and sparser and scattered, upright lobelias appeared, ringed by clumps of groundsel with their hairy upturned bracts. Numerous little rock hyraxes appeared in twos or threes to peer nosily at us. As the path went up and up and up, the wind became infused with the raw electric odour of approaching cold. By late afternoon we had reached a rocky plateau. At last we scrambled over a laval mound and there was the hut – a simple box of corrugated iron with an outhouse, on the far edge of a large square of gravelly sand.

We had brought red lentils and chocolate to eat. The red lentils would not cook at altitude – after an hour on the stove they were still obdurately stone-like. We ate the chocolate, spread a piece of cardboard on the wooden sleeping platform and climbed into our sleeping bags which we had zipped together for warmth. The air in the hut was frigid and our out-breaths were converted into misty nebulae, but inside the bags it was tolerably warm. In the middle of the night Cyril began to shake and moan. He retched intermittently until the early hours of the morning.

When we woke up we made some tea and then set off, descending from the little plateau where we had spent the night. The land up here was very marshy. We passed a number of beautiful glacial tarns. Here and there a drifting breeze had whipped their marmoreal surfaces up into a pattern of white horses. The tarns were almost turquoise in colour. We spotted a couple of little malachite sunbirds pecking for grubs at the waterline. It was difficult to imagine anything surviving in that water.

We squelched over the bog for over an hour, after which we came face to face with an immense sheet of bare brown rock and sand marked with cairns. The vegetation and its attendant friendly rock hyraxes disappeared abruptly. We started to tackle it, moving slowly and painfully up the face. By now I also had altitude sickness, so we were both quite faint and vomited frequently. I kept my conscious thought trained upon the action of lifting a foot, finding a place to put it, pushing up on the muscle and repeating the action with the other leg, over and over and over.

In another few hours we had reached the snow line. I crammed snow into my mouth to reduce the taste of bile. Eventually we reached a ridge, lost our way, reached the right ridge and dropped a few hundred metres. From there we regained the lost height and a bit more by climbing up a very slippery but snow-sheltered sand scree. Now we were almost on the doorstep of the Austrian hut, a pretty little wooden structure built by Austrian POWs in the Second World War and reminiscent of an Alpine shelter. In the background was our destination, Point Lenana. We lurched into the hut and passed out.

During the night my altitude sickness intensified. I kept stumbling out into the freezing snow flurries to be sick. When this had happened for the fifth or sixth time in quick succession, there seemed little point in returning inside. I crouched on the veranda in my parka, shivering uncontrollably and rubbing at my aching calf muscles. I made a distinct mental note that high altitude climbing was not going to constitute a major new interest. At that point a family of yeti loomed through the snow.

In fact the yetis were Japanese, with Kikuyu porters. They came inside the hut, stamping their boots and making a lot of noise. They had left base camp at Naro Moru at some ungodly hour and were now resolved to press on to Lenana before daybreak. The leader of the Japanese had a moustache and an air of do or die.

'Going up!' he announced grimly.

I watched their retreating backs numbly, and was prodigiously sick once again.

At dawn they reappeared, looking haggard.

'Good views up there?' I asked.

They did not reply, but sank exhaustedly against the hut wall. I noticed that the moustache of the leader was layered up with tropical sleet. I stared out of the window at the remote pinnacle above us. I had that feeling one has before diving into the sea in winter, only much, much worse.

Later in the morning we started out from the hut and began to grapple our way up the glacier, past a frozen lake and a snow cave which was full of gleaming blue-white icicles. Eventually

216

we were out on the ice face clawing our way up. Point Lenana was completely obscured by mist, but I knew we were almost there.

I was starting to hallucinate. A little stone on the snow seemed to be growing and receding, growing and receding. My vision blurred and then focused again. I staggered. When I looked up the point was completely invisible. I was surrounded by a blanket of fog. I could not see Cyril. Was he in front or behind?

'Cyril?'

No sound in the glacial silence. The fog flooded gelidly around my face.

'Cyril!'

'Here. I'm here.' He was only a few yards away, turning around in disorientation.

'Christ. I can't see a thing. Which way is the hut?'

'Behind me, I think.'

I caught on to his sleeve. The mist softened a little and I did catch a brief glimpse of a corner of the hut. I stood there for a moment, torn. I so badly wanted to reach the top. But Mount Kenya is responsible for fifty per cent of the world's cases of cerebral and pulmonary oedema. I did not really know what I was doing. A few months ago my brother must have faced the same decision. In my mind I saw my mother, my father. I did not have the right to play around with my life.

'We'd better get down,' I said to Cyril at last. 'We'll never figure out the route in the mist.'

After we had descended for a few hours we turned back and looked up. The morning light was lucent and clear. Point Lenana stood out sharply against the cobalt sky. There was not a shred of mist on her. From where we had been it would have taken us about another half hour to reach the summit.

La Ilaha Illa Allah

After the Lenana ascent I was feeling rather out of sorts. I longed to be on a beach and do the gentle, lazy things one does on beaches, which are very much more my milieu than snowy mountains. Cyril was of the same inclination, so we only passed a night in Nairobi before boarding a train bound for Mombasa.

The station was not overwhelmingly busy. At the third class end there was the usual commotion of weary baby-laden mothers struggling with their outsized parcels. First and second class were quiet. Suited black businessmen and groups of Indian girls in saris wafted in and out of the train, making final arrangements and embracing relatives.

I made my way to the second class women's cabin to which I had been assigned. It was a spacious cabin with four bunk beds and a washbasin – in infinitely better nick than any other train I had been on outside South Africa. The two lower bunks were already occupied by other *wasungu* women who acknowledged me briefly. One was tall and fat and the other was short and fat. They were engaged in a fierce discussion. I listened with half an ear. Obscurely, it seemed to be all about lamp lights.

The train began to pull out. At first we travelled through slums and shanty towns. Ragged gamins waved from the banks

218

and rubbish tips. Then we cleared the town and chugged out into the Athi plains. The diamond light of late afternoon slanted through the open window and the rich grassy breath of the savannah flooded the cabin. I leaned my cheek sleepily against the window pane, watching the plains roll by until the sky turned saffron, dulled into grey and finally a dusky navy, through which the brilliant stars sparkled. A Sotho nanny who had once looked after me at my grandparents' farm when I was very young, told me that God pulls a blanket over the sky at night so that human beings can sleep. But the world is so old and the blanket so well used that it is full of little holes where the daylight continues to shine through.

The cabin lights came on. The other two *wasungu* were still raging on about lamp light. From their accents I guessed they were Canadians.

'You're absolutely right,' said the tall fat one. 'In the whole of Nairobi I don't think I saw one building with adequate wheelchair access.'

'My God, they're so in need of a strong-voiced wheelchair lobby,' said the short fat one.

I wondered where all the wheelchairs were going to be coming from in the first place. Most of the people I had seen in Nairobi who needed wheelchairs were crawling about on their knees. In Africa the maimed and deformed suffer because there are no resources. But however hideous their injuries, they are still accepted as a part of the community – free to marry, to live their daily life, free from whispers, free from the averted eyes and dreadful, hooded stares that handicapped people in the West must endure.

Presently the two women noticed that I was listening and sought out my name and nationality. They told me that they were students of recreational management from Toronto on vacation. I had never heard of recreational management but I didn't let on. One of them had a master's in it, and the other one didn't, but wanted to. She was doing a related paper on access routes rights, she informed me, pronouncing it rowts. I blinked. At our universities we studied things like philosophy and botany.

'What do you do, Sarah?'

'Nothing.'

'You must do something! What would you like to do?'

'Write.'

'Oh, yeah? What do you write?'

'Diaries,' I muttered.

They looked at each other.

'What's the South African attitude towards enforcing ramp rights?' enquired the short one doing the related paper.

'We're going to be protecting all human rights in the future,' I said defensively.

They both looked at each other again – wearily.

'That's so typical of world attitude,' said the short fat one sadly. 'Nobody wants to give the wheelchair-bound a lobby of their own.'

I resumed my seat at the window and continued to stare meditatively out at the stars.

'These *wasungu* from overseas are very different,' I thought to myself parochially.

In the morning Cyril came over from the men's cabin and we went to have coffee in the dining car. I noticed that some of the plates were still monogrammed EAR & H – East African Railways and Harbours. I started to tell Cyril about how in the old days the tracks would be thick with game on either side and the train would stop so that passengers could have dinner at wayside bungalows. Later four-course dinners were served on board with vintage wines to wash them down. At this point I was interrupted by an elderly waiter who had been lingering nearby.

'Yes, everything you say is true. I have been serving on the railway since I was a boy of fifteen years.' He sat down comfortably on a nearby chair. 'More coffee, *Bwana*? More coffee, sweet lady? Yes, yes, the railway is a long story. I remember the very first time that . . .'

Together, we plunged down the byways of history until, looking out of the window, I began to see copses of the coastal coconut palms and the first tantalising splash of azure.

We did not stop at Mombasa but transferred instantly on to the bus bound for Malindi. Cyril had the seat next to the window and I sat next to him. The aisle seat was empty. We drove out of town. Presently we crossed the bridge over Kilifi Creek. At that point, a young man who had been sitting near the back of the bus stood up, walked down the aisle and sat down in the empty seat.

'My name is Suleiman,' he said.

I said hello.

'I am a very educated man. I have completed the whole primary school and most of the secondary.'

I said congratulations.

'I come from a family of great virility. My father has seventeen children. And ten are sons. We are all very educated.'

'Your father must work very hard,' I commented politely, 'to educate seventeen children.'

'Oh no,' laughed Suleiman. 'Only the sons are educated. The daughters are not educated in the least. They cannot even read or write.'

I looked at him in surprise.

'Education is not good for girls,' he hastened to add. 'But my sisters are well cared for. The beautiful ones are married. The ugly ones will care for my father in his old age.'

It was difficult to know how to respond.

At last I said, 'Your mother must be jolly strong to produce seventeen children.'

'The work is shared,' explained Suleiman. 'My father has had four wives.'

'Do they all live together in the same house?'

'No no,' he said reprovingly. 'My father is an educated man.

He has not had them at the same time in the Muslim way. He has divorced them one by one as they have become old and ugly.'

I was beginning to find him very objectionable. I wished he would go away. But the road wound on and on and he prattled away in the same vein, fixing me with his intense stare.

Finally he addressed himself to Cyril for the first time.

'I would like to invite your friend to visit me at my home in Malindi. Do I have your permission?'

Cyril looked alarmed and shot me a glance.

'Do not worry. I am a very educated man.'

'Ask her,' said Cyril uncomfortably.

The boy took this for acquiescence. He settled back in his seat beaming, and put one hand on my knee.

'Your legs are very fetching,' he concluded in contentment. 'I will enjoy receiving you in my home.'

'Oh bugger off,' I said, flicking away his hand.

In Malindi it occurred to me that my dress code would need to be modified for the Islamic world. I stored my shorts away in the backpack and bought an ankle-length wraparound skirt and a vastly commodious headscarf which I hoped would endow me with a suitably matronly aspect.

*

As the ferry slowly rounded the bank, the shoreline came clearly into view, illuminated by an incandescent three quarter moon which hung limpidly in the skies. Now I saw a rough tongue of beach and thickets of coconuts and doum palms. We ploughed on through the inky water. Here was a magnificent Arab house of coral rag and lime, roofed with thatch, standing alone on the littoral, its low walled top floor open to the seaborne airs.

Along the beach men on donkeys wove amongst the mangrove swamps. Now we drew closer and faced a great twinkling spread of lights. Dozens of dhow boats bobbed against their anchorages. The lime-white houses took form against the gloom, casting rectangles of light on to the sandy path above the raised water frontage and shadowing their own exteriors with exquisite tessellations. So eastern, so exotic – lozenge arches yawned out on to the sea and the neat rows of crenellations invited in the breezes. Above them lay the floor-wide balconies hemmed in with undulating walls. Every one was different and every one breathtaking.

This was Lamu.

I leaned eagerly to starboard. It had been a long, rough day. The bus trip from Malindi to Lamu had taken about eight hours over isolated and uneven dust roads. We had not been able to secure a seat, which meant standing in the jam-packed aisle on aching muscles already shot through from Lenana. But that did not matter now. What mattered was that we were here – in this extraordinary town where Africa and the East had intermingled for centuries.

Arab settlements had existed along the East Coast of Africa since the twelfth century. The Arab traders made use of the monsoons to propel their dhows between the Persian Gulf and Africa. Lamu was one of a series of local bases for their trading operations. They brought glass beads, dyed cloth, ghee and porcelain and left with leopard skins, rhino horn, elephant tusks, mangrove poles and slaves.

The coastal settlements were structured hierarchically, with the Arabs monopolising trade and administration and the Africans constituting the labouring class. However, there was a degree of miscegenation between Arab and African, resulting in the very attractive castes who now inhabit the coastal towns.

Up until the fifteenth century there were constant internecine struggles between the various Islamic coastal kingdoms. These were suspended by the arrival of the Portuguese in 1498. The Portuguese dominated the coast for the next two hundred years until they were ousted with the help of the sultans of Oman. They were already weakened by their earlier battles with Sheikh Yusuf of Mombasa who had been captured as a small boy and sent to Portugal for indoctrination in an institution of Augustinian monks. However this plan became badly shipwrecked, for when Yusuf grew up and realised that he had been ripped from the bosom of his family and forced to spend years in a ghastly boarding school he turned savage, re-embraced Islam and killed every Portuguese he could get his hands on.

Following the demise of the Portuguese, the Omani elements continued to do battle amongst themselves until the whole coastal strip came under the control of the Sultan of Zanzibar, Seyyid Said. This coincided with the founding of the spice plantations on Zanzibar and a simultaneous massive increase in the slave trade. Slaving was outlawed by the British in 1907, approximately a century later. But although the British East Africa Company had by then assumed the administration of the interior of Kenya, they never contested the Sultan's claim to the coastal strip which was, in fact, conditionally leased to them. This situation remained the status quo even after Kenya became a British colony. The Sultan only relinquished his rights to the coastal strip at independence in 1963.

In the nineteenth century Lamu grew fabulously wealthy on the proceeds of the import/export trade. After the abolition of slavery, however, the economic advantage of the traders was wiped out and the island became rather less well heeled. The 'discovery' of Lamu by holidaymakers in the latter part of the present century has led to a partial recovery. But the particular timing of this slump, in tandem with Lamu's isolation from the mainland hubs, and the sense of history of the islanders, means that outwardly at least Lamu remains untrammelled by the twentieth century.

I spent my time in Lamu exploring the town and its environs in fascination. We were staying at a place called the Lamu Sea Shore Lodging which stood directly above the dhow docks. Every morning I would awaken at dawn and listen to the strident, haunting cadences of the call to prayer.

La ilaha illa Allah
Muhammadon rasul Allah

There is no God but Allah. Muhammad is the messenger of Allah. I dressed and stole down to the frontage where the first rosy clouds were building on the horizon. The docks were deserted and the tide still out. All the dhows rested on their sides on the sandy beach. Amongst the stranded dhows mewled a myriad scrawny cats, searching for fish scraps. Sometimes the quick tides took a weak kitten by surprise and in the morning the swollen body would be lying there, half submerged in the sand.

I walked towards the mainland, past the simple but beautiful geometrical buildings still shuttered against the night. At the far end was the abattoir and its adjacent scrapheap of cow heads. It was a good place to see marabou storks, who hovered on their ugly legs and battled each other to get at the nuggets of flesh.

Lamu is not a good place for the fastidious. The open channels which convey sewage run parallel to the streets and have been in place for several centuries. The ubiquitous donkeys drop their slushy patties at random intervals. At noon the whole town became infused with heat and we sat beneath the restaurant awnings drinking great tankards of fruit pulp.

In the centre of the town is the massive old fort, once a prison, now a museum. Next to the fort grows an enormous African almond tree and in its shade the barrow boys sold their wares – the sweet confection simsim, and coconut fudge. My Achilles' heel was the Arabic halwa – sweet, translucent and deeply orange – that was boiled overnight in the halwa shop on the southern side of town. The halwa merchant explained the whole process to me one afternoon, but I have forgotten it all except that the base is sesame seed. Every other day I would go back and he would scoop a section from his enamel basin and measure it off on an ancient scale, before packing it into one of the little cornucopias that his son wove from palm fronds.

'*Asante*, my friend,' he thanked me, every time.

The coastal people spoke Swahili as their mother tongue. In the early part of the century the British had adopted the language as the lingual bedrock of their administration and now it formed the lingua franca of the whole of East Africa. It was a hybrid tongue deriving from the polyglot influences that had operated along this coast – part Arabic and African, part English and Portuguese.

In the late afternoons when the heat had diminished we made our way to the beach. On the way we passed young men astride galloping donkeys, belabouring their diminutive mounts with stripped thorn branches, like comic parodies of cowboys. We walked past the electric generator, the hospital and the ginning factory to the beginning of the natural beach. Here the Muslim women would be lounging in the shallow waters, still clad from top to toe in their black bui buis, waterlogged dung beetles of modesty. Sometimes we passed a man striding free in a loose kanzu, and a few yards behind him his wife trotted obediently, bent double under the weight of her burdens. From the outside the women's lives seemed to be nothing but stricture and toil. But apparently they are free to choose their own husbands and even to divorce.

Additionally, there is reputedly a great sense of sisterhood amongst the women which makes it possible for them to be able to keep assignations without discovery. Living as they do without visible identity, they can come and go as they will and will cover each other's backs for this purpose. In fact, a German friend I made told me that once or twice he had been discreetly propositioned by a beautiful woman who suddenly disclosed herself from beneath the folds of a bui bui. I saw this for myself later when the woman in question espied him through the window of a coffee shop. She did not falter one pace in her stride but her sloth eyes fluttered in the shade of the black shroud and she delivered an arch wink.

The women brightened their appearances with brightly jewelled sandals and painted delicate henna tracery on each other's hands. To me they seemed happy, and the wind carried their streams of chatter. But still I wondered how the carefree little girls felt as their menstruation and impending purdah drew closer.

The beach itself was gorgeous – a vista of illimitable sands and fine white dunes which rolled back into the distance. The azure water was warm and still – round the bend it caught the brunt of the ocean and gained a gentle wave.

In the evenings we made our way back to the town, stopping at a stall for a preprandial Coca-Cola whilst we watched the sun sink. Now the town was at its most alert: the southern quarter was packed with kiosks selling *nyama choma* – kebabs on sticks – or the spiced, savoury dough balls called *bajia*. From the waterfront restaurants drifted the succulent aromas of barbecued fish – red snapper or shark, tuna steak or lobster, if you could afford it. But the common fish dishes were cheap, even for us. For Europeans and Americans it must have been monopoly money.

One day we sailed through the Lamu archipelago on a dhow. The dhow was called the Fati Moyin and the boatmen were Issa and Mohammed. The craft was small, strong and functional, with a single lateen sail and no centreboard. Instead, sacks of sand filling the bottom served as ballast.

At first we sailed in the open lagoon and then we came into a channel where the wind dropped. The men began to pole us through with stout mangrove poles, Mohammed's broad foot keeping the rudder on course. The channel was flanked by banks of verdantly green marine growth clinging to submerged black stems. Here and there narrow inlets penetrated the muddy banks and we glimpsed sub-channels through the mangroves. The roots themselves were covered with a tessellated veneer of tiny inedible oysters.

I liked Mohammed, but recoiled when he leaned over to

speak to me. I recorded in my diary that:

> *This chap Mohammed has remarkably variegated teeth in respect of*
> *colouring, ranging from a mild dun to a rich loamy chestnut. He also*
> *supports a secondary set to the rear of these, which has displaced one*
> *or two at daring tangents.*

Mohammed made me giggle. He rolled himself a gargantuan joint and settled back to smoke it, remarking with general severity that Allah made grass grow on the ground, but alcohol was the evil invention of man.

Issa climbed out to the end of a narrow plank at right angles to the prow and rode there, holding out his face to the spray. After a while I begged to try. It's not possible for girls, they said. I said I could do it and if I fell off they had my permission to leave me behind in the ocean. They gave in. When I did not fall off they clapped and I continued to swing along on the plank as it rose and dipped above the choppy water.

Eventually we reached the coral and dived beneath the surface of the water. I swam among the huge and gaudy formations that resembled upside-down mushrooms or the brains of a Cyclops, vividly coloured in blues and reds and purples. All around me darted the astonishing fish, slithers of electric indigo, solid ecclesiastical purples with an undulating yellow fin, big and little fish, cruising armadas of fish that shot away from my exploring hand.

I spent so long mesmerised by the coral that I emerged looking like a plucked goose, and almost hypothermic despite the warm water. Issa caught a snapper and we lay dozily in the acacia shade on a nearby island watching it brown and spit over a woodfire.

By the end of the day I was sated and happy.

'I should come back here to write my first novel,' I thought dreamily, trailing my finger in the silver surface of the sunset waves. In fact I did; I began work on a novel which has turned into this book.

But Lamu was not Eden. It was impossible not to notice the seedy realities that coexisted beside the beauty. The east coast of Kenya has a reputation for being able to offer sex on easy terms, particularly to women.

In Lamu the beach was perennially dotted with hopelessly mismatched couples. Typically, the woman was white and European, plump, fortyish and in the spirited wind of a second youth provided by her package holiday. Her elongated breasts slapped unharnessed against the flat waters of the lagoon. At her side would frolic a scrap of Islamic youth freshly grown into manhood, an informal gigolo or 'beach boy'.

The beach boys were quite standard. They had fine looks and good physiques and somehow managed to streak their wiry hair into twists of blond. They also maintained a peculiar air of nonchalance, even in the most compromising positions. Once I saw a pair of beach boys engaged in a desultory chat, magnificently surmounting the fact that collectively they had at least four hundred pounds of colossal and half-clad German matron puddled on to their laps.

It had been a good twenty years since the first flood of hippies poured into Lamu. The Muslims, with their restrained and ancient culture, must have found the creed of gratuitous sex and drugs deeply offensive.

By now, they had certain unbreachable ideas about whites. The most ingrained was the precept that white girls were slaveringly ripe for sex – at any time and with anybody. This meant that the older men looked down their noses, and the younger men tried their luck. I found their insistent pestering annoying and unwelcome.

On the other hand, watching the cloistered formations of Islamic dung beetles make their way through the fleshy and cavorting Bacchants of Europe, it was very easy to see how they might have reached their conclusions.

*

Meanwhile we had acquired new neighbours at the Lamu Sea Shore Lodging, a British airways hostess and her younger brother. The name of the hostess was Cath. Cath had a halo of fluffy blonde curls, a cheerful smile and a pronounced Midlands accent. She was also, without parallel, the most libidinous woman I had ever met. On the very morning of her arrival she collared a beach boy and retired purposefully into her chambers. The beach boy's name was Abdul. He was young and hale, but it became clear after a few days that his energies were flagging.

The younger brother was a shy, skinny young man, who had to occupy himself whilst his sister was thus under siege. Sometimes he wandered aimlessly up and down the waterfront. At other times we sat on the shared balcony chatting to each other baldly over the too evident creaking of bedsprings, and the breathless, noisy injunctions with which Cath was improving Abdul's technique.

'So how long are you and Cath on holiday together?'

'No, not there. There. There. *There*. Oh, *yes, yes, yes*. Oh lovely, sweetie, *more, more*.'

'Three weeks,' said the etiolated young man gloomily.

One evening we went to the beach with a group of young people. They made a fire of coconut fronds. But I was feeling sluggish and dull and the sweet scent of the burning fibres made my stomach revolt.

Soon it became clear that the succubus of disease had seduced my body with extraordinarily unpleasant results. I alternated between lying exhaustedly in bed, wishing that I could sink deeper and deeper into the pillow, and making desperate dashes for the bathroom. After one of these dashes I sank against the wall. I couldn't get up the momentum to get back to bed. Fortunately Abdul arrived for one of his exhausting love assignations and hoisted me up on his broad shoulder.

At the lowest point of the feverishness, a hated nightmare began to churn through my mind. It was a recurring dream that I had had for years in moments of weakness. I knew the sequence of events with absolute clarity, I could pace myself through its unravelling moment by moment, but still it filled me with horror. There were never any variations on the plot. It was a febrile vision of hyper-reality. It was a dream about school.

My home life as a child had been strict but safe. Nothing had prepared me for the institutionalised sadism of my boarding school. The school still followed the Victorian system where the prefecture held absolute powers over the unanointed and ran the place like a boot camp. The inevitable result was that the final year was sheer hell as the prefects fell like vultures on those of their classmates that they had never liked. In my case, I had had it coming for ages. They must have sniffed out that I was a private dissenter months before they got free rein.

The victimisation that formed the basis of the nightmare was ridiculous and silly. But it was also humiliating. My sin was 'bad table manners' and the prescribed antidote was to spend the remainder of the term on the platform at top table with the smaller offenders, under the eye of my old friend, the head-master. Already under stress from the impending examinations for university, I found this public torment unbearable. Week after week, I would sit hunched and miserable over the sausages, amongst the noisy clatter of knives and forks and the smug 'tips' from the prefects on the niceties of etiquette.

My nightmare took this memory and inveigled it with the macabre. Now when I raised my eyes to the windows I would see a pantheon of ghostly figures pressing against the pane. They were all dressed alike, in the algae-green uniform of the school, but their faces were pallid and horror-stricken. They were trying to tell me something, on the far side of the window they fluttered their insubstantial limbs, it was something desperately important. Only one child did not gesture and gape, but floated apart from the rest. Yet her mournful preternatural eyes were riveted on mine, I felt somehow I knew her, I knew her so intimately that I ached for her sadness. Then suddenly, viscerally, a realisation would descend on me. These girls, these waving ghostly girls were all the misfits of generations past, girls who had been accused of bad manners, who had held poetry in their minds, who had got beyond themselves. My head slammed down and I saw that my own fingers, curling around the cutlery, were discoloured and drained, the pattern of the table-cloth was beginning to loom up through the flesh. Desperately my eyes sought out and found the lonely ghost, she seemed to loom in terror against the pane and then – sickening lurch! – I knew and felt and sensed what we were to each other.

'No! No! No! No! No!'

'Hush, quiet,' said a firm but mellifluous voice. 'Sickness brings bad dreams. But in sickness it is necessary to be calm. So now we will wake and put the dreams aside.'

I opened my eyes and saw a tiny woman in a pale pink gown and bonnet. Behind her Cyril was hovering anxiously – he must have called somebody for help. I reached out my fingers to touch his hand – to thank him – a sensation of pricking in my fingertips – an arm around my back – some liquid being poured into my throat – I tried to speak, but a steady brown hand settled me back on to the pillow.

The next time I awoke I felt much more alert. My eyes opened and then widened because the same curious figure was emerging through the doorway.

'I have taken the blood slides to the clinic and it's not malaria,' she said busily, settling herself in the chair. 'So it must be gastric. This dirty island water! You must be more careful, my dear.' And her wizened, beautiful face creased into a smile. She tugged expertly on a strand of my hair and cocked her head to the ceiling.

'Good, good, a reduction in temperature. I am Fatima.'

'Hello Fatima,' I said, in weak amazement.

Under the care of Fatima I rapidly recovered. She was an extraordinary woman, trained in both Western and Eastern medicine. Born in Zanzibar, she had moved to Lamu after her husband divorced her. Now most of her work was with women in purdah who had contracted the Aids virus. Many of these nominally protected women had been infected through the infidelity of their husbands. Secluded from the world, they were baffled by the onset of the mystery illness. They also had no access to money, so much of Fatima's toil was done gratis.

'Doesn't Islam make you angry?' I asked this brave, intelligent woman.

'No. I am very, very proud of my faith.'

'But the way the men behave! The Ayatollah!'

'But that is not the way of Islam,' she said gently. 'That is the way of men. Islam is a very pure faith. There are very, very few practitioners of pure Islam in this world. And on such a very pleasant afternoon, let us not discuss the Ayatollah.'

By afternoon I was feeling well enough to sit out on the balcony. Cath came to join me after exchanging a lengthy farewell of kisses with her beach boy lover.

'Bye, Abdul,' I called over my shoulder.

'Oh, he wasn't Abdul. He was "Sharp".'

'Oh no,' I said, blushing. 'I've been calling him Abdul for a week! Why didn't he tell me?'

'There is Abdul,' she replied, her eyes twinkling. 'But that wasn't him. That was "Sharp".'

I took this in.

'You have to err on the side of caution, I think,' I said at last, very gauchely. 'They're rather prolific you know, these beach boys.'

'Oh I do, I do! Absolute golden rule. I'm a rubber landlubber.'

That night as I was falling asleep a stark cry broke the silence of the night. My mind, sensitised by fever, picked up and amplified the pathos of the appeal.

'We hate you white people. We hate you white people. Take your money, take all your money and go away from Lamu!'

On the waterfront stood a solitary figure in a ragged kikoi, howling his grievance to the dark. Poor and black, every day he must silently witness the careless pleasures of the rich and white.

Perhaps he was indentured in service to an Arab, as many of the Africans were. Although racial distinctions were not clear cut here, the old Arab families still held a clear monopoly over the wealth, which marginalised and antagonised the blacks. After a while the man's shoulders slumped, he kicked dejectedly at a pebble and then he went away.

After I recovered I became very restless. Consequently, we decided to explore some of the other islands in the archipelago. On the ferry I got into conversation with a rather sanctimonious boy who introduced himself as a Westernised Kikuyu and went on loudly to decry the phenomenon of beach boys.

'What do you think of the behaviour of all these middle-aged women who take them as lovers?' I asked him curiously.

'Oh, they can't help themselves.'

'Huh?'

'White women go mad as they get older,' he explained. 'They're not circumcised, you see.'

He seemed blithely unaware of the fact that I would necessarily be included in his glum prognostication.

The ferry dropped us at Matangawanda and we spent the afternoon walking to the little village of Pate. We were off the beaten track now, to my relief. A villager hired out his roof-top bedroom for our convenience, his pretty daughter cooked a meal of fish and hid her face from Cyril, and small children hid behind the pillars, peeping out at the *wasungu*.

In the morning we struck out again for Siyu after exploring the old Nahabani ruins which nestled in thickets of vegetation on the outskirts of the town. We found the way to Siyu by following the donkey tracks. Now and then we would see a boy shinnying up a coconut palm, or a little hamlet nestling in the sands.

'*Wapi* Siyu?' I asked the rheumy old *mzees*, the old men, and they pointed the way, jaws closing rhythmically on the ubiquitous *mira'a* drug, which is supposed to keep the mind alert if chewed in large quantities. I found it so unspeakably foul that I could never get through more than one stalk.

The sun burned more fiercely. We waded over the watery channel to Siyu, which was criss-crossed with the little breathing roots of mangroves. From Siyu we pressed on to Faza. As we walked through the town a half dozen people spilled out of their mud houses to shake our hands and chat in Swahili.

'Don't understand,' I said from time to time, but nobody minded, they all clapped me on the back and a little old lady got hold of my hand and hung on to it, nodding vigorously and smiling a tremendous smile. Presently we were bustled into a restaurant for ginger tea.

'Dhow,' I said generally. 'Dhow?' Someone must have understood because presently a dhow captain arrived and agreed to take us on to the next island, Kiwayu. Off we bustled again, down to the dhow, with the whole smiling, clapping restaurant contingent in tow, some twenty or thirty people.

'Kwaheri,' I ventured in farewell, and the crowd gave a loud cheer. Off we sailed again into the Indian Ocean to Kiwayu, where we stayed a number of days, camping on the beach and snorkelling all day among the coral pools. In the late afternoons we joined the elderly proprietor of the restaurant to play the complicated African bean in the hole game called *bao*.

When we made the return voyage it was the night of the full moon. There was not a cloud in the sky, the night was warm and the winds were perfect for speed. As we cut through the water a silver gleam of phosphorescence sprayed out on either side of the prow and the moon lay huge and trembling overhead.

The dhow captain began to beat an ancient rhythm on his drum and his crew took up the chant. It was so achingly beautiful that soon my heart was full and my thoughts had turned to mysticism, and then to the mysteries of my own existence. I had the privilege to live this African life, as my brother had also had. He had lived as fully and as wildly as he could and in the end he had succumbed. But if we could not touch, if we could not speak, the cadences of his spirit would still resonate in my being because I would still love, I would always love.

For a moment it seemed as if he was beside me, as if all these influences were the subtle voice of his being – the full fecund moon, the haunting drums, the spray and the silver light, the warm wind on my cheeks, the briny slap of the wet ropes against the wooden hull. I sat mutely, a young woman on a dhow boat in the Indian Ocean, and I allowed my own spirit to be soothed by the sensing of all these immutable things.

All Decent Girls Wear Bloomers

We left Lamu after a fortnight and caught the bus down to Kilifi Creek. We had stayed on a couple of extra days because Cyril had cut his knee open when I tried to help him over an oyster embankment, and he wanted to wait until it had healed. I was completely unsympathetic. It looked like a fairly minor sort of scratch and, besides, nothing ever healed here in the first place without the help of antibiotics, and he did not believe in antibiotics.

The first guest house that we stopped at in Kilifi was called Top Life. Behind the counter was a man with bloodshot eyes and a peculiarly stagnant smell. A duo of women in a half doze lounged behind the counter on low stools. We asked to see the rooms.

'Short time or long time?' enquired the proprietor.

The windowless room had a similar musty pall. Cobwebs festooned every corner. The two iron beds were covered with carelessly crumpled grey sheets.

'I'm sorry,' said Cyril unceremoniously. 'I can't possibly sleep in unchanged sheets. There's an epidemic, you know. And I have an open wound on my knee.'

We left the proprietor staring after us in mystification.

Kilifi is a quiet town with well-preserved Arabic ruins and a

237

wide and navigable river mouth. It is much favoured by wealthy Kenyans who go there to yacht and fish and entertain in the sprawling properties they build for their holiday leisure. But Cyril and I were both eager to get to Zanzibar – The Spice Island – so after only a night in Kilifi we pressed on towards Mombasa where we hoped to find a commercial dhow going south.

Mombasa was once the most exquisite of cities and is still attractive in parts, particularly the staunch edifice of the sixteenth-century Portuguese-built Fort Jesus at the harbour entrance, and the higgledy piggledy sprawl of Mombasa Old Town with its profusion of latticed Arab and Indian houses and wide veranda'ed British colonial buildings. But nowadays Mombasa is overcrowded and down at heel. There are a great number of horn-blaring matatus which play maddening little electronic ditties. The matatu drivers also apparently get their kicks from bawling sexually harassing slogans lustily out of their windows.

Hoot! Hoot toot toot! *Dee da da da dee*. Blare! Hey, Madam Madam look at me! *Dee da da da dee*. I'm here, sister, for a good time. Hey sister! Bleeeep! Bang! Bang! *Dee da da da dee*!

As soon as possible we boarded a large commercial motorised dhow bound for Zanzibar. These infrequent dhows are much preferred to the alternative route, which is a tedious bus journey to Dar es Salaam and then a ferry transfer. For this reason, by the time we staggered out of dock the boat was groaning under a crippling weight of people and their possessions. Fortunately the biggest shipment was one of mattresses which were piled up on the top deck. Presently the moon came up and trailed a bright reflection across the calm surface of the ocean. I settled down and began to play cards with a couple of Australian girls, while Cyril reclined happily on a mattress with his potted Ramtha notes.

There was a happy convivial atmosphere on board. What there was not was a toilet. Or rather there *was* one, but it was situated in the hellish cavity of the covered deck below, where the luckless and jam-packed purdah women had been getting sick to their stomachs for hours. One of the Australians ventured below and returned looking horribly nauseated. Her friend adopted a look of grim determination which increased as the hours passed.

Fortunately, by now I was an old hand at dhows and had mastered a discreet, difficult, but not impossible procedure which I delicately called 'The Illusion'. 'The Illusion' involved some nonchalant perching on the furthest extremities of the boat. I tried to guide the in extremis Australian through the mechanics, but she lacked the necessary agility. In fact, she came within a hair's breadth of plummeting into the watery depths. So in the end she, too, was obliged to wade greenly through the purdah muck.

We docked in Zanzibar in the early evening in time to participate in the sumptuous ritual of 'dining in the Jamituri Gardens'. The Jamituri Gardens are sandwiched between the castle and the old fort. At sunset this strip of lawn spawns a horde of trestle tables and food stalls serving kebabs and curries, fish cakes and *bajias*, roasted cassava chips, smoked octopus and ice-cream. An old man cranks the lever of a machine which makes fresh cane juice on the spot. It's the traditional place to wander in the gentle hours of the day, to meet a friend, to watch the sun wane, to eat a piece of this and a little of that. Afterwards we walked home along the dark little alleys. Like Lamu, the wealthier dwellings here had richly patterned and solid carved doors of masterly craftsmanship.

In the morning the Australians arrived to ask if we wanted to make a journey to the less populous east coast in a hired car. We agreed. They had collected a fifth member for the party, a stocky Cockney called Peter. Peter was taciturn, hirsute, and very, very dirty. He was also not terribly vocal. However, since I wound up next to him on the four-hour journey I tried to strike up a conversation.

'What do you do in England, Peter?'

'Smash and run jobs, mostly,' replied Peter. 'Gotter survive, 'aven't you?'

'Gotter,' I said brightly.

On the east coast we stayed at a place called Jambiani. I had started to write a tragi-comedy about gender relationships and spent my days sitting under the coconut palms scribbling. But every few minutes a ragged child would come to tug at my elbow.

'Pen, please' – and a smile of heart-rending hopefulness.

Very soon I was out of pens.

We were back in Zanzibar town in time for Christmas, and learnt that Moi had won the election in Kenya. Being a predominantly Muslim community, Christmas in Zanzibar was an ordinary day like any other. We celebrated it by taking a spice tour of the island with a septuagenarian Indian man called Mr Mitu.

Despite his age, Mr Mitu was possessed of formidable energy. We shot round the island in his truck looking at raw cloves, pepper, liquorice and tamarind trees. Mr Mitu had a particular party trick which was to throw out handfuls of coins as he passed through the villages strung out along the dust roads. This brought the children scurrying out in their hundreds, big and little children, even diminutive round-faced toddlers.

'Mitu!' cried the little things, scrimmaging in our wake 'Mitu! Mitu!'

I felt we were ridiculously like a carload of pale Pied Pipers.

I took a dimmer view of Mitu after he used me for a public medical experiment. My feet, over the last few months, had suffered successive infestations by jiggas – nasty little burrowing sand fleas that lay their eggs under the surface of the skin. The only way to get rid of them is with fortitude and a knife. We had stopped in the shade of a palm whilst Mr Mitu explained the properties of an adjacent iodine tree. I took advantage of the others' absorption to strip off my boots briefly and ease the chafe of the embarrassingly purulent jigga pits.

'Aha!' said Mitu, beaming. 'Jiggas!' He advanced purposefully with a strip of iodine bush and dribbled its viscous and undiluted sap into my sores. He might as well have plunged my entire body into liquid lava. As everybody crowded around to have a look, I smiled wincingly and repressed my desire to run screaming into the thickets.

*

By now I was very eager to return home. My university term was due to begin in a few weeks and I wanted to spend some time with my family before leaving them again.

So after Christmas we set off once more, boarding the train at Dar es Salaam. The women's cabin was relatively empty – there was a mother and baby and a very fat and cheerful young woman wearing a colourful T-shirt. *Rape is a Serious Crime* said her chest. *Wives are for Loving not Beating* read the back. I looked at her curiously. In the male-dominated society of Africa these were defiant statements.

Most of the public transport that included sleeping space was gender segregated in East Africa and I hugely preferred it that way. Apart from offering me a respite from Cyril, I relished the atmosphere in the women's cabins. Again and again I found that the bond of womanhood superseded the antagonisms of race.

There was a warm complicity of purpose in the cabin. I might have been a *msungu,* but I was still a woman. They would give me their babies to hold and entertain whilst they arranged themselves and their possessions, or they might show me the art of plaiting, or giggle at my submission to the children's earnest preoccupations with my hair. Cyril, on the other hand, was unhappily relegated to the uncomfortable and sub-cutaneously hostile silences of the men's cabin.

The train chugged out towards the west. At first we travelled through the shambas where the women toiled endlessly to feed their young. Up and down, up and down, swung their powerful arms as they broke the earth with their hoes, the cannon-ball heads of their new-borns just visible above the stooping backs. Later, the train's path crossed the Mikumi National Park and startled buffalo and elephant galloped away from this noisy incursion of metal.

Inside the carriage the cordial woman in the sloganised T-shirt had introduced herself as Betty. Her English was very good. We shared a bunch of bananas and got to talking. Betty was on her way to Zambia to persuade women there not to submit to the traditional marital practice of dry sex. Dry sex is a technique for making intercourse more pleasurable and stimulating for the man. The woman introduces powerful herbs into the vagina which tighten and shrink the vaginal walls. A dry sex bride fetches a much higher bride price for her father. The problem is that during sex the vaginal walls will always rupture and bleed. Apart from the initial pain the woman must suffer, in a society where condoms are perceived to make a mockery of manhood, there is no possible way in which she can avoid the transmission of Aids if her husband is infected.

Betty was a real battleaxe and I admired her tremendously. As a black woman in the less Westernised African countries it must be a very daunting task to take on these ancient abuses. I was always in two minds about the issues. Because I am a woman, I felt a great empathy with the position of women. But circumcision, marriage rites and the concept of the woman as the beast of burden are inseparably embedded in the matrix of many African cultures.

When the missionaries arrived in Africa they tried to ban the circumcision of women, in the face of tremendous hostility. Elspeth Huxley told the story in *Out in the Midday Sun* of how in the twenties a Church of Scotland missionary was attacked and crudely circumcised – an atrocity designed to keep the outsiders at bay. The elderly woman did not survive.

With the demise of tribal life today it is difficult to establish how widespread the ritual has remained in the latter half of the century. Certainly it has been greatly reduced. But, tellingly, President Jomo Kenyatta, who was a graduate of the London School of Economics, still held that the abolition of female circumcision would irreparably damage the morale and social well-being of his people.

We disembarked at Mbeya and continued south by bus, crossing the border into Malawi at Kaporo.

Malawi at that time was still under the leadership of the self-appointed life president, Dr Hastings Banda. Dr Banda had a consummately Victorian outlook on life. He detested hippies and democracy (probably in that order). And he was determined not to inflict either of these ills upon the nation. Foremost amongst Dr Banda's precepts was the principle that men and women ought not to look like one another. For this reason, the border guards kept a particularly sharp eye out for men with Samsonite tresses. Women were allowed to wear nothing more racy or unisex than a dress which fell decently below the knee.

I had duly donned the wraparound skirt and everything was going swimmingly at the border post. Unfortunately, an ill-timed drift of wind plucked playfully at the hem of my skirt to reveal my cotton-clad shins.

'Attempting to enter the country in men's clothing!' pounced the border guard testily.

'They're bloomers,' I said hopefully. 'All decent girls wear bloomers.'

But he would not have it. He ushered me purposefully into a roadside cabin until I could show him that my shins were as naked as the day I was born.

The next lift that we got was on the summit of a top-heavy maize truck. Here we had to cling like monkeys to a latticework of ropes in the teeth of a howling wind. Unfortunately, the wrap-around skirt billowed out behind me like a full spinnaker, much to the merriment of the other passengers. After some twenty minutes of struggle I reflected that I was now doing far more to compromise the national mores of decency. None of the cheerful young men on the back of the truck looked like government agents. I got back into the subversive trousers.

We arrived at Nkatha Bay on beautiful Lake Malawi on the morning of the 31st of December. There was quite a crowd camping on the beach – and they were all beginning to phase into the bibulous frenzy synonymous with New Year's Eve.

A group of them paid for a vigorous young billy goat to be brought up from the village. When he arrived they didn't want to kill him before the evening as they had no place to store the meat. So the poor old billy was tethered to a sweet thorn near our camp where he remained for several hours, bleating pitifully and sweating a pungent and unpleasant deathstink. At last they came for it and, seizing the animal by its legs, fore and aft, they made a deft nick in the jugular. Ruby plumes of blood pumped four foot into the air, a last wail of protest from the goat, a final desperate plunge of the convulsing body.

An hour later the goat was skinned and on the spit, the rich odour of fresh roasting meat filled the air, and small African children squabbled over the skins and entrails which they had been given.

We bought a bottle of horrible local wine and wandered along the beach drinking it. Cyril fell asleep early and I sat cross-legged outside our tent, watching the iridescent sky darken over the great sheet of water. Down on the beach there were fireworks and revelry, the sand was littered with discarded bottles and cans and the air suffused with the sweet acrid scent of burning marijuana. Great ribald cries and peals of helpless laughter rose from the crowds. But I did not yet feel ready to join in an atmosphere of merriment.

I turned my head to look at Cyril, whose sleeping features were visible through the fly net. I had noticed in the last week that as our journey drew to its close, his features were becoming diaphanous and misty. It was as if he had already entered the past, as if he were undergoing a transition into memory.

Whatever he might do tomorrow, or the next day, I would accept without rancour because already I was berthing on the far shore of the sea of cloudy pain that had been my months with Cyril.

A great clamour went up from the revellers. The New Year, 1993.

A single curved pod dropped from the sweet thorn and bounced off the taut canvas of our tent. I looked up into the branches of this generous tree in a continent that has lost too many of her trees. In my mind the past months rolled by, one after the other.

'*Annus horribilis*,' I said softly to the sweet thorn.

It had been, entirely and devastatingly, and yet again it had not.

*

After the New Year we made a bus journey to the border with Zambia, and then another bus journey to Lusaka. This second bus journey was far and away the most arduous one I have ever made. In fact, though, I have never regretted having made it, because it was such a very classic example of an African bus journey.

There was a popular fiction that the bus was due to leave at ten in the morning. In truth, it left at four in the afternoon. We spent the intervening hours drinking lukewarm tea and eating goat in a roadhouse, keeping one eye on the terminus.

At four the bus did leave, but got only as far as the outskirts of town where it broke down. The driver revived it sufficiently to get us back to the terminus where we exchanged buses.

The same thing happened. After a bit of head-scratching someone seemed to recollect that there might, in fact, be another bus. The third bus was the oldest bus I had ever seen, and also the noisiest. But it got us reliably out of town and on to the national road. I was rather reminded of my writer's habit of having a great collection of pens, all of which worked only a little.

But by now I was not thinking about buses. I was thinking that there was clearly something unsavoury about that roadhouse goat. I doubled up on the floor and made little protesting whines, and the superannuated bus made little protesting whines, and thus we carried on.

Fortunately – and on the brink of disaster – it transpired that I was not the only one with roadhouse syndrome. A gaggle of anxious mamas who had also taken refreshment were making anguished requests of the driver. Presently we pulled up at a roadside toilet and I shot out in the vanguard of the goat-stricken mamas.

Everything would have been manageable at this point, except that as I reached the bathroom I heard a high-pitched shrieking that was unmistakably Cyril's. Because he had stopped making this sound months before, I instantly assumed that there was trouble or that he was being hurt. I doubled back to find him. In fact, he was simply jiggling on the spot and letting off steam and excitement.

Now the bus was hooting impatiently, and the bathroom was sealed up with mamas. I think I picked up a loose plank of wood and tried to hit Cyril with it, but he fled precipitately back into the crowd of passengers. Since the driver had never had any concept of how many passengers he had, it was your own indaba if the bus left without you. I followed Cyril on board, cursing him roundly all the while.

Much later, after dark, we finally stopped at another bush toilet. As I was emerging from this one I was greeted by a weird symphony. Cyril was still in his mood of generally maddening rambunctiousness. He had climbed into the aisle and begun to chant my name raucously into the night. After a while the Africans, with their natural sense of rhythm and musicality, took it up. So when I rounded the corner I found the ancient old African bus tottering on its two axles, whilst inside a hundred joyous choristers chanted my name, again and again, into the hollow stillness of the night.

'*Oh, Sarah, Sarah, Sarah. Oh, Sarah, Sarah, Sarah. Oh, Sarah, Sarah, Sarah.*'

I climbed slowly up the steps and advanced on Cyril, half amused, half exasperated.

'You're such a loon, you know.'

'*Loon! Loon! Loon!*' sang the bus.

'You're quite quite mad.'

'*Mad! Mad! Mad!*'

'Eighteen months, Cyril. *Eighteen months* and I still don't understand you a bit.'

'*Bit! Bit! Bit!*'

He giggled and eased himself into his seat.

I sighed. There was less point in lecturing him than there was in chastising a toddler. Whatever I said, he would still be led by his maniacal, irrepressible, enthusiastic responses to life. There was always a quality in my dealings with him that made me feel like somebody's horrible old opprobrious aunt.

I was perennially absorbed in the condition of African public toilets. To say they were horrid doesn't really do justice to the situation. I found them to be completely – and affrontingly – politically incorrect.

This did not apply to African toilets proper. The traditional African toilet – influenced by the coastal Arabs – consists of a rectangular hole in the ground over a deep pit. These simple, low maintenance outhouses are usually in fairly good nick. The axe that I had to grind was with the porcelain structures of the West, which still proliferate across the face of Africa. These may have done good service to the pale bottoms of administration in former times. But the problem is – in countries like Zambia and Tanzania – that they universally foundered after the disappearance of the last colonial plumber thirty years ago.

This would not matter in the least, except that people still continue to use them. Or rather, not so much use the toilet, which is unusable, but the space around the toilet – the floors, the walls, even the cemented walk-ups outside.

It always amazed and disturbed me that a peasant who had shamba at her disposal crying out for night soil, might choose instead to defecate on a filthy and stinking strip of cement, simply because it was a few yards away from some defunct old chipped porcelain cavity. And this situation had ludicrously arisen because fifty years ago some white man had proclaimed the area 'toilet' and had built a flimsy edifice upon it.

The bus struck out again upon the road and we trundled along until the driver decided it was time to rest upon his oars. He drove off on to a sandy strip beside the road, killed the engine and got off the bus. Then, without further ceremony, he lay down in the sand and went to sleep. So did everybody else.

In the morning I woke up with a pounding headache and a smutty taste in my mouth, dirty as a street gamin and thirsty as hell. The bus wouldn't start. The driver tinkered unremuneratively with the engine for some hours. A nearby baby gazed at me unflinchingly through the numerous flies on his eyelids. Eventually the engine was repaired and we struggled on for most of the morning until, at the summit of a particularly steep hill, the whole bus reverberated with a tremendous series of bangs and stopped short.

It was quite apparent that we would not be going anywhere for a while. I cut into the bush, found a waist-high pool of water, took a bath and washed my hair and clothing. Then I returned, much refreshed. Suddenly I noticed that there was not one, but three buses stranded on the summit of the hill. I made enquiries. It turned out that one bus had been waiting for two days and the other bus for four days. Nobody quite knew what they were waiting for.

We hitched into Lusaka on the next truck, along with the richer passengers. The poorer ones could not afford to as they had already spent all their money on the bus ticket. But they did not seem unduly worried at the prospect of losing a few days on the road. Time, in Africa, is not a valued commodity.

They do not parcel it out, as whites do, and pull at their hair if things are not running smoothly to the minute. Today is today, but there is always tomorrow or the next day. Something might take an hour or it might take a hundred hours, but in the end it will come to pass.

More African time elapsed on the evening train bound for Livingstone. I woke in the morning and found we had not budged even a yard – I was staring out on to the same dismal Lusaka platform that had been the last thing I looked at the previous evening. The station official I consulted was equally mystified. Usually the train moved on during the evening, he agreed, but somehow not this time. I retired gloomily to our squalid, waterless, tepid cabin. Much later I discovered that the delay was due to a derailment. We finally pulled out twenty-four hours late of schedule.

In Livingstone we met up with Honore once again and stayed for an evening in an outside cabin on her land. She was as acerbic and self-reliant as I remembered her.

That night I had a parting gift from Africa. A scorpion stung me squarely on the heel as I was traipsing barefoot between the outside cabin and the main house. I knew that I had been stung from the dull throbbing that persisted through dinner and preparations for bed, but at midnight I woke, soaked with sweat and seized with torrential vomiting – wave upon wave of vitriolic nausea – as if my entire intestine was trying to force itself out of my mouth. The force of it tore the back of my throat, filling my mouth with blood. We had a bottle of purified water; I soon finished it and groped in the dark for more.

'Cyril, Cyril,' I said, panicking. 'I've been stung, I'm sick and the water's finished.'

'Go and drink from the river.'

'But it's dirty! And the crocodiles.'

'Then drink from the toilet,' he answered, in a flash of ill feeling.

Too desperate for water, I threw all dignity to the winds.

'Oh *please*, Cyril. Please, I'll die if I don't drink something. I can't move. I'll pay you, I'll give you anything I own, I'll borrow money from my parents, just say what you want – it's yours.'

My crassness startled him into full wakefulness. Grumbling, he went away and came back with a full bottle.

I forgave him because he no longer existed, his words were the memory words of our past. Besides, I knew that he never meant to be cruel or malicious. He fell into the trap of cruelty frequently and without struggle, but only because he had never yet developed an understanding of the concept.

Honore, typically gruff, did not hold with my scorpion story in the morning.

'It was a jam sandwich,' she said succinctly.

I wondered how many stings her hoary old legs had sustained over the years. Mine swelled up to a glorious size and took on the texture of plasticine so that I could sink my finger in it up to the first joint and the depression would stay intact for hours. Gratifyingly, it remained in that condition for a week – just long enough for me to be able to startle my mother with it.

We left Honore's and travelled on into Botswana, past the bush savannah and great baobabs of the Makgadikgadi pans, past the thickets of mopane, past dusty tracts overgrazed by cattle, until we came to Gaborone and crossed the border into South Africa. At once the *Zeitgeist* of the territory altered. Now there was a broad and even tarred road, cleft by a firm white stripe and flanked by cat's eyes.

It was midsummer, seven months since we had first set out. Maize fields in a greening adolescence held up their heads to the sharp sunlight. The driver of the car that we were hitching with stopped at a corner shop in Zeerust for cold drinks to thwart the heat.

It was just an ordinary corner shop – the bored cashier was beaded with sweat, and a knot of army boys joshed each other over the mild girlie magazines. A modification to the censorship laws had just permitted the revelation of nipples for the very first time; hitherto they had been concealed by a little black star. But Cyril and I moved in breathless delight amongst the bright, laden shelves, touching the myriad cans and packets and bottles with our fingertips, in a consumerist fever of desire. I bought a newspaper, a chocolate milkshake, liquorice strips and candy buttons. I held the sweets in my hands for a long time, just looking, before I tore open the plastic.

Outside, the countryside rolled by in a haze of maize fields, interspersed with bush and the gate posts of private lodges.

'Keep left. Pass right' warned an orderly bottle-green road sign.

I bit my lip, filled with an almost stupefying love for this raw, savage, troubled nation that I had the great good fortune to call my own. A few years ago our prospects had looked so bleak. We were not yet out of our trials, but now we had the extraordinary forgiveness and vision of Mandela and the reformist pragmatism of De Klerk in which to vest hope. At last I could believe that we would draw back from the brink of ruin, at the eleventh hour.

All my life I had been part of a parochial and blinkered nation, at the foot of Africa but not a part of Africa. Now I had seen for myself the great matrix of the North to which we were inseparably linked. I opened the newspaper. There were the usual squabbles, the rash of murders, the ongoing agony of negotiations, and a good few pages given over to the national mania of rugby. I leaned my head against the window and shifted on the seat whose dark plastic was growing uncomfortably warm under an intense, brilliant sunlight which would last for several months to come.

I was home.

Aftermath

For a long time I did not talk, or indeed even think very much about my via dolorosa in Africa. It was such a deeply private time that I could never have imagined that I would ever want to write about it. But when every novel that I tried to write crumbled in its first chapters, I realised at last that it was my own experiences which I was yearning to express.

Whilst we had been away, one of the little parrots that my mother was nurturing died. I took the other one away to university with me, but she sickened not long afterwards. I sought the advice of a vet, but he could not save her.

Soon afterwards a man in a safari suit appeared on the doorstep. He was from the veterinary services, and he wanted to know where I had got the parrot, which had suffered from a disease never before diagnosed in South Africa.

I was so taken aback that I stammered out some pathetic excuse in a lather of guilty fright, which he seemed to put down to female vagueness. He explained to me, avuncularly, that parrots like these came from a very dangerous country in West Africa, that they were protected, and that they were meant to be accompanied by a lot of paperwork.

I had an urgent desire to confess, to get it off my chest, but I remained silent, partly out of fear, but partly because I could not tell him the whole story in a few sentences. Besides I saw in his eyes what I was to him – a dizzy young blonde in a sundress, hovering on bare feet. Would he have believed me?

I did return Honore's money with a note saying that I had not been in my right senses, but I knew that this was the one thing I had done in my life for which I would always feel culpable.

And what happened to Cyril? After we returned to South Africa, I left him and went to stay with my parents for a week before travelling up to my new university in Grahamstown. On the way I stopped at a South Coast nature reserve where there was a reunion of the Purple Bubble, to which I had invited him. He was so taken with the nature reserve that he decided here was the place where he could live in peace and harmony with nature for ever. I was doubtful. It was all very well to sneak in for a night or two, but the authorities might object to a permanent fixture.

But Cyril was convinced, so one morning I took him into the nearest town for supplies and then dropped him at the road head. He sauntered jauntily along the track to his new life and I gunned up the engine and drove away to mine. Presently it occurred to me that I was now a free agent.

'Well, well, girl,' I said musingly, looking at my visage in the overhead mirror.

I plunged into the university term. At first it all seemed exceedingly strange, but later it became commonplace. Gradually I grew less frenetic and keyed-up, and began to feel my way into this safe and orderly world. I cut lectures to surf, spent nights writing essays by lamplight, and long hazy evenings in pub discussions.

One day Cyril arrived. Nature had assailed him in the onset of the mosquito season and covered him in rosy spots, so he had decided to move on. We had nothing to say to each other. I was unable to deal with his intrusion into my new life and greeted him with rank hostility. He left the next day and went to live on a remote sheep camp owned by the family of one of the Purple Bubble, where he scared the jackals away in exchange for a weekly carton of vegetables. That was the last I saw of him for some time.

However, the following Christmas when I was staying with my parents, my mother appeared with an anxious and half-forgotten expression on her face.

'*He's here*,' she hissed tersely.

'Who?'

'*Him!*'

Cyril was dressed in copious trousers coloured in raffish whorls and loosely gathered at the ankles and waist. I, conversely, was having a Marks and Spencer day in a matching waistcoat and tailored bermudas in pastel green. I hailed him warmly and we went down to the shopping mall to look at the lurid Christmas decorations, the tinsel and baubles and iridescent streamers. The shopping scene infused Cyril with vibrant life – he skipped and *jetéd* between the aisles and eventually he stopped at the centrepiece fountain and executed a series of delirious pirouettes.

'Cyril!' I whispered urgently, relapsing into the past. 'Do stop! Everyone is looking at you! You haven't even got any shoes on.'

'Hey man!' he laughed. 'What does it matter? They should get right! You've gotten so straight.'

I laughed too. I had to laugh – with the rough affection that I would retain over the years for this crazy, impetuous, giddy child-man with whom I had undergone such unlikely travails. I laughed for the impulses of youth, the great social leveller which whispers hotly in our ears that we might do whatever we want and to hell with the consequences. I laughed because he was what he was – such a wild creature of the wind, such a floating fragment of sea eddies following on the tides of his whims. Whatever sober avenues I might trundle along in life, he would always remind me that once I had been adrift.

After that, I never saw him again.

A year later I decided to go to England after all, even though it was too late for A-levels and Oxford. I went up as far as Kenya overland, this time travelling alone. Sometimes I passed a place where I had been before, and the past would come upon me in a wash of sadness and comprehension. Here I had been, I had done this and I had felt that, and now I felt it again in muted shadow as the geography of memory corresponded with the history.

When I reached London my memories were foremost in my mind. I picked up a pen and allowed them to flood into script.

It has been over five years now since my brother died. Sometimes in a conversation with a casual friend a direct question must elicit the fact of his death. Then the friend looks jittery and the conventions of chit-chat are ambushed. They ask when and I say five years.

'Oh, five years ago!' they say, greatly reassured, and rescued from the brink of human intimacy. 'Oh, not recently then.'

And then I know that they have never carried a death of their own.

Whilst I have not been able to share the passing years with him, the past is still mine to hold close. But my unravelling future tinkers with the frozen bygones. Suddenly I will see a half-remembered conversation in a different light. The memory of high jinks, of a joke, of an insult, flashes through my head and I realise with a start that I am now the age he was then. Then I see through the eyes of both the man and the girl. In this way mysteries clarify and sour recollections become sweet.

In fact, the most treasured of my memories was once my very bitterest. I had fired off a protesting letter at his treatment of me – I have always found it easier to express what I feel in writing. At that point he requested an interview in the family sitting-room.

The sitting-room is high-ceilinged, thick-walled and cool –

part of the Georgian frontage to the house – and filled with stinkwood cabinets and exquisitely crafted yellowwood escritoires. The walls are ranged with solid Dutch oil paintings of venerable gentlemen in stiff collars, or surly Roman centurions.

I hunched on the sofa in a sundress that flourished in dahlias.

'You treat me like I'm an idiot,' I said stiffly.

He was pacing before the fire grate; he paused and swung on his heels to look accusingly into my face.

'But you are an idiot! You're such a *confirmed* little idiot.'

I demurred, twisting the tulse beads at my neck.

'You're an idiot now,' he repeated, converging on me and seating himself on the sofa. 'But you're not going to be an idiot for ever. One day – some day – you're going to grow up and do something worth while with your life.'

Life is a pitched battle between constraint and desire, and passion is the gilded weapon we have to fight with. What my brother left to me, magnified and distilled by his death, was the example of a life lived passionately and the challenge to journey the path towards my own elusive dreams.